Reflections
of Canada

**Peter Wall Institute for
Advanced Studies**

REFLECTIONS

OF

CANADA

ILLUMINATING OUR OPPORTUNITIES
AND CHALLENGES AT 150+ YEARS

edited by
Phillipe Tortell, Margot Young,
and Peter Nemetz

Peter Wall Institute for Advanced Studies
University of British Columbia
Vancouver BC
www.pwias.ubc.ca

Cataloguing data available from Library and Archives Canada
ISBN 978-0-88865-267-6 (hardcover)

Edited by Phillipe Tortell, Margot Young, and Peter Nemetz
Produced by Page Two
www.pagetwostrategies.com
Cover and interior design by Peter Cocking
Cover photo by Nicholas Taffs
Frontispiece photo of the Parliament Buildings,
Ottawa, Ontario by Nicholas Taffs
Printed and bound in Canada by Friesens

17 18 19 20 21   5 4 3 2 1

PETER

WALL

INSTITUTE FOR ADVANCED STUDIES
THE UNIVERSITY OF BRITISH COLUMBIA VANCOUVER

Contents

Foreword

David Johnson
Governor-General of Canada

AS GOVERNOR GENERAL of Canada, one of my great privileges and responsibilities is to help celebrate our country and the people who call it home. This year, which marks the 150th anniversary of Confederation, is one of special celebration. However, it's important that, even as we celebrate and honour our remarkably diverse and successful country, we avoid the trap of complacency and self-satisfaction. After all, we can and must do better on so many important issues. My mandate as governor general has focused on encouraging Canadians to help build a smarter, more caring nation, a broad focus which recognizes that, fortunate as we are to live in this country, there remain many areas for improvement and that require our sustained and thoughtful attention.

This collection of essays, which gathers contributions from some of Canada's brightest minds on a wide variety of social, environmental, economic, political, scientific and cultural topics, marks an important contribution to our sesquicentennial celebrations. In recent years I have often asked Canadians to consider what their gifts to Canada will be on the occasion of its 150th birthday. This volume offers us a timely and relevant gift of thoughts and ideas on some of the most pressing issues of our time. There is a great wealth of insight and analysis within these pages that gives us all much food for thought as we reflect upon Canada in this milestone year and look towards our shared future. I thank the contributors and everyone who played a role in bringing this volume to fruition.

Preface

Santa J. Ono
President and Vice-Chancellor of the
University of British Columbia

I HAVE THE privilege of being the fifteenth president of UBC as the university enters its next century. My move to UBC was, in a sense, a homecoming: I was born in Vancouver while my father was a UBC professor of mathematics. But the move was also a positive choice to join an institution known around the world as a leader in research, education, and social engagement.

Perched on a peninsula jutting into the Salish Sea, UBC's Point Grey campus sits in a breathtakingly beautiful setting, with views up Howe Sound, to the downtown high-rises of Vancouver and North Shore Mountains, and across the sea to the Gulf Islands. This site is the traditional, ancestral, and unceded lands of the Musqueam people, members of the Coast Salish Nation. This fact reminds us daily that the future of Canada must be one in which we engage honourably with Indigenous peoples who have lived on this land since time immemorial. Our university and others are called to play a critical role in shaping a just, equitable, and prosperous society, and we must engage deeply in scholarship and commentary that touches on issues of reconciliation and other pressing concerns facing Canada on the 150th anniversary of Confederation, and beyond.

This book brings together some of Canada's foremost thinkers to contemplate the future of this country, with all its multi-faceted challenges and exciting opportunities. The authors bring a variety of voices and perspectives to reflect on the past 150 years and offer new insights on complex issues. This collection captures the diversity and creativity of scholars at UBC, while also drawing upon a range of voices from other Canadian universities and from community partners with whom the scholars are engaged. The essays showcase critical understanding and appreciation of our society and the biophysical world we inhabit, as it reflects upon the history and future of Canada.

The collection of essays and photographs comes out of the Peter Wall Institute for Advanced Research, a UBC institute that was founded twenty-five years ago to promote interdisciplinary research and intellectual dialogue. Scholars at the Institute come from across the UBC campus and around the world, engaging each other, and the public at large, in deep discourse on critical issues. The Institute has achieved a remarkable record of research accomplishment and community engagement. It has upheld the ideals of free and open intellectual exchange that are the hallmark of a university. The work of the Institute demonstrates the transformative power of interdisciplinary collaboration in solving complex problems and advancing the frontiers of knowledge. With the assistance of his co-editors, Professors Margot Young and Peter Nemetz, Institute Director Professor Philippe Tortell has assembled a collection of essays that sparkle, challenging us to mark this moment in Canada's history with careful, insightful, and diverse thought.

Introduction

Philippe Tortell

MY PERSONAL HISTORY has given me glimpses and snapshots of Canada over the past four decades. I was born a Canadian, but I wasn't born in Canada. After bouncing between France, Quebec, and Algeria, I landed in suburban Toronto by the time I was eight. The face of Canada was rapidly changing when I arrived in the 1970s; immigration reform had begun to reshape the ethnic and cultural landscape of the country, and, even as a young child, I remember the friction, uncertainty, and, yes, racism of those years. Later travels would take me to Italy (for high school), then back to Quebec (university), where I experienced the separatist fervency in the lead-up to the second sovereignty referendum.

Around that time, events surrounding the Oka Crisis also awakened my awareness of the struggles for Indigenous recognition and respect in this country. Over the next five years, studying in the United States, I continued to watch, from a distance, as other events unfolded in Canada. Globalization was rapidly shrinking the world, and Canada was trying to redefine its place on the international stage. I began to appreciate Canada's distinct identity, and the deep, yet subtle, cultural and social differences that separated my country from the proverbial elephant parked along its southern border.

Upon returning to Canada, I put my shoulder to the academic wheel—teaching courses, running a research program, and undertaking various administrative duties at the University of British Columbia. After more than a decade at UBC, in 2014, I spent the first of two years as Wall Scholar at the Peter Wall Institute for Advanced Studies. This marked the beginning of a major transition in my approach to research, and a significant expansion of my scholarly horizons. The Institute was established to promote the free-ranging exchange of ideas; it is a place where passionate scholars and artists could engage in creative risk taking and experimentation, striving for intellectual transformation. Its first Distinguished Professor, Michael Smith, was a Nobel Laureate, and a pioneer of the molecular revolution that underpins much of modern biological research and medicine. Over its twenty-five-year history, the Institute has hosted many other world-renowned scholars whose work has helped to transform the way we think and live. By promoting a deeper understanding of our societal, political, and artistic culture and fostering developments in chemistry, mathematics, environmental studies, and many other disciplines, work at the Institute has touched on and shaped many facets of our collective lives.

So, the 150th anniversary of Canadian Confederation seemed like a perfect opportunity to ask how the scholars and scholarship of the Peter Wall Institute could inform critical questions facing this country. How might we reflect on our communal history, while imagining a forward-looking future? What could we say about Canada that hadn't already been said before? Quite a lot, as it turned out.

This volume represents the end product of an intensive process of reflection and dialogue among leading Canadian scholars, and a variety of other important voices from across the country. We began, in October 2016, with a series of lunch meetings at the Peter Wall Institute, where we engaged in lively discussion of critical issues facing Canada. From the outset, it was clear that the project would not simply celebrate Canada. For how could we, in the era of Truth and Reconciliation, gloss over the most difficult moments of our collective past? Rather, as we reflected on our accomplishments as a country, we sought to embrace the pain, tragedy, and follies of history, to re-envision a different path forward.

From our initial discussions, we cast a wide net. Contributions came in from a number of UBC scholars, and we approached others, within and beyond academia, who have particular expertise in key areas. All of the contributions were subject to a peer-review process to ensure accuracy and rigour, and edited to achieve broad accessibility, while respecting the diversity of language and styles used by the contributors. The result now before you is a collection of many contrasting voices. These voices are sometimes dissonant, and they do not fit cleanly into a single coherent narrative. As with the cultural mosaic we call Canada, this book is built from many small shiny pebbles, each reflecting its own light from a particular corner of the complex landscape of our nation.

Yet, strong themes emerge. Perhaps first and foremost is the theme of diversity—cultural, ethnic, linguistic, racial, and more. Canada prides itself on this diversity, although our collective actions too often tell a different story. The opening poem, by Canada's Poet Laureate George Elliott Clarke, reflects a similar aspirational vision of Canada as a "kaleidoscope" of colours reflected through a "stained-glass igloo." Other contributions pick up this theme with a focus on multilingualism in Canada, reflecting on the need for Canada to preserve and develop its linguistic capital.

Several contributions reflect on Canada's relationship with Indigenous peoples, and on the legacy of systematic abuse through the residential school program. The use of "150+" in the book's title acknowledges the complexity of the anniversary of Canadian Confederation: Indigenous peoples have been here long before Canada, and the very idea of "Canada 150" has generated critical debate. Thus, a number of essays consider critically the challenges we face as our country grapples with its colonial history. These essays look unflinchingly into the past, while also urging a better future based on the resurgence of Indigenous cultures and languages, and a more ecologically sustainable and politically just approach to the management of natural resources.

Canada's relationship to the world is also the focus of several of the authors, who examine how our country is positioned on the world stage and how our national character has been influenced by (at least sometimes) welcoming citizens of the world to our shores. There are a number of contributions that focus on Canada's rapidly changing physical and ecological landscape; these authors engage with challenges to air and water quality, declining natural resources and biodiversity, and the massive environmental changes occurring across our vast Arctic territory. Some authors provide guidance on how Canada can meet its international obligations to mitigate climate change through innovative technological and financial approaches.

Other authors engage with our social landscape, considering a range of important issues, including poverty and food security, privacy, and social justice. The political framework for Canada is taken up by authors who reflect on how we govern ourselves as a democratic nation, and on the shifting relationship between Quebec and the federal government, as seen from contrasting perspectives. As the demographics of our population change, several contributors help us to imagine a healthy Canadian society of the future, where citizens of all ages, ethnicities, and cultures enjoy the highest possible quality of life and health care, irrespective of income or social status. The role of Canada as a significant global player in technological innovation is also considered, with examples drawn from quantum computing and sustainable architecture. Finally, to round out the themes, there are several contributions on Canada's cultural heritage, from galleries and museums to theatre and literature. All of the contributions reflect our sense of ourselves as a nation as we look back to our history and forward into the future.

If the words in the collection are beautiful, so too are the images. The photographs in this volume were selected from several hundred submissions to a national photo contest that ran between November 2016 and February 2017. These images are literal snapshots of Canada, taken from across the country and representing a diversity of artists and perspectives. As with the essays, these remarkable photographs reflect the places and people of our nation, as captured in the split second of a lens shutter.

Of course, it is not possible in any collection to capture everything one might say about a country as diverse, complicated, and vast as Canada. With 150-plus years under its belt, Canada is many different things to many people. This collection represents a narrative in progress, much like Canada itself. The words and images in this volume tell their own story and, in doing so, contain the threads from which the collective visions of our country can emerge.

Reflections
of Canada

Divers à dessein

George Elliott Clarke

Ce que nous construisons, que nous avons construit,
C'est un igloo fait d'un vitrail dont les couleurs
Chatoient aux lueurs d'un spectre incluant moi et lui,
Avec nos accents distincts, le mien et le leur.

« Mosaïque », « kaléidoscope », des mots vibrants
Qui nous décrivent au chaud, blottis et confortables,
Inukshuks qui aimons d'un amour intégrant
Et ne croyons pas nos enfants dorés coupables.

C'est notre Canada, fulgurante nation –
Un refuge accueillant, la ferme et la cité.
Notre igloo arc-en-ciel produit l'Exaltation :
Rêve sans prix éclatant de Diversité.

Traduction : Robert Paquin

Diverse by Design

George Elliott Clarke

What we are building, what we've been building,
Is a stained-glass igloo, where all colours
Shimmer, lighting the spectrum, including
Supple accents—hints, tints—that are all ours.

"Mosaic," "Kaleidoscope," these vivid nouns,
Also picture us, warm, snuggled in our quilt,
Where we breathing inukshuks love beyond bounds,
And in our gilded children see no guilt.

That's our Canada, this dazzling nation—
A welcoming shelter, farm, and city.
Our rainbow igloo radiates Elation:
Priceless dream—our gleaming Diversity.

Practising Reconciliation

Jillian Harris, Alex Maass, and Andrew Martindale

IN THE PAST few years, the horrific reality of Canada's Indian Residential School (IRS) system has begun to seep into the collective consciousness of the country through the testimony of Indigenous Canadians to the Truth and Reconciliation Commission of Canada (TRC). This collective acknowledgement of grievous injustice looms large on the 150th anniversary of Canadian Confederation.

Mandatory attendance was legislated at residential schools as early as the 1890s and was enforced by 1920 in all parts of the country. The schools were in operation for more than 130 years, until 1996 when the last school closed in Saskatchewan. They became the subject of the largest legal settlement agreement in Canadian history, negotiated in 2007 on behalf of former students with the federal government of Canada and the churches that administered the daily operation of the schools.

Disease and malnutrition were present from the start and continued throughout, to the point that IRS students were seen as viable test subjects in the 1950s by government scientists conducting medical experiments on the effects of nutritional deprivation. That many students did not survive is a truth long known by the country's Indigenous population but not one commonly understood by other Canadians. The death rate was especially high in the early years due to epidemic diseases accompanied by denial and deliberate neglect by government authorities, poor conditions leading to school fires, and accidents that occurred during the forced transport of children to the schools. It was not uncommon for runaway attempts to result in drowning or death from exposure.

Consider the words of Duncan Campbell Scott, Canada's deputy superintendent general of Indian Affairs from 1913 to 1932. In 1912, he wrote:

> It cannot be gainsaid that in the early days of school administration in the territories, while the problem was still a new one, the system was open to criticism. Insufficient care was exercised in the admission of children to the schools. The well-known predisposition of Indians to tuberculosis resulted in a very large percentage of deaths among the pupils. They were housed in buildings not carefully designed for school purposes, and these buildings became infected and dangerous to the inmates. It is quite within the mark to say that 50 percent of the children who passed through these schools did not live to benefit from the education, which they had received therein.[1]

Most of these children were buried in small, unofficial cemeteries on or near the school grounds. Often parents were not notified about the death of a child; in some cases, parents or descendant families still do not know where their children or relatives are buried. Over the past several decades, these small, generally unmarked burial places are increasingly disappearing.

The legacy of these schools and the suffering they inflicted continues to reverberate within Indigenous communities today. The task of remediation and reconciliation must fall to all Canadians. And it has only just begun.

The final report of Canada's Truth and Reconciliation Commission has charted the path forward for us, stating that "reconciliation requires political will, joint leadership, trust building, accountability, and transparency, as well as a substantial investment of resources." Discussion is not enough:

> Together, Canadians must do more than just talk about reconciliation; we must learn how to practice reconciliation in our everyday lives—within ourselves and our families, and in our communities, governments, places

of worship, schools, and workplaces. To do so constructively, Canadians must remain committed to the ongoing work of establishing and maintaining respectful relationships.

Here we present a conversation between three scholars who work in partnership to locate the burials of children who died at the Indian Residential School on Kuper Island, now called Penelakut Island, in the Salish Sea. We discuss our collective efforts in collaboration with the Penelakut community to remediate both the physical and spiritual damage wrought by this notorious residential school.

HARRIS: The Kuper Island Indian Residential School was torn down by the people of Penelakut and its cornerstone thrown into the sea, but the memories of it still remain standing. People still see shadows of children who died there and still hear their voices. They died of disease, they died by their own hand, or they were killed. My father attended that school and nearly died there from neglect, and his stories haunt me to this day.

MARTINDALE: The horrors of Canada's Indian Residential School system have been documented through the research of and testimony to the TRC. The legacy of these places and the suffering they inflicted continues to reverberate within Indigenous communities. Indigenous resilience in the face of state-sponsored institutional abuse and the many individual criminal acts the state facilitated is evident in the ongoing Indigenous effort to document their history. Though Indian Residential Schools have closed and the TRC has completed its mandate, the task of remediation has not ended. Perhaps it is just beginning.

HARRIS: My father died without ever having dealt with the abuse he suffered there when he was a child. In the late 1990s and early 2000, when I was the elected chief of Penelakut, people would approach me to tell me that they were hearing children crying and sometimes laughing. On many occasions, people would see shadows moving through the place where the school building was located; sometimes the shadows of the children would be peering in the windows of the homes built near the school site.

MAASS: The Kuper Island residential school on the west coast of British Columbia was a notorious place among Indigenous people, with one of the highest number of recorded deaths of any school in the residential school system nationwide. The Canadian government had a long-standing policy not to return the bodies of children to their home communities but rather to bury them in nearby cemeteries, often on the school grounds. Some of the site plans for the schools include cemeteries, indicating that deaths among schoolchildren were expected and planned for by government officials.

HARRIS: The experience at Penelakut during my term on Council still haunts me. I want to find the remains of children who did not get to go home. I am upset that the institutions that caused the injury to our community have not been strong enough to claim their part and stand with us to bring relief to the wandering souls and their families. Historic trauma must be understood for its cause and for its remedy. Many people will not come to our island, even for traditional gatherings, because they are still haunted by their own painful memories or those memories that are inherited.

MAASS: This industrial school, with its unconscionable death rate, included a large farm and grounds and many outbuildings, all of which were later incorporated into the reserve lands belonging to the Penelakut Tribe. Today, the health and daycare centres are built on its ruins. Although children from many surrounding Indigenous communities attended this school, it has particular resonance for the Penelakut community, in large part because they continue to live daily with its unresolved impact. The TRC's Missing Children and Unmarked Burials project recorded 167 student deaths during the eighty-five years of the school's operation between 1890 and 1975. In those records, a place of burial was found for only four children, and these were passing references in journals or letters rather than exact locations. The school closed in 1975, and the building was demolished in 1980. Nothing remains of the original building or the many outbuildings associated with the school except for a few flights of concrete stairs opposite the government wharf.

HARRIS: What I would like to see is a meeting with our community to talk about what community members have experienced; scientists need to be able to see what we see. This is cultural safety [as recommended in the TRC report] and it points to cultural competency on the part of the officials and scientists who want to help us. Community members, especially traditional ritualists, must be a part of the plan to embark on this search journey; every tribe has a way in their traditions to deal with death, and officials and scientists must come to terms with these local approaches in order for the work to be done in a whole and satisfactory way.

MAASS: Work began at the place Elder Florence James had identified on our first visit to the island in the fall of 2012. Although this small cemetery had become completely overgrown and obscured, it was never hidden from the memories of the survivors of the Kuper School, who had walked past it daily as children. The youth arrived at the site on their bicycles with tools of various kinds to cut brush and later helped operate the ground-penetrating radar equipment. Monty Charlie brought his Bobcat to the site and helped to cut the larger brush with his chainsaw. Elder James smudged the site before work began and stayed to watch over the proceedings and provide guidance while we worked. Three days' work eventually revealed a small cemetery plot with a low stone border dating to the early 1900s. Several small stone crosses were also uncovered, along with a clearly marked headstone belonging to Father G. Donckele, a Belgian priest and the principal in charge of the school until his death in 1907. While this small cemetery appears to contain the burials of school staff, records indicate that at least two children, a young girl who died of a sudden illness on September 3, 1922, and a boy who died of meningitis on March 3, 1924, were also buried "in our little cemetery." The cemetery reference in these records is very probably to this place, located southwest of the former Kuper Island school.

MARTINDALE: In addition to the visible burials of the school staff, we located twelve apparent unmarked burials in rows behind these, most of them the size of children. Monty told us that there was a young girl buried nearby, beside the apple tree; he remembered when she died and how she was quickly buried. We found her, as well.

HARRIS: My community is still coming to terms with the historical trauma of the school, but our leadership must also work to address ongoing needs such as economic development. On the one hand, I appreciate archaeology and the science that will help us, but, on the other hand, I am asking how our traditions will help to heal the pain and grief—the memories—of so many who grieve in silence.

MARTINDALE: Our work is not primarily archaeological, despite the practices we engage in. Working together is as important as what we find. Archaeology is simply a medium through which we, as a partnership of non-Indigenous and Indigenous people, are seeking pathways of remediation that may advance the hope of reconciliation. We listen, we learn, we do what is asked of us, and we stay only as long as we are welcome. We accept the inheritance of our citizenship and the conclusions of the TRC that non-Indigenous Canadians committed cultural genocide on Indigenous peoples.

MAASS: In the case of the IRS system, by deliberately separating children from their parents, Canada consciously attempted to assimilate the children and undermine Indigenous family and community structures, leaving some villages effectively childless. Referencing the UN Convention on the Prevention and Punishment of the Crime of Genocide, some legal scholars and Indigenous leaders argue that these culturally mediated efforts designed to prevent group continuity amount to physical genocide under international law.

HARRIS: I spoke to an Elder who I knew was a traditional funeral worker and asked what we should do. She knew that it was not a matter of looking for remains but rather of embarking on a spirit journey to rescue the ones who still wandered in the memory of the Kuper Island Indian Residential School. It was then, through a spiritual medium, that we began to see the many children who did not get to go home. We were guided to some places where children had fallen. It was only the beginning of the spiritual work of recovering our lost children; many families still grieve for the children who did not make it home. People living on Penelakut Island are still being bothered; the pain and grief continues.

MARTINDALE: Although our partnership makes use of archaeological and archival methods, we recognize that the greatest damage to people exists on a spiritual plane and in the relationship between Indigenous and non-Indigenous Canadians. Thus, our message to non-Indigenous archaeologists—and to Canadians in general—is that reconciliation starts with self-examination and a willingness to acknowledge and find meaning in the spiritual truth of Indigenous knowledge. Our story reminds us of one of the founding principles of multiculturalism: the limits of our understanding are not the limits of all that can be known. The TRC noted that simply knowing the truth about the past is insufficient for reconciliation. Instead, the non-Indigenous community must learn and practise respect. The spiritual resonance of Indian Residential Schools is clear to all people. True reconciliation can arrive only when all Canadians are able to accept that truth.

Anniversary Reading

Sherrill Grace

Literature is the unique bearer of a unique cargo—the cargo of the human imagination.
TIMOTHY FINDLEY, "Turn Down the Volume"[1]

JANUARY 2017: I am rereading two famous Canadian novels: Margaret Atwood's *The Handmaid's Tale* (1985) and Timothy Findley's *Not Wanted on the Voyage* (1984). I first read them shortly after they were published, and I have taught them many times over the years. So why read them again, and why now, when others are rereading Orwell's *1984*?

Because, like Orwell, Atwood predicted a dystopic future in a vision of what America might be like for women and what Canada could represent in such a future. Because Findley warned us about the dangers of autocratic rule and the abuse of language to tell a big lie and produce violent exclusion and oppression; those not wanted on the voyage of Noah's ark are all those who don't agree with Noah. They are, in Primo Levi's words, "the drowned," not "the saved." Because, in 2017, on the 150th anniversary of Canadian Confederation, we are asking ourselves where we stand and how to defend democratic values of tolerance, inclusion, and peace, and because literature does crucial work in the world by helping us imagine a better world. Therefore, my suggested anniversary reading begins with these two cautionary tales, before I turn to Yann Martel's *101 Letters to a Prime Minister* (2012).

Where Atwood and Findley warn about a world in which human rights are denied and reading is forbidden, Martel encourages us to think about the present and future by reading great works of literature, some of which are by Canadians. Over four years, he chose books to send to Stephen Harper, and I applaud Martel's message. Read now, he insisted, while you can, for the joy of reading. Read widely and read Canadian to learn what our writers say about who we are and what roles we can play in the twenty-first century. Every reader's recommendations are personal, of course, and the books I suggest are among those I find most stimulating. The key takeaway is that we read literature and that, this year, we read Canadian.

Although I haven't the space to name 150 books, I hope my recommendations will inspire you to make your own discoveries and compile your own list. Findley never abandoned hope for the human race because he believed, as Samuel Johnson did, that we must "make prayers against despair." My prayers are for more books, especially Canadian books, which help me explore being Canadian and sustain my faith in the power of imagination.

Canadian literature has a long and distinguished history that arguably began in the eighteenth century and has developed in spectacular ways. From works of fiction, non-fiction, and poetry written by white European colonizer-settlers in central and maritime regions of the country, our literature has expanded to include a rich diversity of voices and perspectives on the land, on cities, and on identity. Today we can read works by writers living in and thinking about the entire country, from coast to coast to coast. The stories of First Nations, Afro-Canadians, and new immigrants are now included. We can enjoy books in every genre imaginable—historical fiction, fantasy, detective novels, graphic novels, children's fiction, biography, and autobiography—and we can read translations across French and English Canada. If you read one book a day through 2017, you would get only a taste of what is available.

Where to begin? One place might be with works by the writers we have recently lost. In many ways, 2016 was a traumatic year; for Canadian literature, it saw the deaths of Austin Clarke, Leonard Cohen, and W.P. Kinsella, and it would be hard to name three more different writers. Clarke's *The Polished Hoe* (2002)—a Giller Prize winner—is not set in

Canada, but it explores the tragedy of colonialism and celebrates memory, imagination, and the strength of the human spirit. This novel will shock you and remind you to treasure human rights and democratic freedoms. Cohen's *Beautiful Losers* (1966) will take you back to 1960s Quebec nationalism with a narrator who has "stumbled on the truth about Canada" (43) and is obsessed with an "Indian" saint. Cohen's poetry and songs, like *Flowers for Hitler* (1964) and "Democracy" from his 1992 album *The Future*, will remind you to not forget the past and to safeguard the future. Kinsella's *Shoeless Joe* (1982) is less serious than Clarke's or Cohen's books, but it will entertain the baseball fans among you, while addressing corruption in sport.

Another place to begin your anniversary reading could be with Martel, especially if you value a wise guide. Martel sent books by several important, award-winning Canadians to Prime Minister Harper, including *Generation A* (2009) by Douglas Coupland, *The Tin Flute* (the 1947 English translation of Bonheur d'occasion) by Gabrielle Roy (a masterpiece about a family in Montreal's Saint-Henri quartier that belongs on everyone's list), *Scorched* (*Incendies*) by Wajdi Mouawad (2011), *Selected Poems* (1981) by the late Al Purdy, a founder of modern Canadian poetry with a vernacular Canadian voice like none other, and Chester Brown's graphic novel *Louis Riel* (1999). In fact, Brown's portrayal of Riel is a fine entry point into a wealth of writing about this iconic Canadian figure, who is the hero of the Harry Somers and Mavor Moore opera *Louis Riel*, commissioned in 1967 for another anniversary and receiving a major Canadian Opera Company revival this year. Talk about uncanny timing and timely reminders! Riel stood for human rights and resisting state power; the opera celebrates his vision for a diverse Canada in which love and respect conquer race hatred and the rhetoric of fear.

Runaway (2004), one of Alice Munro's collections of short stories and a Giller Prize winner, was also a pick for the prime minster, but, since 2009, when Martel sent the book to Ottawa, Munro has won the Nobel Prize for Literature, so you might choose to spend several weeks reading all her fine stories. Other prize-winning books could join Munro on your reading voyage, beginning with Madeleine Thien's 2016 novel about a Chinese-Canadian woman discovering her past and the silencing of her ancestors in *Do Not Say We Have Nothing* (winner of both the Giller Prize and a Governor General's Literary Award [GG], and a Man Booker finalist). Consult the CBC online lists, check out "Canada Reads," or look for "Heather's Pick" in the bookstores. You will find *The Illegal* (2015) on those store shelves and read a story about freedom, identity, and long-distance running by Lawrence Hill, author of the prize-winning 2007 bestseller *The Book of Negroes*, which is also now a successful TV serial. Where *The Illegal* considers the fragility of human rights in a fictional setting, *The Book of Negroes* brings black history—with all its courage, achievement, and suffering—home to Canada.

Martel was too modest to send the prime minster any of his own books, but I think he should have. My recommendation is *Beatrice and Virgil* (2010), not because it is about Canada (although the main protagonist is a Canadian writer) but because, like *Not Wanted on the Voyage*, it is a fable about what happens when the rhetoric of intolerance metastasizes into violence. Martel's writing is beautiful; his subject, however, is the Holocaust.

Perhaps you cannot face such grim issues in fiction when there are plenty in real life, and you want lighter reading. No problem. For a timeless, gentle book about growing up on the Prairies, read W.O. Mitchell's *Who Has Seen the Wind* (1947). Or read Roch Carrier's 1979 classic story about our national sport and a Quebec child's mortification with having to wear a Toronto Maple Leafs sweater, *Une abominable feuille d'érable sur la glace (The Hockey Sweater)*. Better still, watch the NFB animated film and let Carrier read it to you and your kids. For a thoughtful look at growing old, try Margaret Laurence's *The Stone Angel* (1964). If you like love stories, read Marian Engel's *Bear* (1976; you'll be surprised), or Frances Itani's *Deafening* (2003; you'll be moved to tears), or Jane Urquhart's *The Stone Carvers* (2001; many kinds of love prevail here over war and prejudice). Why not explore the landscapes and stories of the Canadian North with early masters like Pierre Berton or Farley Mowat (his *Never Cry Wolf* [1963] was adapted into a delightful family movie)? Or be more adventurous and travel with Aritha van Herk to *Places Far from Ellesmere* (1990); her *The Tent Peg* (1981) and *No Fixed Address: An Amorous Journey* (1986) will also carry you north and delight the feminists among you along the way.

If family stories are your thing, then you have much to choose from, and these books will explode your ideas about who is family. Start with Carol Shields's *Unless* (2002), a small masterpiece that mothers who lose children will appreciate, or with Findley's *The Piano Man's Daughter* (1995) for an impressive historical journey across four generations of settler-Canadians, whose lives mirror a changing country. One of my favourite family novels, also a profound meditation on the North, is Tomson Highway's magisterial *Kiss of the Fur Queen* (1998). I think this is one of the best novels ever written by a Canadian, and it will open your eyes to the world of Cree people, their treatment in residential schools, their artistic ambitions and brilliance, and the fate of their homeland—the North—in twentieth- and twenty-first-century Canada. You may also enjoy *All My Relations* (1990), edited by Thomas King. According to King, the idea of community is fundamental to First Nations' literature, which involves landscape, group, and family history. Surely this is true for all people.

But I must also mention novels about the two world wars. Such books are increasingly popular these days as we remember the horrors of the Great War. Canadians have written some of the best novels about both wars in the English language. The obvious place to start is with Timothy Findley's *The Wars* (1977), a GG-winning novel, never out of print, and now listed as Canada's book for the world's required reading on the TED-Ed Blog. Then read Jack Hodgins's *Broken Ground* (1998), Joy Kogawa's *Obasan* (1981), Colin McDougall's *Execution* (1941; the 1989 edition), Alan Cumyn's *The Sojourn* (2003), Michael Crummey's *The Wreckage* (2006), Joseph Boyden's *Three Day Road* (2005), about two Cree soldiers in the First World War, Michael Ondaatje's *The English Patient* (1992; also a successful film), and Anne Michaels's *Fugitive Pieces* (1996), a heartbreaking reflection on intergenerational trauma within a Toronto Jewish family.

When speech becomes hate speech and anger becomes ideology, it is important to ask how a slide into bigotry and violence can be stopped. In January 2017, most Canadians are asking themselves what they can do, and politicians are rushing to proclaim "Canadian values." But politicians cannot tell us what our values are. We must live those values, learn about them, and explore them here. One way to do this is by reading literature—for us now, in 2017, Canadian literature. Artists do not tell us what to think. They encourage us to think, empathize, and imagine. They take us on journeys of discovery, celebrate our freedoms, and warn against tyranny and forgetting. That's what Canadian writers do. They speak in many voices to express the diversity of Canadian culture. They recreate the dramatic landscapes of our country. They explore our history and describe the complex life in our cities. And they often speak truths to all the powers that be. This is a voyage you want to be on.

Other books I have recently read, besides Atwood and Findley, are André Alexis's *Fifteen Dogs* (2015)—a parable about intolerance set in Toronto—and Joseph Boyden's *Wenjack* (2016), suggested to me by my twelve-year-old grandson. Eden Robinson's *Son of Trickster* (2017) is waiting on my desk, as is Kevin Patterson's *News from the Red Desert* (2016). The next time I check the newspaper or go online I will find new things for my reading list and perhaps for a prime minister's list. One thing is certain: I will continue to learn about being Canadian in 2017 and continue to have faith in Gilles Vigneault's words, from the iconic Quebec song "Mon Pays": "À tous les hommes [et femmes] de la terre ma maison c'est votre maison. [...] Ma chanson ... c'est pour toi."

A Greener Future

Janis Sarra and Sally Aitken

A society grows great when old men [and women] plant trees whose shade they know they shall never sit in.
Greek proverb

AS CANADA CELEBRATES 150 years as a nation, it is an opportune time to consider what we are planting for future generations. In our short history, Canada has benefited greatly from resource exploitation, but that benefit has come with the cost of unsustainable greenhouse gas emissions. If we are to nurture the trees that our grandchildren and their children will sit under, we need to act quickly and effectively to scale up for a green future.

The greenhouse effect driving climate change has been known for nearly as long as Canada has been a country, but many Canadians do not understand the science. In 1824, French physicist Joseph Fourier first hypothesized an increase in Earth's temperature with increasing atmospheric carbon dioxide, and, in 1896, Swedish Nobel laureate Svante Arrhenius mathematically predicted global warming. Today, more than 830 climate scientists from eighty countries have recognized the urgent need to address climate change.[1] Denying its existence is akin to denying gravity, yet climate change skepticism persists. A 2016 survey of Canadians found significant persisting skepticism, with over 50 percent of respondents believing climate change is just a natural fluctuation in Earth's temperatures.[2] Of those surveyed, 37 percent also believed that many leading experts question the role of human activity in causing climate change, and 8 percent believed that climate change is not a problem. These perceptions slow meaningful action and increase risks.

A root of the problem is the temporal scale of climate change, which is a barrier to action. As individuals, we are caught in the moment, the day, the year. Our decisions often do not take into account the long-term effects of our actions. We find it difficult to grasp the gradual but insidious multi-generational effects of climate change. The global average change in temperature each year is small and harder to notice than daily, weekly, or seasonal variability in weather, but it is cumulatively substantial and accelerating, with the past three years being the warmest on record since comprehensive measurements began over a century ago. Canada's Arctic is one place where the manifestations of climate change are most pronounced. This "polar amplification" of climate change is evidenced by maximum winter Arctic temperatures that reached a staggering 30°C above average in 2016.[3]

This same short-term horizon affects our capacity to envision scaling up responses. Our economy is highly dependent on fossil fuel production, sale, and export, making it difficult for many to imagine a Canada less reliant on oil and gas. Yet this sector generates more than a quarter of our greenhouse gas emissions, according to government studies. Decisions of corporations are driven by investors whose objective is to maximize short-term returns. This profit imperative means that oil and gas production continues to increase. Politicians plan within political cycles, supporting the climate policies most acceptable to the businesses that financially support them. We set greenhouse gas targets that are far into the future, with politicians knowing that they will not be held accountable for meeting those distant goals.

A second feature of the problem is the spatial challenge. The human brain has difficulty understanding physically distant events. Cognitive neuroscience has documented that empathy and understanding are increased when we experience change in our own lives. The places where climate change is already causing the most damage, such as low-lying South Pacific regions and the high Arctic, are far from the everyday lives of most Canadians. Dying trees and coral reefs and the loss of both sea ice and biodiversity are too removed from the lives of people who have no emotional or physical connection to these ecosystems. Canadians contribute more per capita to increasing greenhouse gases than people in areas currently suffering the worst effects.

The third barrier is the financial scale. The recent drop in oil and gas prices has focused attention on losses—in jobs and in communities—as energy companies go under. Yet, instead of using this downturn to shift direction and plant seeds for the future, we've been concentrating on financing to bolster the existing sector.

Canadians have begun to develop innovative solutions, but we need to branch out further to seriously meet the challenge of both slowing and adapting to climate change. A maturing tree needs roots that acquire water and nutrients, stems that create a strong structure, and leaves that feed all other parts. Similarly, as a nation, we need to nurture multiple complementary strategies through regulatory, financial, and environmental systems to create a safe and green future that reduces climate risk.

We have begun to see initial attempts at national climate change mitigation policies. In October 2016, the federal government announced carbon pricing effective in 2018. However, a unified method for reaching that goal has not yet been established, and this lack of consensus may lead to highly inconsistent approaches to addressing climate change among provinces. The current patchwork of proposals across federal, provincial, and territorial governments will not allow Canada to meet its commitments to reduce emissions by 2030. We must do better.

Going forward, public policy should support and apply leading-edge science more effectively in the transition to sustainability. Governments can adopt equitable, tailored, and effective climate policies, through reforms in finance and governance, and the deployment of green technologies and infrastructure. We need energy standards that require near-zero emissions across all sectors, including vehicles. The decision in Ontario to ban coal-fired power plants and the national plan phasing out coal are big steps forward for both emission reductions and health. In 2016, the Canadian government's estimate of annual health care costs attributable to pollution from coal power was $800 million.[4] Policies should account for the degree to which regions are dependent economically on fossil fuels and create flexible but firm transition standards that achieve our goals and minimize too-rapid adjustments in the economy. Governments at all levels can lead by example and become carbon neutral in their operations—take, for example, Vancouver's Greenest City initiative.

We should immediately stop the $3.3 billion in direct cash subsidies and tax breaks that the federal and provincial governments give annually to oil, gas, and coal producers, and redirect these funds to renewable energy research, development, and production.[5] We should also support training and employment for fossil fuel workers in renewable energy. According to the *Renewable Energy and Jobs Annual Review: 2016*, this sector already employs more people globally than fossil fuel companies do, and there is substantial room for future growth in renewables in Canada (www.irena.org).

Scaling up communities built for active transportation, such as walking and cycling, will reduce emissions and improve health and well-being. Reducing meat consumption will decrease carbon footprints and have positive health effects. Urban forests that cool cities also improve quality of life, while "green" buildings with lower environmental costs usually come with design features that improve human comfort. We have the tools for these endeavours already in hand.

We already possess the technologies to achieve near-zero emissions. The International Energy Agency (IEA) reported in February 2017 that prices are dropping to the point where solar and wind energy are approaching the price of coal-fired electricity in some places. New technologies are becoming accessible to consumers, such as battery systems for homes and cars, electric cars powered by renewable energy, and solar panels built into roof shingles and sidewalks. Building codes play an important role in changing long-term energy consumption. Energy rebates also help social housing agencies, farmers, and lower-income families transition to alternative energy.

France's new *La loi relative à la transition énergétique pour la croissance verte* (Energy Transition for Green Growth Act) is aimed at reducing greenhouse gas emissions, capping fossil fuel production, and increasing renewable energy usage. French companies and financial institutions must now annually disclose the financial risks related to climate change and how they are implementing low-carbon strategies in all activities.[6] Institutional investors must account for how their investment decisions are contributing to the energy and environmental transition to limit global warming. We must learn from France—and other countries, such as Denmark, Sweden, and Germany—and encourage institutional investors, particularly our pension funds, to adopt strategies toward long-term sustainability. Sweden just announced a target to become carbon neutral by 2045; its proposed Climate Act will cut emissions domestically by at least 85 percent from 1990 levels and offset the remaining 15 percent by investing in green projects overseas.

We can scale up financial support. We can finance all the changes needed through a carbon tax that creates incentive for individuals and companies to reduce their emissions. Such a tax is equitable, as it sets a price on carbon emissions and fossil fuel consumption that everyone pays in proportion to use. It is fair when revenues generated are used systemically in support of green technologies and enhancement of natural carbon sinks.

The British Columbia and Alberta governments have made a start. Recent studies show a direct correlation between the British Columbia carbon tax and levels of emissions; carbon emissions have been reduced by three million tonnes since the tax was implemented in 2008, of which 79 percent is directly attributable to the tax. From 2008 to 2014, fuel use in the province dropped 16 percent. The BC carbon tax is revenue neutral, meaning that the revenue from it is directly connected to reducing the transition costs for low-income people, farmers, and some business sectors. Its revenues are helping to finance climate adaptation, as well. Yet the pricing in BC and other provinces, to date, is too low to result in sufficient change; it requires a scaling-up from current rates, as well as implementing regulations that will reduce emissions.[7]

Studies also show that carbon taxation could have a positive effect on GDP if tax revenues are directed to reducing emissions, retooling economic activity, and helping individuals and businesses transition to lower carbon production.[8] We can support positive developments in financing climate adaptation, such as green bonds, while also working to slow the development of speculative products, such as derivatives, that can work counter to green energy. We could introduce a financial transaction tax, such as the one that the European Union is now considering, with the aim of ensuring that the financial sector makes a fair and substantial contribution to climate adaptation.

Realistically, climate mitigation and adaptation require a mix of public funds and private-market finance, but that mix needs to be scaled and appropriate. The Canadian government has announced it will invest $21.9 billion to phase out coal production and increase green infrastructure such as interprovincial electrical grid improvements. Rather than using public funds to bail out existing companies, the government should take an equity stake as it invests in retooling the Canadian economy to address climate change. In this way, the economic benefits of moving to carbon neutrality will accrue back to the taxpayers who are helping to foot the bill.

Canada can make a global contribution by providing support and leadership. The Canadian government recently announced it will spend an additional $7.5 million over five years to help developing nations address climate change. This relatively modest funding will help emerging nations collaborate with partners on clean energy projects, such as new technologies in the energy, water, forestry, and agriculture sectors. This commitment is important and should be increased and planned carefully. We need to ensure that valuable public services are not lost in those countries because of the demands of private-market players.

We can scale up climate change strategies for agriculture and forestry to decrease emissions and to increase the resilience of crops to climate change. We need to adopt agriculture practices that reduce methane production from livestock and manure, and increase carbon sequestration in soil through reduced tilling and the use of cover crops. Reforestation strategies need to recognize uncertainties of climate change—for example, by planting a diversity of species to increase resilience. Like forest companies, the oil and gas sectors must be held accountable for reforestation. Forests impacted by wildfires, insect and disease outbreaks, and human activities should be rehabilitated but only when restoration results in positive gains in carbon sequestration and storage.

Strategies for biodiversity and species conservation need to take into account climate change and the additional stress it will place on already declining populations. Conservation must also consider the greater need to facilitate and assist species migration as climates warm. Old-growth forests are refuges for biodiversity as well as vast carbon storehouses, and their conservation should remain a top priority. Renewable energy developments need to assess and minimize impacts on Canadian species at risk.

Climate policy needs to be led by all of us. Each sector, business, and consumer has a role to play and a contribution to make to our combined future. These photos by conservationist TJ Watt, who works to protect endangered old-growth forests, illustrate the importance of old-growth forests to our future and the potential of new growth that will benefit the generations to come. In our first 150 years, our nation has pioneered many initiatives that have been beneficial to all Canadians—universally accessible health care is one example. In keeping with our traditions, we should lead the process of scaling-up to remedy climate change and create a greener world, at home and around the world.

TJ WATT

Better Democracy

Maxwell Cameron

CANADA HAS AN exemplary democracy, but it is showing signs of stress as it enters its 150th year. It is not that our institutions are deeply flawed, although they could surely be improved. Rather, our democracy is stressed because we are having trouble sharing the burdens of responsibility at a time when citizens are under pressure to compete in an increasingly market-driven world.

Democratic elections often pose existential choices. What kind of country are we? What do we want to be? And by what means can we achieve our ends? These choices test our collective wisdom. We hope and expect that our fellow citizens will select their representatives in a manner consistent with our collective aspirations as a people. If voters fall under the sway of a demagogue, democracy may be undermined. If a majority chooses a party that a substantial minority finds reprehensible, the value of democracy is diminished for the minority. Citizens in a democracy, unlike in other systems of government, have a stake in the moral character and judgment of their fellow citizens and representatives. This shared responsibility is one of democracy's greatest features. And also one of its greatest challenges.

One of the signs of a stressed democracy is declining voter turnout. According to Elections Canada, voter turnout has declined from an average of 76 percent in federal elections in the 1960s and 1970s to around 71 percent in the 1980s and 1990s, and to 63 percent since

2000. For engaged citizens, participation is a civic duty, which is sustained through civic rituals like voting. For apathetic citizens, voting is a bother. They may not care about the outcome or may think voting makes no difference. Or perhaps they believe that all politicians are the same. Whatever the reason, non-participants refuse to partake in the nation's communal political life. As a result, the public sphere is diminished both by their absenteeism and by what it conveys to others—that voting is a waste of time.

Another sign of stress is the lack of interest in politics. Few Canadians are members of political parties, much less active participants in riding associations. As a result, they have little experience with the political process. Ignorance can be as corrosive as apathy. So-called low-information voters often make decisions based on gut instinct, favouring "truthiness" (what feels true) over the truth. This encourages politicians to act manipulatively, for such voters are vulnerable to fake news, dog whistles, scandal mongering, and vote suppression, all of which occur with growing regularity in Canadian elections.

Caught up in the demands of everyday life, many voters are so focused on the short term that they cannot slow down to consider the impact of their decisions on future generations. Preoccupied with their own problems, they may fail to take a more encompassing view of what is good for them and their community. To be better citizens, we need to cultivate empathy—the capacity to feel and see the world from the perspective of others—understanding, and judgment. Otherwise, apathy, ignorance, myopia, and egocentrism may prevent voters from acting in ways that would have the approval of their own better selves. With greater motivation and knowledge, an apathetic or ignorant voter might come to see the importance of voting—and voting wisely. But how and where do we find our better selves?

Democracy in the classical sense (the Greek word is a conjunction of "rule" and "the people") provides mechanisms through which citizens may become more engaged, knowledgeable, empathetic, and aware of the ways in which their own lives are inextricably bound to the fate of their fellow citizens. These mechanisms include deliberation, judgment, collective decision-making, dialogue, and conflict resolution. The more citizens are engaged in deliberative processes of meaningful decisions, the more they are able to understand the perspective of others and see their own problems in the light of larger circumstances. The end result is that citizens can reach more mature and enduring judgments, and that is why democracy is better than its alternatives: it makes for better citizens.

In a representative democracy like Canada, the opportunities for direct participation in decisions affecting one's self and community are limited. Citizens elect their representatives to govern on their behalf, rather than participating directly in self-government. There are few opportunities to participate in deliberation and judgment, to listen and learn from the perspectives of others, and to make decisions of real consequence. Without continuous reinforcement and opportunities for practice, the character and virtue necessary for active citizenship atrophies, and tends to be replaced by apathy, ignorance, short-sightedness, and selfishness. One of the most powerful objections to contemporary liberal democracies is that they do not provide opportunities for the kind of active citizenship necessary to ensure the vibrancy of the practice of democracy.

It is sometimes said that people get the politicians they deserve. It would be more accurate to say that good institutions alone are not sufficient to ensure virtuous citizens and leaders. As Barry Schwartz and Kenneth Sharpe argue in their book *Practical Wisdom*, a capacity for self-government must be cultivated to ensure voters and their representatives are discerning, judicious, responsible, and generous in outlook. What many Canadians see when they look at their representatives is very different, Alison Loat and Michael Macmillan claim in *Tragedy in the Commons*. They often see pandering, toxic negativity, excessive partisanship, and permanent campaigning. They see parties operating like public relations vehicles for candidates who worry more about how they are perceived in the polls than serving the public good; desire for media attention leads politicians to gratuitously attack each other, undermining trust in both politicians and politics. They see political parties exaggerate their differences, to the detriment of their ability to work together to get results. They see politicians who ignore evidence, devalue science, and make ill-informed decisions. They see the influence of money, which forces politicians to be permanent fundraisers, often at the expense of time they could spend legislating and governing.

Many, though not all, of the defects in contemporary democracies can be traced to features of neo-liberal globalization: the promotion of competition in all spheres of life, the overreliance on rules and incentives, and rampant individualism.[1] The heavy-handed use of incentives and rules promotes the desire for external rewards or gratification, rather than the search for fulfillment through activities like citizenship. A self-centred individualism weakens the bonds of attachment to others and can lead to alienation and, in the extreme, mental health problems. Unchecked competition undermines a healthy culture based on the pursuit of happiness, intrinsic rewards of social activity, solidarity with others, and the ability to work together toward common goods. Such values, which are embraced in many Indigenous cultures and in local and neighbourhood associations, are necessary resources for a vibrant democracy, yet they are under constant threat.

So, what are we to do?

Political cultures depend on practices, and the practice of democracy is a good place to start if we wish to make improvements in our political system. The representative institutions of parliamentary democracy need to be supplemented by participatory innovations that provide citizens with opportunities to acquire the skill and know-how necessary for being good citizens and politicians. Participatory budgeting, which could be adopted in many Canadian municipalities, creates opportunities for engaged citizenship by giving neighbours a say in the allocation of part of the municipal budget. Such innovations provide practical and experiential training for democratic citizenship. Citizens assemblies, in which randomly selected members of the public are given the opportunity to deliberate and propose legislation, are another participatory innovation with the potential to enrich the everyday experience of citizens. Even traditional institutions like schools and universities can do more to prepare people for public life by creating spaces in which individuals can experiment with the activities of representation, deliberation, legislation, coalition building, and conflict resolution. Mock parliaments in high school motivate students to vote when they come of age.

This is not to say that we should not also strive to improve our democratic institutions. For example, some form of proportional representation might mitigate Canada's highly adversarial and hyper-partisan politics. In the short term, hope for electoral reform has been frustrated precisely because of the kind of partisan logic entrenched within the current first past the post system. The failure underscores the need to create well-designed deliberative procedures when crafting reforms—not poorly conceived town hall meetings or superficial Internet quizzes. Even without institutional reform, however, change can come through organizational innovation. For example, Canadian political parties are due for an overhaul. Party discipline needs to be relaxed and more power given to caucus rather than to party leaders. Nomination processes need to be more transparent and better regulated. Parties need to be more deeply rooted in civil society and more democratic in their internal functioning.

More fundamentally, preserving the vitality of democratic practices and institutions demands that we counteract the forces promoting competitive maximizing and individualistic self-gratification. Competitive maximizing may be desirable in the context of business, provided it is well regulated. But when the ethos of competitive maximizing spills over into other spheres of public life, it corrupts and demoralizes institutions necessary for good government. The democratic case for rolling back the rights of corporations is a persuasive one, and we need to seriously rethink the idea of corporate personhood. One cannot attribute to corporations such attitudes as care or responsibility, which are essential for moral agency. Corporations should, therefore, be barred from funding political parties, think tanks, and schools, and their public licence to operate should be conditional upon business practices that advance human needs and environmental sustainability.

To rein in the ethos of competition, it is necessary for politicians to downgrade economic growth and unfettered competitiveness as policy objectives, and emphasize well-being and happiness. Such a "human development" approach offers a powerful alternative to economic growth. Indeed, many countries are beginning to integrate the goal of happiness in policy-making. Bhutan, for example, has pioneered the concept of gross national happiness to replace the gross national product.[2] In Latin America, Indigenous social movements have sparked a lively debate about how to replace a materialistic concept of the good life with *sumak kawsay:* living well, in harmony with nature and others. One way to promote the objectives of such movements is by constitution-alizing rights that enable non-material fulfillment, including a healthy environment, education, high-quality public child care, and health care. Recognizing Canada's Indigenous legal and constitutional traditions opens a pathway to similar sources of the wisdom necessary for collective flourishing.

Canada's sesquicentennial marks an occasion for celebration but not complacency. If democracy is to thrive, it must offer meaningful opportunities for participation and collective decision-making. For a country like Canada, the risk for future generations is not that democracy will be abandoned or overthrown, but that it will be diminished, corroded, and hollowed out by the more powerful forces of the global marketplace. The struggle for democracy is ultimately an effort to ensure that our institutions provide a process through which citizens can find meaningful answers to existential questions. What do we, as a country, wish to do and be? What is good for Canada, as a nation? In seeking answers to these questions, we must strive to perfect our democratic institutions to serve our better selves.

Two Stories

Margot Young and Ed Broadbent

IT IS A MUCH overused phrase, but Canadians, nonetheless, continue to refer to Canada as a "kinder and gentler nation." Events to the immediate south of us may make this seem true, but we should guard against complacency. Looking at Canada on its own, or with a broader lens that pulls other countries into comparative focus, the picture is more complicated.

Indeed, there are two stories to be told about Canada on the 150th anniversary of Confederation. Each speaks to the question of how fair, just, and equal our society is. From one perspective, Canada rightly prides itself on embracing the core values of equality and tolerance. We hear this Canada in Prime Minister Trudeau's February 2017 speech to the European Parliament about Canadian values: "We believe in democracy, transparency, and the rule of law. We believe in human rights. We believe in inclusion and diversity." The other story, however, is darker: it tells a tale of human rights failures, growing inequality, and diminished tolerance. This second frame is captured by the observation from then United Nations high commissioner for human rights, Louise Arbour, in her 2005 LaFontaine-Baldwin Lecture that "poverty and gross inequalities [persist] in our own backyard." How is it, she continues, that "such glaring disparities prevail in a country such as [Canada], a wealthy, culturally diverse, cosmopolitan democracy?"

At stake in each of the two contrasting perspectives is the idea of citizenship—broadly understood—and what it means in Canada. This reference is to citizenship not as a formal legal status, but as an indication of social, political, and legal inclusion in a community. It is a focus that returns us to the insights of T.H. Marshall, a mid-twentieth-century sociologist who, in a famous 1950 essay, "Citizenship and Social Class," formulated the notion of social citizenship, supplementing recognition of political and civil rights with a call for the substantive guarantees of social and economic rights. Social and economic rights are entitlements to the material needs of life—to such things as economic well-being, housing, health care, education, and food security. For Western democracies like Canada, these new rights—core social democratic values—transformed the nature of citizenship.

Marshall's expansion of the meaning of citizenship dovetails with the emergence of modern usage of the term "social justice." Marshall's social citizen is the one to whom social justice is owed. This notion of social justice responds to the ravages of the Industrial Revolution and its laissez-faire economics. And, for Marshall, the linkage with citizenship followed on the heels of the "searing experiences"[1] of the Great Depression and the Second World War. It is worth pointing out that social rights are the result of political struggle led by labour, socialist, and social democratic parties. As Canadian political scientist Janine Brodie argues, social justice demands equality, assigns responsibility for that equality to our public political institutions, and requires just redistribution of the resources required to achieve substantive equality.[2] Without this just distribution, the protections of political liberty and of economic choice are meaningless. Social justice need not necessarily, or only, be cast in the language of human rights. But rights are effective currency for conveying an immediacy of need and the accountability of the state to address marginalization and deprivation.

Alleviation of material inequality thus became a requirement of justice and a matter of state responsibility; recognition of the "social" is counterpoint to the individualism of classical liberalism, and foil to present-day neo-liberalism. And, again as Brodie notes, the ideals of social citizenship and of social justice feed the national identity of Canadians as distinct from "their less caring and less sharing" neighbours to the south.

Canadian notions of social citizenship today are more attentive to how race and gender, for example, configure status in society. Feminists, critical race scholars, and, in the recent Canadian context, Indigenous thinkers have deepened this ideal. For example, citizenship for Indigenous peoples is layered; it is experienced both in relation to the larger Canadian society and from the context of their own Indigenous communities, and, for many, it is intrinsically linked to the land. This more nuanced understanding of social identities and citizenship has allowed keener investigation of the social practices, norms, and rules that grant effective citizenship.

The 150 years since Confederation have seen both high and low points of social citizenship: it is a history of human rights and social justice achievements and failures. The story that celebrates Canada names us as a country of sophisticated human rights understanding and an advanced legal and political system to protect those rights. We hear of twentieth-century Canada active in the field of human rights and social justice. Indeed, as in democracies around the world, the post war period in Canada was a time of growing social consciousness. We are often told of a Canadian's role in the 1948 Universal Declaration of Human Rights: John Humphrey, a former McGill University professor, produced the document's first draft. Enactment of modern human rights law gained steam in this period as the provinces and the federal government, one by one, put human rights codes—protections against discrimination—in place. Ontario's 1944 Racial Discrimination Act was followed in 1947 by the Saskatchewan Bill of Rights Act, the first comprehensive statute. By 1977, every jurisdiction in Canada had a human rights code. With the exception of the broader codes of Saskatchewan and Quebec, these were primarily anti-discrimination laws. In 1960, Diefenbaker's government enacted the Canadian Bill of Rights, legislation granting a range of civil and political rights within federal jurisdiction.

This notion of equality rights–based citizenship went hand in hand with the development of the welfare state and its goal of maximizing the collective well-being of citizens. In Canada, key social and economic programs were launched, aimed at furthering equality and economic welfare: the Canada Pension Plan, Old Age Security, family assistance, unemployment insurance—all gave form to a commitment to social citizenship, delivered through universal social programs. This was the beginning of Canada's modern welfare state. By 1972, our public health insurance system had been created. Begun in Saskatchewan in 1962, the commitment to universal access to health care was now national.

Finally, in 1982, the Canadian Charter of Rights and Freedoms, Canada's constitutional bill of rights, was enacted. Now, at its thirty-fifth anniversary, it's clear that the Charter has ushered in significant changes, and it has altered the language of how we talk about citizenship. In 1989, the Supreme Court of Canada decided its first equality case, *Andrews v. Law Society of British Columbia*. This decision about citizenship and practicing law launched the notion of substantive equality into Canada's legal and political landscape. Substantive equality advances equality beyond merely formal same treatment to nuanced understanding of how context, material circumstances, and identity shape experience of the law and state power. Statistics Canada's 2013 Social Identity Survey found that 90 percent of Canadians regard the Charter to be an important symbol of Canadian identity. (Hockey was lower at 77 percent.) Ninety-two percent said human rights were a shared value. We have come to see government accountability for rights as unexceptional.

This rosy story, however, fades, to be replaced by another. The Charter has been, for many, a disappointment. Those most in need of rights are, too often, those least covered by its protections. Charter litigation is expensive and lengthy. Cases that push at the greatest inequalities in our society—claims for housing rights, decent income supports—have been time after time thrown out by the courts. The poor are Canada's "constitutional castaways."[3] That key partnership Marshall first articulated between civil/political rights and social/economic rights lies neglected by our courts.

And we need our courts because our governments now increasingly disregard the guarantees of social citizenship. The 1990s saw a recasting of the social contract of the postwar years. Austerity became the order of the day, and both federal and provincial governments rolled back social programs, like unemployment insurance (transformed to the Orwellian-named Employment Insurance), legal aid, employment equity, and income assistance. Nascent, much-needed services like a federal public child care plan were cancelled. Even our universal, single-payer health care system is under threat as the business model of health care delivery deploys Charter rights in our courts to dismantle the structures of our system. One symbol of the Canadian difference—the Charter—is used to challenge another—our health guarantees.

As well, taxation has become less progressive as tax credits and deductions increasingly favour the affluent, and as the role regressive consumption taxes and user fees play is enhanced. In the late 1980s and the early 1990s, Canada was one of the OECD leaders in using government taxes and transfers to tighten the gap between rich and poor. By the late 1990s and early 2000s, after cuts to social programs and the taxes that once funded them, Canada had joined those OECD countries with the smallest redistributive impact.[4]

The result is a Canada that, today, is marked by great inequality, a condition that has grown significantly since the 1980s. The Conference Board of Canada recently gave Canada a C grade, ranking us twelfth out of seventeen peer countries in terms of income equality. As of 2010, the richest 20 percent of our population is the only group to have increased its share of national income over the past twenty years. We live in a "second Gilded Age": income and wealth are concentrated in a small percentage of the population—the rich and the super rich—while those at the bottom lie far below acceptable standards of well-being. We are a country of haves and the desperate have-nots. We are, simply, less generous and just a nation.

What does the resulting poverty look like? It has an Indigenous face, for example. A 2016 study found that Indigenous children are twice as likely to live in poverty as non-Indigenous children: the poverty rate for children on reserves is 60 percent. Children of immigrants have a poverty rate of 32 percent. By comparison, children who are non-Indigenous, non-racialized, and non-immigrant have a poverty rate of 13 percent. All of these numbers are too high. And children are poor because their parents—for many, their sole-parent mothers—are poor. Poverty also has a female face. Indeed, those groups most in need of the promise of progressive social citizenship are the groups our economy, government, and courts most neglect. The resulting inequality imperils well-being and challenges our commitment to a healthy society and to fair opportunities for all to develop and flourish in Canada. According to Nobel Laureate Joseph Stiglitz, it is even bad for economic growth.

This second story is in sharp contrast to the first. Yet, both are true, and it is in the tension between the two where our best hope for a just society may lie. Poll after poll shows that Canadians do not like this rising inequality, that we are proud of our human rights heritage, and that we value our country's reputation for tolerating difference and diversity. A survey from 2011 showed that Canadians self-report as accepting of people from different racial, ethnic, and cultural groups,[5] and, in another recent poll, equality, equity, and social justice came first as top Canadian values (25.2 percent).[6] That said, recent polling data also indicate that tolerance may be decreasing: in a poll from 2015, 68 percent of Canadians agreed that minorities should do more to fit in with mainstream society.[7] Of course, answers to a survey are different from behaviours in the real world, but here, the picture is also mixed. Discussions in our political sphere about niqabs, immigration, and welfare rates—to assemble a few disparate examples—are disheartening. However, the warm welcome by so many Canadians to the thousands of arriving Syrian refugees has been very encouraging.

Canada's soul is up for grabs. We need to remind ourselves of the better part of our history and our political culture. Social and economic rights—nuanced by feminists and others—need to re-emerge as common expectations, fulfilled and embraced by both our governments and our courts. Instead of the "secession of the affluent,"[8] Canada must recalibrate its welfare state to ensure the inclusion of the currently marginalized and dispossessed. When we speak of our aspirations for a just society and when we speak to the international community, we must be frank about ourselves but also draw upon our best traditions. The joint telling of the two stories that animate this essay frames Canada's social justice challenges and possibilities. The tension between these different pictures of Canada tells us what we need to do; it tells us that we care that we have failed to become the country we pride ourselves on already being.

above: Masset, Haida Gwaii | MIMI LAM

facing: Koreatown, Bloor Street,
Toronto, Ontario | VICTORIA GENERAL

facing: Burnaby, British Columbia | COLOMBE LANE

above: ASHIK HOSSAIN

A Quantum Parable

Philip Stamp

RECENT REMARKS BY Canadian Prime Minister Justin Trudeau—including a highly publicized press conference about quantum computing in May 2016—have signalled that, on the eve of Canada's 150th anniversary, there is a new wave of determination in Ottawa to put Canada on the world's technological map. In choosing quantum computing as his theme, Trudeau was selecting a hot topic, one very much in the news these days. Moreover, he had in mind a technology that was actually pioneered in Canada, by the company D-Wave Systems, currently based in Burnaby, BC. So, does this herald a new golden age for Canadian R & D?

There is precedent here for some skepticism. For when it comes to science and technology, Ottawa has a long history of talking the talk but not walking the walk—and there are clear warning signs here. In recent months, the controversial MacDonald Dettwiler story has resurfaced in the news;[1] this Richmond, BC–based company managed, during the period from 1990 to 2005, to corner much of the world market in sophisticated satellite surveillance, as well as to design and build the famous Canadarm for the American space shuttle. And yet the company has now shifted its focus to the US, a move that became almost inevitable once the Harper government decided to pull back from investing in aerospace. Canada's future in space has been uncertain for years, even according to reviews prepared by the Canadian government.[2]

Such hesitance from Ottawa is not new. Those with long memories, or an interest in Canadian history, will recall the infamous Avro Arrow story, one of the most remarkable betrayals of a Canadian industry by a Canadian government. Immortalized in the press, books, and a 1996 CBC film entitled *The Arrow* and starring Dan Aykroyd (to date the most-watched CBC show ever made), the Avro story has acquired mythical proportions in the Canadian consciousness and is still worth relating.

In October 1957, Avro was the third-largest company in Canada, employing fifty thousand people, and it had just rolled out the world's most advanced fighter aircraft, the CF-105 Avro Arrow. The Arrow was entirely designed and built in Canada by an extraordinary team spearheaded by Crawford Gordon Jr. How Canada came to take the lead from the world's superpowers, and how it could have gone on to become a big high-tech player, has provided material for historians and journalists for many years. But the reality turned out to be very different. In February 1959, the Diefenbaker government cancelled the Arrow project and ordered all the Arrow aircraft—as well as the blueprints, models, and designs—to be destroyed. The government tried to argue that cash was short and that the future of defence was in missiles. They accordingly bought from the US a collection of Boeing Bomarc missiles, which turned out to be useless. Later on, when the political dust had settled, the government bought sixty-four secondhand Voodoo fighters (capable of less than half the speed of the Arrow), also from the US. The total value of these purchases amounted to more than the cost of the entire Arrow program.

Diefenbaker's actions destroyed far more than just the Arrow project. Before long, almost all of the talent responsible for the company's success had left Canada, with many former employees going on to play key roles in the design of the supersonic Concorde civil airliner and the hardware for the American Apollo and Gemini space programs. The damage to Canadian aerospace, to national self-esteem, and to other innovative technological efforts was colossal and far-reaching. And this history echoes into the current day. In 2017, Canadian aerospace policy is dominated in the news by the attempt to buy, at fantastic cost, a set of sixty-five unproven F-35 fighter planes from Lockheed Martin. Apparently, Canada remains dependent on foreign suppliers for military aircraft; what will happen in the civil aviation sphere now seems to rest largely on the fate of the Quebec-based company Bombardier.

So, given this fifty-year history, we can certainly ask: What hope is there for Canadian high tech on the world stage? And what of quantum computing?

The advent of quantum computation (and, more generally, of quantum information processing or QIP for short) will likely have as great an impact on the twenty-first century as aerospace did on the twentieth century. As one might expect of anything with the word "quantum" in it, QIP is a little harder to understand than flight, but we think the effort is worthwhile. QIP depends on quantum mechanics, the game-changing theory discovered in 1925 by Heisenberg, Schrödinger, and others. Until 1925, it was universally assumed that all objects in the universe, from the smallest elementary particles to the largest cosmic structures, could exist in only one physical state at a given time—what we now call a "classical state." The idea that a molecule could be in several different places at once, or that an electronic circuit could carry two different electric currents at the same time, would have been ridiculed before 1925. However, the nonsensical has now become fundamental—in spite of enormous efforts to show that quantum mechanics must fail, it has withstood all tests and has, along with Einstein's theory of space-time and gravity, extended our understanding of the physical world from subnuclear scales up to the entire universe. The idea that physical systems can be in "superpositions of states"—in several states at once—is here to stay.

Around 1980, the renowned American physicist Richard Feynman noted that such superpositions must also apply to any kind of information, and hence to any information processing system. Thus, a computer could be in a superposition of different computations, a database in a superposition of different searches, a data transmission in a superposition of different coded messages, and so on. The ability to run many computations simultaneously meant that quantum computers would be almost unimaginably powerful. Early ideas included quantum decryption (allowing the decryption of any classical message—past, present, or future—with ease) and quantum encryption (encoding messages beyond the reach of any conceivable classical computer). Other ideas included ultrafast data searches, computations, and optimization (the search among many different scenarios or outcomes for the one best satisfying certain predefined criteria). All of these relied on the possibility of having exponentially many operations going on at once—superposed—in a single physical system.

However, what really counts in a game like this is to actually make a quantum computer—and this is what D-Wave did. Its "quantum optimizer" has now attracted enormous attention, with a cover article in *Time* magazine and the purchase of D-Wave computers in the US by Lockheed, NASA, and Google, as well as by several US universities, the Los Alamos National Laboratory, and a data security company. In response to this success, there have been major investments by a number of large corporations and governments. Within the space of a single year (2016), the European community announced a $1.5-billion research initiative in quantum computing; the Chinese government, in collaboration with Austria, launched a $500-million satellite intended to accomplish global quantum communication; and in an announcement of enormous hubris, Google published a plan for world domination of the new field. It is nevertheless amusing to observers that all the Google and European Union publicity so far has featured photos of D-Wave processors.

Obviously, in a game this big, these are merely the opening gambits—there are still many moves left to play. The D-Wave quantum optimizer is not a full-blooded "gated" quantum computer, which will require solving the difficult problem of eliminating what is called "decoherence," the process by which even tiny interactions of the computer with its surroundings disrupt the very delicate correlations between the different parts of a superposition. Suppressing decoherence requires extraordinary control over these minute interactions, and thus remains a significant challenge. More radical designs—like the "topological quantum computer" advocated by Microsoft—are even further in the future. But this simply means that fortune will favour not only the brave but also the persistent, those in for the long haul.

So will Canada stay in the game? A complaint often directed at Ottawa over the years has been about its inability to engage in ambitious long-term planning, both domestically and in foreign affairs. So far, the federal interest in quantum computing has concentrated on style over substance—the majority of D-Wave's funding has come from the US, and there has been little effort to bring together the Canadian university research community in this field with the R & D effort in Canadian industry (a mistake not being made in other countries). But there is still time for both Ottawa and the provincial governments to focus, to maintain the momentum already gained, and to make sure that an Avro-style hemorrhage of talent does not occur again. For Canada's 150th anniversary, it would be refreshing to see a daring and ambitious effort in this direction, with a clear desire in Ottawa to stay the course.

But herein lies the root of the problem. For great enterprises of this kind to succeed—whether it is an Avro Arrow, an Apollo moon shot, or even an agenda for social change like that advocated by the Truth and Reconciliation Commission of Canada—the participants must feel inspired by what appears to be a lofty goal and believe they can succeed in attaining it. Canadians, however, are not used to the idea of taking on the world and winning (except perhaps in winter sports). To get past this, we clearly need a commitment by the federal and/or provincial governments to give real backing to such enterprises. But, perhaps even more than this, what is required is a change of mindset in the country as a whole. And this is where strong and visionary political leadership can make a big difference: first by inspiring the country to believe that we really can succeed, and then by making sure that small groups of dedicated people get the support they need. It will not be enough here to say "Yes, we can," or to have photo ops about quantum computation. Nearly a dozen other countries are now seriously investing in quantum computation, with a mixture of private and government capital. If we really believe that Canada is capable of playing in such a high-stakes game, then we should also get serious and get on with it—now, before the Canadian advantage is lost and the enthusiasm (and the people) drain away.

Perhaps by the time of Canada's 200th anniversary, in 2067, Canadians will be able to proudly say that their country has finally succeeded in playing (and winning) at the big table. This would befit a country that already has four times the population of both Switzerland and Sweden (two big international high-tech players) and that is projected to have a larger population by 2067 than any European country except Germany. The Trudeau government has promised change—now as we look to the future is the time for Canada to deliver.

Welcome to the Revolution

Kim Brooks

IF YOU WERE able to close your eyes in 1867 and open them in 2017, you'd find that Canada was a surprisingly different place. Women have made sure of that.

The revolution has come along two axes. First, there is the dramatic increase in women's participation in every aspect of public life—from education to the paid workforce, to public office, to science and the arts. Second, there is the effect of that engagement on the way Canada has evolved. If you could close your eyes again, take women's public participation out of the equation, and then open them, Canada would be an impoverished version of itself. We would know less and be less. Writing two thousand words on women in Canada is like asking an author to write about Canada, period.

This essay could be filled with facts showing how the last 150 years have witnessed a revolution in women's equality and making the point that women in Canada have revolutionized who we are. But the point might be more elegantly conveyed by offering the stories of six women: one for each quarter-century of Canada's 150-year (post-Confederation) history. These stories are not representative; they are partial and refractive. They remind us that the revolution is everywhere—from your grandmother, to the theatre in your region, to Parliament Hill, to your neighbourhood school.

More specifically, these stories are designed to take you from sport to education to religion to art to counselling to science and politics. They will carry you from Nova Scotia to British Columbia, with stops in Quebec and Ontario and Nunavik. They reveal something of the range of women's experiences in Canada—coming from low-income and wealthy families, from Indigenous communities and other countries. Each of the six women is extraordinary in her own way, and each could be your mother, sister, grandmother, or neighbour. Naturally, accuracy and completeness in relaying something of each woman's life is impossible: women's stories are rarely captured, and for some of these women, accounts conflict. Nevertheless, the stories reveal the greatness that resides in all women: the possibility to change the world and the gumption to do it in the face of resistance.

The analogy "It's like riding a bike," meant to suggest that something once hard becomes ingrained and axiomatic, has not always been meaningful for women. In the early days of cycling, women's participation was actively discouraged. But Louise Armaindo, who was born in Saint-Clet, Quebec, defied the strictures of her sex and entered the then-still-nascent world of cycling competition. As "the champion female bicycle rider of the world," she had to travel to the United States to compete, against men. Armaindo raced for fifty miles against John Prince in Boston in 1882, losing by a minute. Her real passion, though, was the six-day race. Her racing career is reported to have come to an end in 1896 in Buffalo, following injury in a hotel fire.[1]

If riding a bike was hard for women in Canada's early days, so was learning about its physics or enrolling in any other course of university study. When Margaret Florence Newcombe (later Trueman) entered Dalhousie University, alongside one other woman student, Principal Reverend James Ross asked whether they would be taking master of arts or master of hearts degrees. Newcombe studied English literature and history and carried a Munro bursary. Upon graduation in 1885, she taught at the Halifax Ladies' College and became the school's principal. She retired in 1918 and died in 1935. The Women's Division of the Dalhousie Alumni Association offers an entrance scholarship in her name. Imagine how important it must have been for Newcombe to access university education. The epitaph on her grave in the Cornwallis Reformed

Presbyterian Covenanter Church in West Cornwallis, Nova Scotia, reads only: "First Woman Graduate of Dalhousie University."

Reverend Addie Aylestock's life doesn't start in Nova Scotia, but her path leads there. Aylestock, the first black woman to be ordained in Canada (in 1951), travelled a few career paths. Born in Glen Allen, Ontario, she worked as a domestic servant and dressmaker before graduating in 1945 from the Toronto Bible College in her mid-thirties. Aylestock dreamed of working in Africa. She got as far as Nova Scotia, where she held her first post in Africville, a black community in Halifax. It must have been a substantially different flock from the largely white Methodist church she attended as a child. That post was followed with posts in Montreal, Toronto, and Owen Sound. Reverend Aylestock died in 1998 in Toronto.[2]

Not long after Reverend Aylestock found her calling, Marcelle Ferron became the only woman artist, and one of the youngest, to sign the Refus Global, urging Quebec to open up to the world with the famous call "To hell with the holy-water-sprinkler and the tuque!" Ferron was born in Louiseville, Quebec, in 1924 to a middle-class Québécois family. Osseous tuberculosis left Ferron with a disability. She started her studies at the École des Beaux-Arts, but she left the school (or was possibly expelled) before graduating. After separating from her husband, Ferron ventured with her three daughters to Paris, where she pursued drawing and painting and eventually turned to stained glass. She returned to Montreal, perhaps having been ousted from France. Her stained-glass piece in the Champ-de-Mars metro station in Montreal in 1968 is a major contribution to public art. As Ferron has claimed, "Mon propos a toujours été modeste, je voulais transformer ce mariage de raison en un mariage d'amour."[3] She died in 2001.

We got lucky in 1972 when Baljit Sethi arrived in Canada. Like Ferron, she is an artist.[4] But, despite her love of art and her dream of studying medicine, her counselling talents became her way of making a difference. Precluded from using her education training in Canada, she founded the Immigrant and Multicultural Services Society (IMSS) of Prince George in 1976. Her experiences and expertise with racism informed the multicultural and anti-racism projects she developed. She has documented the experiences of senior immigrants who arrived in Canada as young people.

In search of change, the spirit of the women in these profiles also characterizes the life of Mary Simon. Simon was born in Kangiqsua-lujjuaq, Nunavik, in 1947. She attended a federal day school in Kuujjuaq until she completed grade six. After that she was homeschooled.[5] Simon worked initially as a producer and announcer for CBC North. Her passion, though, as protector of the Arctic become apparent during her service as president of Makivik Corporation and president of the Inuit Circumpolar Conference. It has led her to Parliament Hill, where she is serving as the Minister of Indigenous Affairs' special representative on the Arctic.

Revolution is not the result of a small number of individual women with high profiles working hard, although that can undoubtedly help. It is the consequence of millions of women who have, over the last 150 years, got out of bed (then likely made that bed, the beds of other family members, and breakfast, then washed the dishes, carried out the compost, and packed lunches, all before the day for some people begins) and did what they saw needed to be done. Women like those profiled above. We owe them gratitude.

Disappointingly, in spite of that effort and its effect in transforming Canada, there are many ways in which women's equality has not yet been attained—from pay equity to representation in Parliament. The revolution does, will, and must continue.

Caring for Health

**Paul Allison, Jean Gray, Carol Herbert,
Louise Nasmith, Christian Naus,
Sioban Nelson, and Catharine Whiteside**

FOR THE FIRST time in the 150-year history of Canadian Confederation, Canadian youth may expect a shorter lifespan than their parents. This possibility is reflected in sobering statistics about our inactive lifestyles, rates of obesity, and an epidemic of diabetes and other chronic health conditions found across the country. But if our health is suffering, it's not because we don't spend enough on health care.

Among countries that have comparable accounting systems in the Organisation for Economic Co-operation and Development (OECD), Canada is in the top 25 percent for per capita spending on health care. Total health care expenditure in this country reached almost $220 billion, or $6,105 per citizen, in 2015. This expenditure represents almost 11 percent of Canada's gross domestic product and is the largest single provincial expense in Canada. And yet, many of our health indicators and outcomes lag behind those of comparable OECD countries.

Take, for example, the issue of wait times. Canada has among the longest wait times among OECD peers for specialist services, and all Canadian provinces have longer wait times than the international average. Those who have waited for any manner of non-emergency procedures (think knee replacement) will understand this viscerally.

Measured against other OECD countries, Canada performs poorly in several areas: its infant mortality rate is worse than the average and its adult obesity rate is second only to the US at 18 percent. On a brighter note, Canada does have one of the lowest daily smoking rates and a lower overall stroke mortality rate than most OECD countries.[1]

Why are we spending so much on health care in Canada yet remaining dissatisfied with the outcomes?

We must acknowledge, up front, that good health requires more than an acute-care medical system. Health, it turns out, is more than health care—and evidence shows that health status is influenced by a number of factors outside of the health system. Robust data show that addressing the social determinants of health—including poverty, affordable housing, food security, and geographic and social isolation—is critical to healthy living. On the whole, our governments do a poor job of addressing these critical social and environmental factors that also affect our health. This is particularly true for Indigenous, inner-city, and rural communities, as well as for those people isolated by language or culture, such as recent immigrants.

There are many concrete steps we can take to transform how care is delivered in Canada to better respond to today's health challenges. And many will be surprised to hear that these solutions don't necessarily mean putting more money into the system.

Where to begin?

First, we have to start listening to Canadians, who want to be treated as people, not as individual diseases. They are asking for a more holistic approach to our health care system that ensures equity of access to services.

Historically, the Canadian health care system has been oriented toward the provision of acute care—we visit hospital emergency rooms for urgent-care concerns, for example, or see our doctors if we have specific ailments. Our system functions well for these single disease-focused health issues. But this acute-care model is ill-suited for the management of multiple illnesses and chronic conditions—the reality of our health needs today.

In 2014, close to 40 percent of Canadian adults reported that they had at least one of ten common chronic conditions, including arthritis, cancer, emphysema or chronic obstructive pulmonary disease, diabetes, heart disease, high blood pressure, mood disorders, and poor oral health. Some individuals have a single condition, whereas others suffer from co-morbidities (issues caused by the initial condition, such as renal failure resulting from diabetes) or deal with multi-morbidities (multiple unrelated conditions, such as diabetes, asthma, tooth decay, osteoarthritis, and depression, experienced at the same time). It is a little-known fact that dental decay remains the most common chronic disease among Canadians, affecting the large majority of the population at some stage in life. There are well-established direct links between some oral illnesses and conditions and diseases elsewhere in the body.[2]

Our society and health system have become increasingly geared toward "quick fixes" by "experts." But this model doesn't help people with chronic conditions, who depend on a wide range of experts to provide assistance that is as seamless as possible as they move between primary, acute, and specialty care, and between the public- and private-care sectors. The end result is that too many people with chronic ailments spend too much time going from one specialty appointment to the next, which adversely affects the quality of their lives—and costs the health system large sums in the process. From the patient perspective, there are no real distinctions between primary care, acute care, specialty care, or community care—there is simply health care, which should focus on them as individuals.

Models of health funding have only exacerbated the problem. Our health system is not integrated and still functions in silos. In most provinces, the bulk of health funding has been directed toward hospitals and acute-care delivery, with some shifts into the community. For example, physicians continue to be paid through a separate budget from other health care professionals. The private dental system and other non–publicly funded services, such as physiotherapy and optometry, accentuate the inequalities in care. More vulnerable Canadians—such as the elderly, those with disabilities, those living and working in poverty, and recent immigrants and refugees—are at greater risk for chronic illnesses and their impacts.

The goals of acute-care delivery are also necessarily different from what patients need today to address their chronic health conditions. The trajectory of chronic conditions varies substantially over time, as context, age, life situations, and other factors shift. Chronic conditions are with people for the remainder of their lives. This means that the goal of chronic care, unlike that of acute care, is generally not to cure but to enhance physical, cognitive, and social function, as well as quality of life, and to prevent secondary conditions and minimize distressing symptoms. Again, our current health models fall short.

Going forward, how can we best address the needs of chronic-care patients within the Canadian health care system?

The challenge in achieving the care goals for people with chronic conditions is not so much determining what to do but being clear about the priorities and bold steps that are necessary to make it happen. Policies and decisions must be informed by sound research that, in turn, can be used for on-the-ground adaptations to improve practice and care. And the patient and their family should be at the centre. At present, service provision is too often dictated by professional needs and driven by professional associations or regulatory bodies. We believe that scopes of practice for health professionals should follow models of care that best meet community and population health needs. In other words, we need health care delivery that's based on the patient profile, not the professional profile.

How do we get there?

The Canadian Academy of Health Sciences (CAHS) recommends that primary health care providers and teams act as the critical hub for a comprehensive, person-centred, integrated model of care. This would help to improve health care–system efficiency, improve patient outcomes and satisfaction, and, most importantly, enhance quality of care.[3] However, such a model of care delivery would require a shift to team-based, interprofessional caregiving. By placing the emphasis on health teams rather than on individual health practitioners, we could then provide the needed comprehensive services in a more seamless way for those with chronic conditions. A team-based approach would help to coordinate care with acute, specialty, and community services throughout the patient's lifespan.

To achieve this, we must first recognize what we need. Currently, we have limited understanding of whether we have the right configuration of scopes of practice and professionals with appropriate skills to meet the current and future needs of the population. Health workforce planning is being undertaken by federal and provincial governments, often using a profession-specific lens based on old models (e.g., doctor–population ratios). These models should factor in population health needs, contextual realities (rural versus urban), and measures taken to make sure that professionals work to their full scope of practice.

Second, we will need to provide extra training where it is needed. For example, nurses with additional training could serve as nurse practitioners in specifically defined areas and achieve good outcomes and high patient satisfaction. In a similar vein, physicians could perhaps be given basic training in oral health to meet basic dental needs in rural communities that lack dental services. Or maybe pharmacists could expand their prescribing authority.[4]

More flexible funding arrangements for family physicians and specialty consultants are required, including funding team-based practices rather than individual physicians, and offering a variety of funding mechanisms for general practices. Currently, funding models in Canada reinforce the fragmentation of the system, particularly through governance structures that separate acute and primary care. Many provincial payment systems for family doctors, such as the "fee for service" model, also drive short office visits, often limiting patients to discussions of only one issue per visit. Going forward, additional incentives, such as payment mechanisms to reward effective practice, could be significant motivators for improved outcomes. Provinces are introducing a number of such initiatives—for example, payments for achieving specific screening targets—but these remain currently limited to pilot projects that may or may not become widespread in the future.

Quality measurement should promote excellence in chronic-care management, such as timely, comprehensive, and coordinated care; continuity of care; and easy access. A culture of accountability is needed, in which primary care providers from all health professions recognize the importance of measuring their performance, comparing their patient outcomes to those of their peers, and changing their behaviour accordingly.

The task for reimagining our health care systems should not simply fall on service providers and government funders and managers. Rather, patient self-management also needs to be supported. The goal of care for individuals with chronic health conditions is collaboration between informed and engaged patients, family members, and a coordinated health care team. The emphasis on self-management requires patient–professional partnerships that involve supports for self-management that are appropriate for people's conditions and circumstances.

Improvements in technology will help us along this path, too. As electronic health records become common, tools that assist in shared decision-making will evolve and be of benefit to both practitioners and patients. Systems of this type use science, informatics, incentives, and professional values and beliefs for continuous improvement and innovation. Data are captured, analyzed, and fed back into the health care system to alter and improve care.

Putting patients first, integrating social and health services, focusing the medical model of health services delivery to interdisciplinary teams, and enabling shared decision-making between patients and professionals will be critical to the health of Canadians in the next few decades. With concerted effort and will, we can build upon the achievements of the Canadian health care system and create a healthier society by the time of Canada's bicentennial in 2067.

The Future Arctic

Edward Struzik

WHEN A 187 km highway from Inuvik to Tuktoyaktuk is opened to traffic in 2017, during Canada's sesquicentennial year, it will be the first public road in North America to link the south to the Arctic coast. Long dependent on ice roads, delta waterways, and airplanes to move people and goods in and out, the 850 residents of Tuktoyaktuk will be celebrating. So will the revenue-starved Government of the Northwest Territories, which has been dreaming of a highway to the Arctic since it first achieved responsible government in the early 1980s.

The highway promises to create forty long-terms jobs, save the town of Tuktoyaktuk $1.5 million in cost-of-living deliveries, and increase tourism. But the main reason for the $300-million taxpayer expenditure is to make it easier for the oil and gas industry to get equipment and material in and out of a community in which it has worked intermittently since the 1970s. According to one study conducted for the Government of the Northwest Territories, the industry stands to save between $347 and $516 million in expenses over forty-five years once the road is built.

On the 150th anniversary of the country's birth, there is no doubt that Canada could use a few strategically situated roads to resources and a port or two that will make it economical to get those resources to market. But a road to a coastal community that is sliding into the sea because of rapidly thawing permafrost, rising sea levels, and receding sea ice isn't the answer.

Prime Minister Justin Trudeau's decision to ban future oil and gas exploration in the Arctic in December 2015 was a good start to setting a new course for the future of the Arctic. Canada's costly attempts to forge the future of the Arctic on oil and gas has offered no significant returns since 1975, when government subsidies to the oil and gas industry first began. Some $1.5 billion was spent to establish Petro-Canada as a Crown corporation, and the federal government has since invested billions of additional dollars in incentives and subsidies to encourage oil and gas companies to search for, and develop, energy reserves in the polar regions of the country. This trend has continued to the present day. In 2008, for example, a new federally funded program (Geo-mapping for Energy and Minerals) was initiated to bring petroleum geologists to the Arctic each year. To date, this program has spent nearly $200 million of taxpayers' money to help the energy and mining industries find new sources of fossil fuels and minerals in the region. Under the current funding protocol, money will continue flowing until 2020.

The problem is that, almost without exception, none of this energy has ever made it to market over the past forty years. Many have blamed the failure of Canada's Arctic oil and gas strategy on Judge Thomas Berger's Mackenzie Valley Pipeline inquiry in the mid-1970s, which recommended a ten-year moratorium on oil and gas and pipeline development. Others have blamed unresolved land claims and a complex permitting process that have slowed approvals for a more recent pipeline construction project. But the real reason is different. Arctic oil and gas has never made it south because of the high cost and logistics associated with piping it out over land, or shipping by sea to market. The pipeline that Justice Berger considered in the 1970s would have been an economic disaster. Bob Blair, one of the pipeline's builders, said so years later. The second Mackenzie Valley Pipeline would have fared even worse. In 2008, the proposed pipeline would have required gas prices to be in the range of $6 to $8 per gigajoule (GJ) of energy to break even. That looked good then, when gas prices temporarily soared above $13 per GJ. Since then, however, the price has sat in the range of $2 to $5. Recovering the costs of a $20-billion pipeline would require prices up to triple current values. There are few signs that oil and gas prices will return to levels that will make it profitable to develop reserves north of the Arctic Circle.

In the meantime, climate change is ending the Arctic as we know it and transforming it into something completely different. Since the 1970s, when energy companies redirected their efforts northward, air temperatures in the Arctic have risen by 3.5 to 5°C, and sea-ice area has declined by about 12 percent per decade. Increasingly, more ice is being melted and exported out of the Arctic each summer than gets replaced the following winter.

A warmer and shorter ice season will result in less time for polar bears to hunt seals and more time for mosquitoes and flies to take their toll on caribou. As sea levels continue to rise, powerful storm surges will result in massive seawater intrusions that could imperil millions of birds nesting in freshwater Arctic deltas and coastal wetlands. Sooner than later, low-lying coastal Inuit communities, such as Tuktoyaktuk, that are sitting on rapidly thawing permafrost will have to be relocated, just as the Alaskan community of Shishmaref is about to be.

We are already seeing the rippling effects of some of these changes throughout the Arctic ecosystem. Capelin, not Arctic cod, is now the dominant prey fish in Hudson Bay. Salmon and other southern fish species are moving in and out of the Arctic as sea ice recedes and sea water warms in the summer months. Killer whales, which were once absent from the Arctic, are beginning to prey on narwhal and beluga. Polar bears at the southern end of their range are getting thinner and producing fewer cubs. Some are now mating with grizzly bears and producing hybrids. Trees and shrubs are overtaking tundra landscapes. And tundra and boreal forests are burning bigger, hotter, faster, and more often.

So what does the future holds for the Inuit and First Nations people of Yukon, the Northwest Territories, Nunavut, northern Quebec, and Labrador, whose cultures grew out of a close association with this frigid world? Those cultures are already in a state of rapid economic reorganization and social readjustment. Many people have either stopped or reduced their consumption of caribou and walrus, not because they prefer store-bought beef and pork, but because the caribou and reindeer populations are collapsing, and the receding sea ice is making it difficult for them to hunt marine mammals.

There is very little that can be done to stop the Arctic, and the rest of the world, from warming in the next half century. So much greenhouse gas is being emitted now that it will take centuries to halt the warming that is currently taking place. That's not a reason to give up on curbing greenhouse gas emissions, though, and it's imperative that mitigation measures be pursued aggressively. There is, however, both merit and powerful economic argument to be made for the implementation of adaptation strategies. Using scientific and economic data, as well as traditional Inuit and First Nations knowledge, we must manage the end of the Arctic world as we know it so that the new Arctic will bring a more prosperous future for northern peoples.

What constitutes the future Arctic is a wide-open question that can be answered in several ways. But expectations that northerners live with toxic abandoned mine sites (Giant Mine in Yellowknife) or hydroelectric dams (Muskrat Falls in Labrador) that introduce methylmercury into the food chain should not be part of that future.

The Arctic needs an affordable and efficient air and road network that can bring tourists and investors in. It needs to have food security that goes beyond subsidizing the transportation of southern foods northward. It needs renewable energy to replace diesel, which is prohibitively expensive and polluting. It needs a better form of post-secondary education that combines traditional knowledge with Western scientific knowledge. It needs a forward-looking ecological conservation plan that will ensure a future for polar bears, caribou, walrus, narwhal, beluga, and other Arctic species.

Commercial fishing may play an increasingly important role, as is the case in Greenland, where the government recently launched an experimental fishery to exploit recent increases in mackerel abundance. The comparison with Greenland, however, may not be entirely appropriate, since the Greenland coast is bathed in warm Atlantic-origin waters, whereas the Canadian Arctic is predominantly influenced by colder polar waters. Low-impact mining may also have a place in the future Arctic if a way can be found to get workers to live in the North so that the money they spend and the taxes they pay can stay there.

Tourism in the Arctic may well play the biggest and most immediate potential role for driving the Arctic community. Adventure, sports, and leisure tourism are among the fastest-growing forms of tourism in the world,[1] but they have never amounted to much in the Canadian Arctic outside the Yukon Territory and northern Manitoba, where tourism enjoys modest success. In the Northwest Territories, the number of outdoor adventurers recently dropped by nearly 40 percent, from thirty-one hundred people in 2012-13 to nineteen hundred in 2013-14. In Nunavut, spending on fishing and sport hunting has declined by over $6 million between 2007 and 2011. Parks Canada, which controls some of the most scenic real estate in the entire Arctic world, has made woeful attempts to lure tourists north.

In 2014, only eight people visited Aulavik National Park on Banks Island, where two-thirds of the world's muskoxen are located. Quttinirpaaq, on Ellesmere Island, did better than it did the year before, when only five people showed up. But not by much. Just twenty-three people spent the time and money to fly to the magnificent glacier-covered mountain park on northern Ellesmere Island that year. Even Tuktut Nogait—which has the magnificent La Roncière waterfall on the Hornaday River, the spectacular Brock River canyon, and one of the largest caribou calving grounds in the world—has been striking out. There have been years since the park was established in 1998 when fewer than five people showed up.

Parks Canada is not entirely to blame. Our vast geography is clearly partly responsible. Reaching Canada's most remote northern locations is prohibitively expensive and logistically daunting for all but the richest and most daring among us. That is why investing in infrastructure and transportation is likely to provide better economic returns than continued encouragement and subsidies of oil and gas development. This is an important point in the lead-up to 2021, when the Trudeau ban on Arctic oil and gas exploration is up for review.

Making the choice between tourism and oil and gas may not be an easy one. But the town of Churchill, Manitoba, was compelled to consider this very question a few years ago when the idea of a pipeline transporting Alberta's bitumen to its failing port on the west coast of Hudson Bay was floated. The town flatly rejected the idea, fearing that it could hurt its tourism industry and imperil beluga whales and polar bears.

Like most Arctic communities in Canada, Churchill is largely Aboriginal and not connected to the south by any road. But its businesspeople hit the jackpot more than thirty years ago when they and the town's leaders embarked on an ambitious plan to turn the troublesome polar bear population into an international tourist attraction.

The plan that the Churchill Polar Bear Committee penned in 1977 resulted in what amounted to a polar bear jail for so-called "problem bears" that would otherwise be shot. A more humane protocol for deterring bears was recommended. Opportunities for tourism and wildlife viewing were envisioned. Scientists were encouraged to come and study the animals, the permafrost, and the climate. The plan was not perfect by any means, and unofficially it has been a work in progress to this day. There has, however, never been anything quite like it in northern Canada.

With a little help from the Canadian Department of Tourism and the Government of Manitoba, the polar bears of Churchill became a hot tourist attraction and a cash cow for the town's businesspeople. Each year, media such as *National Geographic*, *Audubon*, the *Smithsonian*, the *New York Times*, *Time* magazine, London's *Daily Mirror*, and *Le Figaro* devote considerable space to the subject in magazines and documentaries. In 1984, the editors of *Life* magazine sandwiched a five-thousand-word article about Churchill's polar bears in between one on the Shroud of Turin and another on the twentieth anniversary of the Beatles coming to America.

Had Churchill not gone that route thirty years ago, there would be nothing left to drive the local economy since OmniTRAX, an American company, shut down the port in the summer of 2016. It's a story that the people of Tuktoyaktuk have seen before and one that residents of Faro, in Yukon, experienced in the 1980s, when owners of the lead-zinc mine there left them with one of the most contaminated sites in the country.

The Canadian government is spending well over $1 billion cleaning up abandoned mine sites in the North. It has invested billions more in incentives, subsidies, roads, and geological mapping programs to encourage the exploration and exploitation of Arctic energy and mineral reserves. Roads to resources have their place. But it's also time the government shift its investment priorities to ensure that the economic returns are long-lasting and of benefit to northerners.

Medicare

Robert Evans

THE FEDERAL GOVERNMENT'S Canada Health Act (1984)—the cornerstone of Canada's universal, publicly financed health insurance programs—faced powerful opposition in many quarters when introduced. The act, which consolidated and clarified earlier federal legislation, was criticized by organized medicine, large and small business, private insurers, provincial governments, and the diverse advocates for the wealthy. There was, however, one significant constituency strongly in support: the people of Canada.

The act was passed unanimously. The opposition Progressive Conservative Party (as it was then called) was looking forward to taking power from a deeply unpopular government. To the dismay of many of its supporters, it supported the bill and avoided the political trap of being seen as "against Medicare."

This episode demonstrated the strength of public support for the most popular, and arguably the most successful, public program in Canada. But opposition, narrowly based but strategically placed, has never gone away. Nor will it, since Medicare embodies genuine conflicts of economic interests, as do all public health care programs.

These conflicts play out along three axes:

Who pays? How are total system costs allocated across the population?

Who gets? How does access to, and quality and quantity of, care vary among patients?

Who gets paid? How and to whom are total health expenditures allocated as incomes?

Where a country's system lies along each of these axes determines both the distribution of its costs and benefits, and its relative efficiency, effectiveness, and cost in responding to the health needs of the population.

Canada's Medicare is primarily financed from general taxation. Contributions are thus more or less related to ability to pay. And access to and use of care are determined, with many qualifications, by professionally judged relative need—current or projected health status. Political struggles over who pays and who gets are largely fought out over the mix of public revenue sources—more progressive (e.g., the income tax) or regressive (e.g., British Columbia's medical services "premium"). But always in the background are efforts to introduce user fees or other sources of private financing. Such measures would increase the relative burden at lower incomes, while reducing contributions and improving access higher up and expanding income opportunities for (some) providers.

The question of who gets paid is largely dictated by the same professions that were in place when the system was established—doctors, nurses, other professionals. The great weakness of Medicare is that major stakeholders have been able to protect their reimbursement entitlements in the face of any threatening reforms.

That said, the major health sectors left out of Medicare—dentistry and particularly ambulatory pharmaceuticals—have evolved to be much more costly and inefficient. (A universal Pharmacare program on Medicare lines could reduce total expenditures by over $10 billion annually.[1]) Medicare's great strength is that it has limited the growth of the vast corporate bureaucracy that, in the United States, now claims hundreds of billions of health dollars in pure waste.

Of course, Medicare, like most large and complex institutions, is far from perfect. It is not only incomplete in its coverage and resistant to obvious reforms, it is dogged by seemingly intractable excessive waiting times for certain non-emergency procedures. These genuine problems are traceable to fragmented and contested management rather than "underfunding." Too many stakeholders, with overlapping and sometimes conflicting interests, have their hands on the controls. Any shortcomings are emphasized either to call for ever more money or (by Medicare's traditional opponents) to argue for pseudo-reforms that would simply roll back Medicare's achievements. That struggle continues.

Canada's first universal public program was launched in 1947. The avowedly socialist government of Saskatchewan, drawing on the *Beveridge Report* in Britain and flush with funds from wartime prosperity, introduced a program of tax-financed reimbursement for hospital services covering all provincial residents. Much has happened since, but broadly speaking this was the template for Canada's current federal-provincial health insurance system.

The federal-provincial structure is, however, dictated by constitutional constraint. Jurisdiction over most health care matters is allocated to the provinces. Establishing a public hospital insurance program was thus within the constitutional authority of the Saskatchewan government but beyond that of the federal government. A federal program would have met immediate and successful legal challenge.

These constitutional issues are not ancient history. They are at the heart of the current wrangling (in January 2017) between the federal and provincial governments over sharing the control and the costs of health care, on which more below.

Yet, the Saskatchewan program turned out to be extremely successful. Several other provinces subsequently introduced more limited variants. The federal Hospital Insurance and Diagnostic Services Act (HIDS) of 1957 was the workaround that enabled the federal government to put its fiscal shoulder behind emerging provincial efforts. HIDS created a joint federal-provincial program in which each province established and administered a public hospital insurance system conforming to federal standards of coverage, in return for federal reimbursement of roughly half the program's costs. In this way, the basic structure of the Saskatchewan program (universality, comprehensiveness, public financing, and administration) could be extended across the country. By 1961, all provinces had accepted the federal offer and had a conforming plan in place.

(Subsequent efforts to undermine and destroy Medicare have accordingly targeted the federal contribution.)

To this point, Medicare's evolution was (relatively) non-controversial. Concerns about federal intrusion into provincial jurisdiction were mollified with federal money, and the new system had strong public support. There was widespread agreement that hospitals needed more funding, and doctors in particular were mostly quite happy to see more public money flowing into the public "workshops" where they carried on (and billed for) their private practices.

Latent opposition flared up dramatically, however, when the Saskatchewan government introduced "stage two," public coverage for physicians' services in and out of hospitals. By the 1960s, physicians were working in a much more favourable economic environment. Patients had more money, private insurance was spreading, and doctors' incomes were rising. They, and certainly their representatives, recognized that negotiating fees with a single government payer would be more challenging than dealing with individual patients or with the physician-sponsored insurers predominant in Canada.

Powerful opposition also came from commercial insurers across North America that had expanded rapidly in the postwar era. They were offering private, employment-based coverage at attractive premiums because they marketed to a low-risk target population and their premiums were subsidized indirectly through the income tax. Private insurers could see an increasingly large and lucrative market disappearing.

The opposition culminated in the famous Saskatchewan "doctors' strike," a collective effort to force the government to abandon the plan. The economic interests became entangled with ideological differences, class distinctions, and, from across the border, Cold War red-baiting. Deep divisions were opened in the community that were slow to heal. In the end, the strike was settled and Saskatchewan's medical insurance program was established. But concessions were made that had long-term implications.

With Saskatchewan's medical insurance program in place, debate shifted to whether the federal government should again offer cost-sharing to promote nationwide coverage with federal standards and guidelines. A decisive factor in that debate was the massive report of the Royal Commission on Health Services (the Hall Commission) in 1964.

Justice Hall concluded that it was not remotely possible for the private insurance industry to provide universal and comprehensive coverage. Employment-based coverage largely excludes the highest-cost users of care—the elderly, the poor, the disabled, and the chronically ill. Private insurers, Hall argued, could at best cover the relatively healthy, who make up most of the population but not of the care needs and costs. Universality and comprehensiveness would require either a universal public system along Saskatchewan lines or side-by-side public and private systems. The public would cover the high-risk, low-resourced populations while the private insurers—with tax-based public subsidies—would cover the low-risk and relatively well off (and profitable).

Hall also observed that private insurance was unambiguously and inherently much more expensive than publicly funded systems. A large proportion of expenditures was absorbed by administrative overheads, marketing, claims adjudication, and private and corporate profits. These provide no care for patients; they are sheer waste.

Faced with Justice Hall's report, as well as powerful advocacy from many other quarters, the federal government passed the Medical Care Act, coming into force in 1968. It provided federal cost-sharing, on a slightly different formula, for conforming provincial programs insuring the costs of physicians' services. By 1971, all provinces had programs in place.

But, by 1971, health care costs had been escalating rapidly for over a decade, absorbing an ever-growing share of national income. Public, or at least government, priorities had shifted from system expansion to "cost containment" and "value for money." The competing (and equally misleading) political rhetorics of "underfunding" and "spiralling costs" have been with us ever since.

Whatever the impact of health care on health, total health care expenditures (public or private) will always exactly equal the total incomes received directly or indirectly from its provision. Cost containment necessarily limits someone's income aspirations. Conflict is inevitable.

Perhaps remarkably, the Medicare programs were relatively successful in limiting cost escalation. The contrast with the US is dramatic. Prior to 1971, the two countries were on parallel expansion paths; thereafter, they have increasingly diverged. By now, Americans are spending over 50 percent more than Canadians on health care, per person and relative to national income. Are they healthier? No, less healthy on most metrics. Do they receive more care? Some, yes, others much less, but on average, no. Where does the money go?

Roughly half this huge gap finances a vast private bureaucracy. Justice Hall was right: private health insurance is inherently expensive and wasteful. The other half supports higher prices, and higher incomes for well-placed individual and corporate providers. Single payers have more bargaining power. Other national systems have since learned this lesson; the US remains an obdurate outlier.

But the endless Canadian tug-of-war between payers and payees, and the efforts by some payees to open additional (i.e., private) revenue sources, have for half a century been a major distraction from initiatives (and there have been many) to improve the efficiency and effectiveness of patient care. Everyone supports these goals in principle, until they threaten someone's income. Official commissions and academic studies routinely conclude that Canada's health care system needs more management, not more money. The echo comes back: "More money!"

There has been progress. A hospital system once grossly over-bedded has been dramatically downsized, with significant health benefits. But physician-to-(age-adjusted)-population ratios continue their half-century upward march, leaving perceptions of "physician shortage" unabated. This distorts financial priorities; doctors must be paid. The confluence of economic and professional incentives has fed an explosion of diagnostic testing and imaging, outrunning questions of health benefit.

At time of writing, however, there are two new developments of particular interest.

First, the federal minister of health has announced that in the future the federal grant to the provinces will be escalated by 3 percent annually, no longer at 6 percent. But an additional 3 percent will be available for underserviced priority sectors such as mental health. This attempt to steer, not merely sustain, Medicare and to shift the national discourse from "How much?" to "For what?" could be very promising.

Second, a recent book offers an excellent guide to "what's working and what's not in Canadian health care, and what to do about it." Drawn from clinical experience, the "six big ideas" in Dr. Danielle Martin's

Better Now share a common theme of "more management." But the required manager must come from the primary care practitioner. No MBAs need apply.

"Return to relationships" is the most subtle of these "big ideas." The primary care practitioner is at the hub of a network of relationships extending outward to the other people and institutions involved in care, and backwards to the patient's family and life circumstances. If these relationships are solidly rooted in trust and clear communication, clinical decisions can be better targeted, more effective, and ultimately even cheaper. But these relationships must be kept in good repair, from both sides.

Universal Pharmacare: a payment system along American lines, with mixed public and private insurance and self-pay, produces American results: very unfair, very expensive, and a threat to health. Many are denied drugs they need; many receive drugs they do not need—both for well-understood economic reasons. But if Pharmacare reduced expenditures, it would reduce total pharmaceutical incomes by an identical amount. So, we do not have Pharmacare.

"Don't just do something; stand there!" and "Do more with less" both respond to the clinical predilection for intervention, reinforced by the payment system. But all interventions, diagnostic or therapeutic, carry risks. Even simple tests can lead into a "spiral of investigation" that is potentially dangerous, as well as costly and painful. And "unmet needs" are better and more safely met by redeploying existing resources than by the knee-jerk response of "more money."

The conditions in which people live and work are ultimately more important for health than access to even the finest health care. Poverty is unhealthy; its elimination requires at least a basic minimum income.

All these things are known. There is no shortage of good ideas in Canada, nor of successful pilot projects. But they seem to die out; they do not "go viral" and spread system-wide. Danielle Martin's "The anatomy of change" addresses this pattern.

Much to be proud of in Medicare; much to improve.

Regarding China
中加關系

Alexander Woodside and Diana Lary

THE FIRST CHINESE immigrants to Canada arrived in the 1860s, just before Canadian Confederation. Over the ensuing 150 years, the relationship between Canada and China has matured significantly, evolving as a major factor in the Canadian economic, political, and cultural landscape. Yet, successive governments have struggled to clearly articulate a national strategy for engagement with China. Indeed, in a recent book about the relations between Canada ("a middle power in middle age") and China (the imperial "middle kingdom"), former Canadian ambassador David Mulroney lamented Canada's apparent inability to develop a long-term vision for its interaction with China.

The lack of clear strategy for engagement with China is not a new issue. It has haunted Canada's relations with China since before Confederation and has much to do with two interconnected factors. One is Canada's location between two empires—the United States to the south, and China to the west. The other is Chinese immigration to Canada. The interconnection between Canada and China can be viewed in light of the stories of the formidable individuals, Chinese and Canadian, who have shaped the relationship between the two countries.

Early Chinese reformers were determined to incorporate Canada into Chinese political life. The brilliant scholar Kang Youwei 康有為 (1858–1927) advised the emperor of China to prepare for "the age of the

Pacific" by giving China a constitution and a parliament. He explained the Canadian system of government as a republic cleverly disguised as a monarchy, a powerful parliamentary government that tolerated the "empty" leadership of a king. His efforts failed, and he fled abroad, coming to Canada in 1899 and again in 1904. During his time in Canada, Kang encouraged local Chinese communities to become an overseas pressure group for change in China, establishing a trend that continued throughout the twentieth century.

Relations between Canada and China in the early twentieth century were undermined by the racist policies of the Canadian government. The growth of Chinese communities in Canada was prevented by exclusionary policies, first a series of head taxes and then the ban on Chinese immigration in 1923.

The Chinese community in Canada was particularly active in resistance to Japanese imperialism in the 1930s. The mass educator Tao Xingzhi 陶行知 (1891–1946) devoted his energies to global opposition to Japanese imperialism. He spoke in theatres, schools, and city halls across Canada, demanding Canadian assistance to China in resisting Japan. He wrote a love poem to "Canadian friends." In it he celebrated Niagara Falls; its "thrilling music" sent "a wise message from Canada" that humble individuals, like separate drops of water, could combine to create a force to defeat aggression.

Canadians, in turn, were eager to bring their belief systems to China— although these were religious, not political. China was the major focus of Christian mission work, and thousands of missionaries from Canada went to China, starting in the late nineteenth century. These Canadians often combined religious missionary work with practical pursuits such as medicine and dentistry. Some, including the Reverend James Menzies, immersed themselves in Chinese culture. Menzies played a key role in the momentous discovery of China's earliest written archives, the oracle bones.

Canadian missionaries also played a significant, though perhaps unanticipated, role in the political life of China. In the 1930s, they rallied to the aid of Chinese civilians as Japanese armies advanced through the country. Quebec Jesuit missionaries found themselves on the front line in May 1938 and gave sanctuary to tens of thousands of desperate people. Dr. Robert McClure (United Church) organized mass refugee relief in the Yellow River Valley.

As the twentieth century went on, several factors further eroded the relationship between Canada and China. The Japanese conquest cut off connections between China and Canada during the Second World War, and this separation continued after the Communist Party took over China in 1949. During the ensuing thirty years, there was no contact between Chinese Canadians and their families in China, and no trade or diplomatic relations. Doctor Norman Bethune was the only Canadian known in China, and was immortalized by Mao Zedong in an essay that lambasted his supporters for lacking the dedication shown by the "doctor from afar."

Canada-China relations went into a deep freeze, caught up in global geopolitical machinations. During the Cold War, Canada was captive to American hostility to the People's Republic of China (PRC), and to what Lester Pearson called in 1951 the "hysteria, prejudice, and immaturity" of American debates about China policy. In his memoirs, Pearson writes that Canada did not dare to recognize the Communist Chinese republic between 1949 and 1970, or vote for China's admission to the United Nations, for fear that the United States would withdraw from the United Nations. Keeping the US in the UN was more important to Canada than the "incongruity" of excluding China from this body.

But the political winter was short. Canada was one of the first Western countries to resume diplomatic relations. It did so in 1970, while the Cultural Revolution was still raging. Canada sold wheat to China, which was the only interaction permitted by Beijing at that time. The real resumption in relations had to wait until China turned against Maoism, ended its isolation from the world, and adopted the Four Modernizations (early 1980s). In a short time, China went from extremes of collectivization to extremes of capitalism, and its economy has grown exponentially since then, while its influence in the world has risen dramatically. But this growth has come with vast increases in inequality and corruption, and mounting social and environmental problems. Although China remains ruled by a Communist party, and Mao Zedong still looms over Tiananmen and on every piece of Chinese paper currency, Canada, a democracy, now looks to many observers like a more socialist society than China.

The political thaw in Canada-China relations led to the resumption of Chinese immigration to Canada in the 1980s. The first wave of immigrants was of ethnic Chinese from Hong Kong, before the 1997 return of Hong Kong to "the embrace of the motherland." Recently, the largest movement has been from the PRC—that is, mainland China. These successive recent waves of migration have created several Chinese worlds in Canada, reflecting different regional and political origins. Language is a key identifier. Cantonese is the spoken language of immigrants from Hong Kong and Guangdong Province. Those from the PRC and Taiwan speak Mandarin. The elegant traditional written form of the language 繁體字 is dominant in Chinese-Canadian communities rather than the pared-down characters 简体字 used in the PRC. English is the main language of those long settled.

Given the long and complex relationship between Canada and China, it is not surprising that there are distinct and sometimes contradictory Canadian attitudes to China. In government, business, and universities, attitudes are positive—even rosy—stressing trade, immigration, and recruitment of students. In the wider society, however, there are rumbles of negativity about China, as manifested in complaints about rising house prices, money laundering, Chinese-only signs, and the import of fentanyl and other toxic chemicals. These attitudes share an indifference to Chinese history and culture.

The future of Canada-China relations will reflect major issues in China. While economic growth in China continues, its political system is frozen. The gradual moderation of the totalitarian regime hoped for by Canadian governments has not materialized. Instead one man, Xi Jinping 习近平, holds the top four positions in China. The return to administration by mandarins makes the state efficient but does not guarantee the solution of fundamental problems: the growth of economic inequality, the oppression of ethnic minorities, the lack of human rights. These problems are recognized in Canada. In 2010, Grand Chief Ed John, of the Tl'azt'en Nation, presented a totem pole to the Qiang people in recognition of their suffering in the 2008 Sichuan earthquake, a gift from one Indigenous people to another. The winner of the 2016 Governor General's Award for fiction was Madeleine Thien. Her novel *Do Not Say We Have Nothing* is set in two disastrous periods that cannot be discussed in China—the Cultural Revolution and the Tiananmen Massacre.

In the twenty-first century, China is trying to resemble something familiar to Canadians: the American empire, with its hundreds of overseas military bases and its sense of its cultural and historical exceptionalism. The two extremisms of "left" and "right" of the Mao period have been replaced by the two extremisms of uncritical admiration of things American and a strongly nationalist ambition to compete with, and supersede, American power. China has created a global bank (the Asian Infrastructure Investment Bank) to rival the American-dominated World Bank. The Chinese e-commerce giant Alibaba challenges Amazon. China is also developing a military-industrial complex that matches the American one. Beijing now talks of a Chinese "Monroe Doctrine" for the South China Sea.

There is the real danger that Canada could, once again, become hostage to tensions between the American empire under President Trump and its imitator and would-be successor, China. Canada must avoid becoming embroiled in American-Chinese relations, or worse, as Prime Minister Mackenzie King wrote in 1948, becoming the "cat's paw of United States policy" in eastern Asia. Canada will have to learn how to live with a China that is both an ancient civilization and an ambitious but vulnerable contemporary great power. China's foreign relations are rooted in history. From its ancient civilization, China has inherited a culture that includes great concern with dignity in international relations. Part of this sensitivity to "face" and pursuit of status in international relations derives from what Chinese commentators call "one hundred years of humiliation" at the hands of Western and Japanese imperialism. Pierre Trudeau was (and is) popular in China because he gave China "face" in 1970 by recognizing China, despite US attempts to isolate it internationally.

The Canadian tradition of quiet diplomacy, pioneered by Pearson in the 1950s, has never been more important. Canadians need to be aware that the vulnerabilities of the Chinese state, with its huge population and its limited natural resources, sometimes inspire the Chinese elite to see resource-rich, population-poor Canada as an antidote, in quasi-utopian terms. To take one example, urban growth and construction projects like dams and reservoirs have led to the disappearance of twenty thousand natural villages each year in China in the early twenty-first century.

This means the shrinkage of farmland and the displacement of at least 150 million peasants who cannot be absorbed into overcrowded cities. Chinese commentators have fantasized about exporting tens of millions of these so-called surplus people to Canada and other countries around the world. Adrienne Poy Clarkson's triumphant ascent as Canada's governor general is cited as evidence of Canada's receptiveness to Chinese migrants. Although Canada is unlikely to accommodate many of the displaced people, we should expect sustained immigration from China. And there will be refugees from China seeking political asylum and—quite soon—fleeing urban pollution in China for Canada's clean air.

As Canada celebrates its 150th anniversary, we face old issues. If a national vision for Canada's relations with China is difficult to create, it may be partly because we still have only a limited understanding of what holds the Chinese state together. Finding a positive long-term vision for Canada's interaction with China demands major increases in our understanding and appreciation of Chinese history and culture.

Canada has an important role to play in supporting Chinese participation in global civil society. Leading by example, we should encourage greater Chinese participation in international organizations and institutions that promote political, economic, cultural, and scientific co-operation. Rather than viewing China as a rival power that must be "contained," we must harness the capacity of China to promote global ideals of shared responsibility and co-operation. Canada can and should build on its long-standing relationship with China as a path to global well-being over the next 150 years.

Our Most Precious Resource

John Richardson, Hans Schreier, and Leila Harris

CANADA IS FORTUNATE to have one of the largest endowments of freshwater in the world. These waters have provided for our peoples, stretching back to a time well before the idea of Canada itself. Our freshwaters have served as trade routes for First Nations and other later travellers in all manner of vessels (from canoes to freighters), while also sustaining communities with drinking water, fish, and many other foods and products. Beyond the essential role of water for our economy and livelihoods, freshwater is also an important symbol of our national identity and a backdrop to our lives. Think of the cottage on the lake, or hockey on a frozen pond. Think also of the many iconic Canadian works of art and literature (including a previous incarnation of our $20 bill) that feature freshwater imagery. Seen in this light, water may be considered to be the very essence of Canada.

And yet, Canadians often take water for granted, resulting in some significant challenges to what might be our greatest national resource. The past 150 years have seen important shifts with respect to freshwater use and management, with rapidly increasing consumption of freshwater for irrigated agriculture, power generation, and many other commercial and recreational activities. The twentieth century, in particular, was an era of big projects to dam rivers and divert water for hydroelectric power production, to supply water to municipalities, or for irrigated agriculture—all drastically altering the Canadian landscape. These projects have powered our economies and connected people, while allowing economic growth and prosperity for many. But this progress has often been accompanied by significant environmental and socio-economic environmental impacts, including filling in of wetlands, channelization of streams, diversion of entire catchments, downstream effects of dams, and wastewater pollution. Moreover, land-use change and development have created a need for flood defences (e.g., dikes on rivers) that protect human settlements but often have detrimental impacts on ecosystems.

In the face of mounting pressures on freshwater resources around the globe, Canada has been a pioneer in research dedicated to protecting water quality and freshwater ecosystems. Investments by Canadian governments in the past created and supported a world-class group of freshwater scientists and monitoring networks, including globally famous research sites such as the Experimental Lakes Area. Through research at this and many other locations, Canada has made major strides forward on water protection and management, including significant mitigation measures for acid raid impacts and the demonstration that phosphates in detergent were a major cause of freshwater pollution. In fact, Canada has been, and continues to be, a global leader in providing the scientific basis for wise water management. Yet, despite our plentiful freshwater resources, and our capacity for leading scientific research and engineering, Canada still faces many water access and quality issues.

Older Canadians will remember the era of acid rain, which affected our lakes and streams because of the elevated levels of industrial contaminants in the atmosphere. The effects of acid rain are still detectable, even though the rains themselves have returned to a more normal acid level. We will live with the legacy of this pollution for a long time. For instance, one long-term consequence is the removal of calcium in the soils and water through chemical reactions with acidic rain, resulting in the limited availability of this important mineral for the bones of fish and the shells of crustaceans and clams in eastern lakes. The calcium will only be slowly replaced through the breakdown of rocks, highlighting the long-term impacts of environmental degradation. We might better protect our ecosystems and resources by anticipating and avoiding such detrimental outcomes from the outset, rather than by attempting to fix the damage retroactively. The challenge is that these long-term impacts are often invisible to the untrained eye.

Indeed, the appearance of freshwater is often misleading—we can look at relatively clear water and fail to see the changes to water quality and aquatic ecosystems. This apparent transparency can belie the truth about contaminants carried from the air and land into our waters, as well as the changes to water temperature and the timing and continuity of flows that are important to many species at local scales. The challenge might be too much water at a certain time, resulting in flooding, or droughts during the hot summer months during prime agricultural season. At times, it may seem like feast or famine. And these challenges are likely to become more complex when considered in light of ongoing and future climatic shifts, and shifting demographic trends. It is thus necessary that we anticipate the consequences of growing populations, warmer climate, and more variable precipitation and lower snowpack expected with climate change.

Another persistent challenge relates to variable and uneven water access and quality across our country. Water is not distributed equally across Canadian provinces and territories. Consider that 60 percent of the rivers flow north, while most of the people live within one hundred kilometres of the Canada-US border. Moreover, biophysical considerations also play into locally differentiated conditions. For instance, groundwater contamination in regions such as southwestern Ontario and central BC, among others, impair water quality in a manner that is difficult to remediate. Some features, such as the mountainous topography of some areas of the country (e.g., for major municipalities in BC), allow for stronger protection of source water in ways that would be impossible for other major metropolitan areas that are highly populated and already host intensive agriculture and urban land uses. Many areas are not as fortunate to have secure water supplies.

While many parts of the country still have abundant and high-quality water supplies, water security is a real issue for a significant number of Canadians. Smaller communities are particularly vulnerable in this regard because of a number of factors, including a host of governance and institutional considerations. For instance, First Nations' drinking water has a fundamentally different regulatory and institutional structure than that of other communities. The net result is all too familiar to Canadians watching the evening news. Many communities are simply not able to enjoy safe, secure, and affordable access to water for drinking and other household needs. How could a community anywhere in Canada have to live under an extended boil-water advisory?

These challenges highlight broader governance issues that result in highly variable water management and drinking water regulation and treatment across the country. In particular, Canada is one of the only industrialized countries lacking a uniform national regulatory standard for drinking water and wastewater treatment or monitoring. While the federal government is involved in navigation in freshwater bodies, it has no direct role in drinking water regulation and quality assurance. As a result, regulatory concerns are left up to individual provinces and territories, or even, sometimes, to individual municipalities. This creates a highly variable patchwork of quality, access, and requirements across the country. There are also clear data and monitoring gaps with respect to Canada's freshwater resources. Risk assessment and monitoring is ad hoc, and data are often collected in a way that cannot be easily shared, even between agencies of the same provincial or municipal government. Among the things that are most needed are foresight, coordinated planning, and reliable and consistent data.

It is also important to note that the challenges to Canada's freshwaters permeate well beyond our national borders. We export "virtual water" in the form of agricultural products sent to regions of the world. Some agricultural products, including beef, are tremendously water-intensive, since irrigation to produce alfalfa and hay use large amounts of water, and livestock husbandry itself often produces contaminants (nutrients, antibiotics) and pathogens that directly affect freshwater ecosystems. It can take up to fifteen times more water to produce a kilogram of beef compared with an equivalent weight of grain, while the process also produces significant amounts of greenhouse gases and nutrient problems in runoff from poor manure management. These challenges highlight how protection of Canadian freshwater resources can be intimately linked to our role as a global trading nation. Thus, the challenges are great—but solutions do exist.

Considerable efforts are now underway to promote integrated watershed management through "source-to-tap" and "one-health" approaches that recognize the linkages between ecosystem health and water quality, while minimizing the downstream costs of treatment and pollution mitigation. Water protection needs to start at the source, with increased focus on preserving small streams and wetlands that are all too often filled in or diverted into ditches, tile drains, and pipes. Mitigating environmental degradation in these key source water regions would significantly offset the need for expensive water treatment and flood protection.

As urban expansion continues rapidly over the coming decades, the vision for green cities should include major efforts to reduce the water use in cities through use of efficient devices, smart meters, and public education, in addition to governance reform at all scales. At the same time, we need to revolutionize the way we deal with stormwater and flooding problems. Rather than piping and conveying urban runoff directly into streams, we could invest in stormwater detention systems, enhanced protection of water-absorbing vegetation around edges of freshwaters, constructed wetlands, rainwater harvesting, and the building of rain gardens that allow water to infiltrate the soil. Indeed, many of these solutions are already being deployed in a variety of Canadian communities. Some of these measures include individual contributions to storing and using rainfall, such as rain barrels and cisterns, and reductions in the amount of paved areas where water runs off immediately. Municipalities have constructed retention ponds and encouraged protection of wetlands in many places to reduce the rate of water entering streams and the size of floods simultaneously. A costlier solution, which has been applied in some areas, is the construction of reservoirs to store water for later use and help regulate the release of potential floodwaters downstream.

There are also clear opportunities for Canada to move forward on water protection through shifting agricultural and livestock management practices. For instance, there is the potential for Canada to increase food exports, since global demand is increasing and few other countries have sufficient land and water resources. We could focus on producing high-value and water-efficient food products, with less emphasis on livestock exports and with the aim to minimize water-quality impairments and greenhouse gas emissions. One can use technological advances, including drones and remote sensing, to monitor the health of crops over the growing season, and water-smart irrigation devices that are revolutionizing food production. Canada is emerging as a leader in this area, and there is strong potential for future economic opportunities.

Research has shown that the infrastructure that delivers and releases water to streams, lakes, and groundwater has been neglected and is in need of a major overhaul if we hope to reduce impacts and improve the health of the aquatic ecosystems. Better communication and more effective strategies to allow all users to connect to sources, whether streams, lakes, or groundwater, will likely be a key action moving forward toward a more water-secure future.

While an overwhelming majority of Canadians appear to value freshwater as a key resource, it is also evident that we need to do more—socially, scientifically, and governmentally—to recognize and protect the value of water to Canada. We need to commit to stand on guard for the environment in ways that sometimes slow the rate of land conversion and economic exploitation, leaving space for water and natural filtering of water in the soils. This begins with realizing that water is not unlimited in supply and can be easily impaired by our direct and indirect uses of both freshwater and land around it. Freshwater can be easily exploited and damaged by private interests, extraction, deforestation, mining, and similar efforts. We need to face these challenges by assessing the cumulative impacts of these activities to ensure continued access to clean and abundant water for people and ecosystems. Protecting our freshwater heritage will be a beautiful reflection on Canada's past 150 years—if we have the collective will.

Kananaskis, Alberta | NICHOLAS TAFFS

Calgary, Alberta | MARION BUCCELLA

facing: Yellowknife, Northwest
Territories | GARY CLENNAN

above: Outside of Dinosaur Provincial
Park, Alberta | NICHOLAS TAFFS

Clearing the Air

Chris Carlsten and Michael Brauer

THE ASSEMBLY OF First Nations describes air as a life-giving force that allows existence from our first breaths. Ancestors have long viewed the wind as "the intermediary plain connecting the spirit world to our own." As a vital connector, air facilitates transformational mental and spiritual journeys. Canada's massive open space has been a buffer to degradation of this precious, voiceless, boundary-free resource. But that buffer is fragile and tenuous, and our atmosphere needs ongoing care and vigilance.

Air is fundamental to life and yet easily taken for granted. The less our air is made visible by smog and other pollutants, the better it is for health. As we often carelessly add substance to air through combustion, we produce toxic particles that have a harmful impact on more than just the vast surface area of our lungs. We must embrace the challenge of keeping air clear and, at the same time, make air visible to Canadians.

For most of the twentieth century, the general public did not consider ambient air quality in Canada to be a serious concern. However, efforts by figures such as Dr. David Bates (a former dean of medicine at UBC) began to change this perception. In 1972, Bates and his colleagues published the first *Citizen's Guide to Air Pollution*, and this was followed by the establishment of the Clean Air Act several years later. This act was significant in mandating the first National Ambient Air Quality

Objectives, which established limits on air pollution. Growing concern for the potential health impacts of air pollution in Canada arose in part from demonstrable ecosystem effects of acid rain, as well as early recognition of atmospheric contamination in remote locations, including national parks and the high Arctic. Canada took international leadership on global initiatives to protect the atmosphere, including a prominent role in developing the 1987 Montreal Protocol to combat stratospheric ozone depletion, and the inaugural 1998 intergovernmental negotiating committee on persistent organic pollutants (e.g., dioxins, DDT, and PCBs). In 1999, the Clean Air Act was subsumed into the Canadian Environmental Protection Act (CEPA), which reflected the mounting evidence of the hazards of airborne particles and ozone as major components of summer smog. In 2001, airborne particles were declared as toxic and included in the CEPA List of Toxic Substances.

The Canadian Constitution delegates health, including air pollution control, as a provincial responsibility. Provincial legislation specifies permissible rates of emissions from pollution sources, and objectives for environmental concentrations of pollutants, while the federal government regulates transportation and has standing to intervene over transboundary pollution concerns. This results in a complex and interjurisdictional regulatory framework that can pose challenges to effective management of air pollution.

To support the regulatory community, Canadian research has made substantial contributions to our understanding of the important human health impacts of air quality. In the early 1970s, groundbreaking Canadian studies documented links between episodic summer smog in southern Ontario and increased hospitalizations for respiratory disease. Dr. Bates, in particular, was masterful in translating these research findings into tangible messages for government officials, policy-makers, and the broader Canadian public, significantly raising awareness of air quality as a critical national issue. In the 1980s and especially the 1990s, the pace of research regarding adverse effects of air pollution in Canada accelerated sharply; there was a growing appreciation that the cardiovascular system—in addition to the lungs—was dramatically affected by inhaling toxic air. Health Canada took a leading role, including in the application of advanced statistical models that improved our ability to connect pollution levels with disease. These efforts led to the development of the Air Quality Health Index, an innovative tool (now also used in Hong Kong) to communicate the risks of air pollution to the public. In the past fifteen years, Canadian researchers have continued to make significant contributions, including greatly improved estimates of air pollution exposure and documentation of the staggering global health impacts of poor air quality.

Relative to many countries, Canada has some of the best air quality globally, with our cities among the cleanest in the world. This is due to five main factors: low overall population density; a high level of socio-economic development; a service-oriented economy in urban areas replacing manufacturing; resource extraction, and processing; resource extraction being focused in remote areas (away from most population centres); and coordinated efforts to manage air quality. Air pollutants such as lead and sulphur dioxide have decreased by more than 95 percent since 1970, while particles and volatile organics (less remediable by changes in fuel standards) have decreased by approximately 50 percent. Not only has this led to significant health improvements, as noted above, but it has granted additional benefits in terms of improved visibility, ecosystem health, and agricultural yields.

But Canadians have not always enjoyed high standards of air quality. Even as recently as the middle of the twentieth century, it was common to have smoke-belching industries in the heart of densely populated areas (Figure 1). Up until the 1990s, beehive burners were commonly used to combust waste material from saw mills, without any pollution control. Similarly, domestic waste incinerators and open burning were permitted in urban areas, leading to high levels of pollution, including toxic furans and dioxins.

Significant improvements in Canadian air quality over the past century reflect Canada's development as a high-income, technologically advanced economy whose citizens value environmental quality as a right. Canada's approach to improved air quality differs from the heavy regulatory and litigious process in the United States, and is focused on multi-stakeholder air quality management. The Canadian process brings together all relevant stakeholders within a defined airshed to develop and implement a plan to manage the local air quality. This

FIGURE 1. View of mills and log booms on False Creek, Vancouver, 1936. *James Crookall.*

includes identification of major pollution sources and quantification of their impact, a plan for gradual improvement (including air pollution control technology), zoning changes, and legislation to restrict specific combustion practices. Progress toward improved air quality is then monitored and the plan regularly revised. Canada was the first country in the world to instill the principle of "continuous improvement" of air quality in the establishment of Canada-wide Standards in 1998. Continuous improvement reflects current understanding that there is no "safe" level of air pollution, and avoids the practice of polluting up to a specified regulatory limit. Further, by "keeping clean areas clean," the principle stresses the need to improve air quality in all locations in Canada.

Despite the comparatively excellent air quality throughout most Canadian communities, air quality continues to impact the health of Canadians. The latest estimates from the Global Burden of Disease suggest nearly eight thousand Canadian deaths annually (approximately 3 percent of the total) are related to air pollution, ranking tenth among all risk factors for death in Canada. Air pollution causes more death than motor vehicle collisions, suicide, and HIV combined. So we're not in the clear yet.

Moving forward, we must recognize that urban traffic-related air pollution, from both private and commercial vehicles, continues to have health impacts, from heart disease to childhood asthma and lower birthweights. Approximately 30 percent of Canadians live in close proximity to high-traffic roads, where levels of air pollutants are roughly threefold higher than those found elsewhere in urban areas. Nearly one-third of Canadian elementary schools are located in these same high-traffic pollution zones, putting growing children at risk. In many smaller communities, and even in major cities, residential wood combustion is another major source of air pollution. Unfortunately, there has been only slow adoption of advanced technologies to burn wood more efficiently and cleanly, especially in smaller Canadian communities. Furthermore, we are increasingly affected by global pollution sources, including trans-Pacific pollution carried through the atmosphere or by the combustion of fuel on large container ships, which are among the most egregious particle emitters.

Without question, one of the great challenges for Canada over the coming century will be the transformation of our economy from fossil fuel dependence to net-zero carbon emissions. The same combustion sources that contribute to global warming are also the major sources of health-damaging air pollution. As a founder of the Climate and Clean Air Coalition, Canada plays a leading role in global efforts to reduce emissions of pollutants and provide near-term climate and human benefits. We look forward to a future where air quality will be preserved and all will have access to clean, renewable energy sources. Until then, a warmer climate portends worsening of air quality. Over a relatively short period of time, we have witnessed growth in the frequency, magnitude, and severity of wildfires in Canada, along with an extension of the length of the fire season. Devastating fires in Fort McMurray and Slave Lake are recent examples, while generation of huge smoke plumes that affect major cities, and indeed large portions of the continent, are now becoming regular summer occurrences. Smoke from forest fires is clearly linked to increased deaths and exacerbation of lung disease, creating an additional burden on local health resources. This is the reality of a warmer climate.

Virtually all Canadian (and indeed global) population growth in coming decades will happen in cities, and it is clear that all aspects of urban life need to be refocused through a lens of environmental impact, including air quality. Regional sprawl, along with car-focused and short-sighted civil planning, is still widespread around the world. Thankfully, Canadian cities, and Vancouver in particular, provide world-leading examples of the promise of sustainable urbanization. The Vancouver model—with increased population density, better and cleaner public transportation, pedestrian thoroughfares, and bicycle lanes—is now being replicated worldwide. Today, half of all trips in Vancouver are made by walking or cycling. The city has set a major goal of being the world's "greenest city" by 2020 and relying on renewable resources for all of its energy by 2050. Meeting this goal will require an integrated approach between government, private, and citizen sectors, and steadfast commitment.

As we look to a future in which we maintain a high Canadian standard of healthy living while decreasing our carbon footprint and reversing the escalating harms of global climate change, we need to be creative, humble, and interdisciplinary. We must bring all stakeholders to the table in a thoughtful and forward-thinking effort to avoid any deterioration in overall air quality. Embracing innovative smart sensor networks and citizen science may help identify remaining pollution hotspots and uncover unappreciated sources, while robust health-monitoring programs can help identify vulnerable populations and mitigate severe health impacts. There are, however, clouds on the horizon—in particular, the speed at which we transition from fossil fuel dependence and automobile-centred development lags behind the rapid pace of climate change, with its impacts on wildfires and summer smog. With these challenges, we must draw from the strengths of our experience and incorporate innovation to support a brighter future.

What then can Canada teach the rest of the world? We have shown that a model of continuous improvement in air quality, based on multi-stakeholder management and engagement, can succeed in spite of obstacles, while coexisting with economic development. The Vancouver example provides a North American model for thoughtful interdisciplinary promotion of healthy densification to develop cities in a way that promotes sustainability. Perhaps most significantly, Canada has developed a strong national consciousness and coherent philosophy supporting the right of all citizens to a healthy environment, now and in the future.

Un avenir confédéral

David Sanschagrin

L'IDENTITÉ DU CANADA, traversée par la diversité ethnoculturelle et sociopolitique, est longtemps demeurée vague. La fédération de 1867 est issue d'un esprit de modération et de compromis entre élites coloniales, notamment les partisans d'une union fédérale et ceux d'une union législative. Elle unissait politiquement deux cultures qui devaient garder leurs spécificités (droit privé, religion, langue). Quant aux opposants, ils reçurent des pressions de la part de Londres ou furent achetés avec des promesses d'obtenir des postes clés au sein du nouvel État fédéral. Malgré d'importantes crises[1] et en dépit de l'existence des pouvoirs unilatéraux de l'État fédéral – nécessaires à la construction d'un empire commercial et d'un chemin de fer pancanadien –, l'élite politique et cléricale québécoise a accepté la légitimité de la fédération, tant que le gouvernement central n'empiéterait pas sur les compétences socioculturelles. Mais c'est ce qu'il fit, d'abord par l'édification d'un État-providence, puis par le rapatriement de la Constitution en 1982 sans le consentement de l'Assemblée nationale du Québec.

Si le caractère vague de la définition du Canada permettait l'existence de multiples interprétations, la réponse donnée à la question de son identité, institutionnalisée en 1982 à l'initiative du premier ministre Pierre Trudeau, rend son avenir incertain. Loin de l'esprit de modération et de compromis de 1867, le nouveau Canada découle d'une réforme constitutionnelle profonde qui met de l'avant le multiculturalisme, le bilinguisme officiel, une certaine justice sociale, l'égalité provinciale, ainsi que les droits des individus et des minorités sociopolitiques. Une tare importante caractérise toutefois ce nouveau Canada, car l'égalité provinciale et les droits individuels s'opposent à d'autres principes fondamentaux. Le fédéralisme est désormais considéré comme une pratique institutionnelle dépassée, l'autonomie gouvernementale des minorités nationales est écartée et les droits socioéconomiques deviennent secondaires face aux droits civils et politiques traditionnels. Pour un grand nombre de Québécois, le Canada hors Québec vit son moment national unitaire et veut établir une union sociale et économique fonctionnelle, en centralisant les pouvoirs décisionnels à Ottawa. Depuis les années 1970, l'opposition provinciale aux visées d'Ottawa est perçue, à tort, comme un rejet du progrès social et des droits de la personne.

Sans tenir compte de leur identité et de leurs valeurs propres, on demande à l'ensemble des citoyen(ne)s, doté(e)s des mêmes droits individuels, de donner leur allégeance à une société pancanadienne, dont le centre national est Ottawa, l'idéologie est libérale individualiste et la langue dominante est l'anglais. Les membres des Premières Nations et de la nation québécoise sont donc appelés à ranger leurs valeurs plus collectivistes et à se fondre, en anglais de préférence, dans un grand tout canadien. L'allégeance des citoyen(ne)s issues de l'immigration ou appartenant à la catégorie officielle des minorités visibles, réuni(e)s par le concept de « multiculturel », est quant à elle tenue pour acquise. Or, le multiculturalisme, qui suppose à tort l'absence d'une nation majoritaire canadienne, est une catégorie dénuée de pouvoir politique et économique, qui n'a pas amené de redéfinition majeure du fonctionnement des institutions de pouvoir et de la hiérarchie sociale au Canada. De plus, selon Will Kymlicka, la définition officielle d'un Canada multiculturel, bilingue et chartiste sert le nationalisme canadien, en vantant la réussite d'un pays présenté comme un modèle de gestion de la diversité aux yeux du monde[2].

Cependant, ce marketing du nouveau Canada fait oublier les autres éléments plus sombres de l'histoire de ce pays, dont premièrement les politiques d'immigration racistes sous forme de quotas, de taxes d'entrée et d'exclusion. Deuxièmement, la conception élitiste de la démocratie et la méfiance envers toute participation populaire de la part de la classe politique. Troisièmement, les camps de travail durant la Deuxième Guerre mondiale où l'on a interné les Canadien(ne)s d'origine japonaise, allemande et italienne soupçonné(e)s de déloyauté. Quatrièmement, l'utilisation étatique répétée des pouvoirs d'urgence qui suspendent les libertés civiles. Cinquièmement, le long et continu combat que les femmes doivent livrer pour atteindre une pleine reconnaissance sociopolitique. Sixièmement, la répression dont furent victimes de la part de l'État les groupes contestataires de gauche dès 1919 et jusque dans les années 1950. Septièmement, les embûches constantes qu'ont éprouvées les syndicats dans la reconnaissance toujours précaire de leur droit associatif. Huitièmement, la discrimination et le racisme systémique dont furent victimes les francophones et toute personne qui n'était ni britannique ni protestante. Finalement, la spoliation des terres des Premières Nations, leur aliénation et leur enfermement dans des réserves, en attendant leur assimilation en tant qu'individus à la société canadienne.

La réconciliation entre classes, minorités ethnoculturelles et nationales, ainsi que majorité nationale ne passe pas par une amnésie des luttes et des injustices au profit d'un discours rassembleur et optimiste, alors que les francophones subissent toujours le poids du bilinguisme, que leur assimilation se poursuit au Canada[3] et que la situation sociopolitique des Premières Nations est scandaleuse. La reconnaissance et la compensation des injustices n'impliquent pas seulement un changement de ton, mais aussi une transformation profonde de l'idée du Canada ainsi que des rapports de pouvoir.

Depuis le rapport interventionniste et centralisateur de la Commission royale d'enquête sur les relations fédérales-provinciales (1940), le Canada hors Québec construit sa nouvelle nation pancanadienne, qui répondait à des demandes sociales et à un besoin identitaire tout en intégrant en son sein les minorités nationales. Pour la nation québécoise, le choix se situe entre l'assimilation et la lutte politique, jusqu'à la sécession. Comme le disait Justin Trudeau dans la Déclaration du premier ministre du Canada, à l'occasion de la fête du Canada (2016): « Aujourd'hui, nous célébrons le jour où, il y a exactement 149 ans, les gens de ce grand territoire se sont rassemblés et ont forgé une seule nation et un seul pays – le Canada. » Le Canada n'est donc pas une fédération multinationale.

L'evocation récente par Justin Trudeau d'une identité canadienne postnationale[4] ne change rien à la donne, car la promesse d'une identité universelle de la part des nations majoritaires est aussi un appel à l'assimilation des minorités nationales[5]. C'est cette même vision assimilationniste[6] qui a contribué à l'éveil du nationalisme autochtone à la fin des années 1960, lorsque les Premières Nations sont devenues une force politique aspirant à être reconnue « de nation à nation » et refusant autant l'histoire officielle unitariste (un Canada, une nation) que le contre-discours dualiste (le pacte entre deux peuples fondateurs) promu par le Québec.

Le nationalisme sur le territoire du Québec a connu deux moments libéraux progressistes (le républicanisme patriote et la Révolution tranquille) cherchant à redéfinir le régime politique et ses liens avec la Couronne (britannique hier et canadienne aujourd'hui), suivis de défaites majeures (militaires en 1837–1838, constitutionnelles à notre époque) qui ont mené à une déroute, à la fermeture de l'horizon politique et à un repli conservateur culturel, comme voie de retraite préservatrice.

Rejetant le nationalisme de l'idéologie de la survivance, la Révolution tranquille, animée par un néonationalisme progressiste, fut aussi un moment de modernisation politique et de progrès social. Elle répondait au projet d'édification nationale canadien et s'inscrivait aussi dans un contexte mondial de décolonisation. Il fallait d'abord redresser la situation socioéconomique des Blancs francophones. La Commission royale d'enquête sur le bilinguisme et le biculturalisme, lancée par le premier ministre Lester B. Pearson en 1963, révélait qu'ils subissaient une discrimination socioéconomique systématique au Canada, surtout au Québec. Ils étaient les porteurs d'eau du capital anglo-protestant et on leur commandait de parler la langue « civilisée » du maître.

À mesure que le statut sociopolitique du français s'affirmait, la Révolution tranquille devint aussi peu à peu pluraliste. D'abord, c'était officiellement la langue, et non l'identité ethnique et religieuse, qui devenait l'élément d'appartenance nationale. Puis, les divers gouvernements, en sécularisant le milieu scolaire, encourageaient l'intégration des personnes immigrantes dans les écoles françaises. De plus, le gouvernement du Parti québécois (PQ) lançait les premiers jalons d'une politique interculturelle en 1978, qui prenait en compte l'existence d'une nation majoritaire au Québec et permettait l'intégration en français des personnes immigrantes dans le respect de leur diversité culturelle[7].

Du référendum sur la souveraineté de 1980 jusqu'à celui de 1995, des défaites constitutionnelles majeures freinèrent cet élan progressiste et pluraliste. Les élites politiques québécoises, péquistes et libérales, rencontrèrent une fin de non-recevoir à la fois de la part du peuple québécois (qui dit non deux fois à l'indépendance) et du gouvernement fédéral (qui refusa le fédéralisme asymétrique), ainsi que de la population du Canada hors Québec (pour qui l'égalité provinciale est synonyme d'uniformité). D'un côté, le nationalisme pancanadien, qui suit son évolution centralisatrice, ne peut accommoder les revendications du Québec sans miner sa propre existence. De l'autre, malgré la baisse du soutien à la souveraineté, de plus en plus de citoyen(ne)s s'identifient davantage – voire exclusivement – comme Québécois(e)s et plus des deux tiers de la population sont insatisfaits du *statu quo* constitutionnel et souhaitent une sortie de crise satisfaisante[8].

Cette impasse constitutionnelle, combinée aux effets pervers de la mondialisation néolibérale, a nourri la montée d'un conservatisme culturel. L'économisme néolibéral, important depuis 1996 au Québec, sert tant les fins des péquistes (démontrer qu'un Québec indépendant est viable financièrement) que des libéraux provinciaux (développer l'économie en attirant des investisseurs étrangers). Au Québec comme au Canada, la progression d'un courant nationaliste conservateur – liant institutions libérales et valeurs traditionnelles – entraîne un rejet des enjeux qui divisent l'opinion, comme la diversité ethnoculturelle, le féminisme, les luttes sociales. Ce nationalisme inquiet perçoit de multiples menaces envers l'« identité québécoise » et est obsédé par la décadence du « sujet national québécois », comme si une telle entité pouvait être figée dans le temps et se reproduire en vase clos en « assimilant » tous les éléments étrangers venus s'y greffer. Or, ce nationalisme conservateur est contraire à l'idée de l'intégration dans le respect de la diversité, qui implique que la majorité nationale est aussi appelée à évoluer sous l'influence des nouveaux arrivants.

Pour la frange conservatrice du nationalisme québécois, la « communauté nationale » semble se réduire aux « Français de souche ». Mais un projet qui ne parle qu'aux seuls Blancs francophones est inadapté au Québec moderne. C'est aussi condamner l'un des véhicules de la Révolution tranquille, le PQ, à l'insignifiance politique à long terme en raison de la croissance de la diversité ethnoculturelle et du désintérêt des jeunes pour les enjeux identitaires et souverainistes, qui leur préfèrent les questions sociales et environnementales.

Le PQ, sans avoir pu faire le plein d'un vote nationaliste conservateur, se retrouve en porte-à-faux avec sa propre aile progressiste et pluraliste. Perdant des votes en faveur de la gauche indépendantiste (Option nationale et Québec solidaire) et de la droite autonomiste (Coalition Avenir Québec), le PQ est affaibli, cherche avant tout à regagner le pouvoir et est incapable de reprendre l'initiative sur le front constitutionnel.

Voyant le danger de raviver la flamme nationaliste par des demandes constitutionnelles qui se verraient refusées, le Parti libéral du Québec (PLQ) a depuis 20 ans évité ce terrain miné, arguant que le « fruit n'est pas mûr ». Le PLQ élève donc comme des victoires historiques de simples ententes administratives, qui ne modifient en rien les rapports de pouvoir entre le Québec et le reste du Canada. Si le PQ a peu cherché à mobiliser les citoyens autour de l'indépendance depuis 1995, le PLQ n'a pas non plus beaucoup promu l'idée fédérale au Québec, contrairement à ce qu'il faisait du temps de ses anciens chefs comme Robert Bourassa. Le nationalisme québécois est alors de retour à une position défensive stérile et impuissante, pris entre un impossible fédéralisme asymétrique dans le cadre canadien et une inatteignable indépendance, du moins à moyen terme.

Pour le Canada hors Québec, le rapatriement de 1982 a été un moment de renouveau national qui a complété son indépendance face à Londres, a sacralisé son identité moderne et a promis, pour plusieurs, de mettre fin aux injustices passées. Le Canada hors Québec cherche maintenant à bâtir une union économique et sociale fonctionnelle dans laquelle les membres des minorités nationales sont invités à se fondre. Les nationalismes québécois et canadien suivent donc des trajectoires parallèles et irréconciliables.

Avec l'inévitable renouvellement générationnel du nationalisme québécois, un possible scénario serait l'apparition d'un mouvement pluraliste pouvant mobiliser une base populaire pour soutenir un projet de société progressiste, mais aussi donner un nouveau rapport de force à une renégociation constitutionnelle avec le reste du Canada. Pour être viable, le résultat de telles négociations devrait prendre en compte les aspirations réciproques du Québec et du Canada hors Québec. C'est-à-dire permettre au premier de continuer à développer une société francophone, progressiste et pluraliste et, au second, de poursuivre son projet d'édification nationale pancanadien. Autrement dit, dans l'esprit de la formule de Samuel Laselva, il s'agit de respecter « la volonté de vivre ensemble et la volonté de vivre séparées » de ces deux sociétés. Or, la seule position qui puisse accommoder le Québec et le reste du Canada tout en maintenant entre eux un lien politique est la confédération : une union d'États souverains qui ont choisi d'agir de concert sur un ensemble d'enjeux cruciaux en mettant en commun des compétences générales (défense, monnaie, etc.), qui sont déléguées à un gouvernement central, tout en conservant leurs pouvoirs locaux (éducation, santé, etc.). Le gouvernement central jouerait un rôle de coordination et de soutien pour les États membres, mais demeurerait subordonné à ces États souverains desquels il émanerait. Ainsi, le Canada, en tant que multination issue du compromis de 1867, pourrait réaliser pleinement sa vision d'une société à la fois progressiste et pluraliste.

A Confederal Future

David Sanschagrin

FOR MUCH OF its relatively short history, Canada's identity has remained vague, characterized by ethnocultural and socio-political diversity. The federation of 1867 was born out of a spirit of moderation and compromise between colonial elites, most notably between supporters of a federal union and those favouring a legislative union. It politically united two founding settler cultures, while enabling them to keep their specificities (private law, religion, language). Opponents to the union were pressured by London to endorse the arrangement, or bought with the promise of key postings in the new federal state. Despite significant crises,[1] all concerned parties eventually accepted the legitimacy of a federation endowed with central government unilateral powers that allowed the building of a cross-continental railway and a commercial empire, so long as this government didn't encroach on socio-cultural powers.

But encroach that central government did, first by building a welfare state, and then, with Prime Minister Pierre Trudeau's patriation of the Constitution Act, 1982, brought about without the consent of the National Assembly of Québec. Since the vague definition of the Canadian federation had allowed for multiple interpretations, the Constitution Act, 1982 has contributed to an uncertain future. Departing from the spirit of moderation and compromise of 1867, a new Canada emerged in 1982 from these far-ranging constitutional reforms. As a result, federal public institutions began to emphasize multiculturalism and official bilingualism, paired with a limited conception of social justice, provincial equality, and the rights of individuals and socio-political minorities.

One could argue that this new Canada has a profound flaw, since provincial equality and individual rights can be seen to be at odds with other fundamental principles. The result is that federalism has been reinterpreted as an outmoded institutional practice, recognition of national minorities is obviated, and traditional civil and political rights are given precedence over socio-economic rights. For many in Quebec, this new foundational moment meant that the rest of Canada had embraced a unitary conception of the federation, seeking a more functional social and economic union with decision-making power centralized in Ottawa. Since the 1970s, opposition to this vision of Canada has been wrongly perceived as a rejection of social progress and human rights.

The constitutional reforms of 1982 have meant that, regardless of their identity and values, all Canadian citizens, imbued with the same individual rights, are asked to give allegiance to a Canadian society whose national centre is Ottawa, whose ideology is liberal individualism, and whose dominant language is English. This has also meant that members of the First Nations and the Quebec nation must put aside their more collectivist values in order to blend, preferably in English, into a Canadian whole. The allegiance of citizens of diverse immigrant origin, or of those belonging to visible minorities, is taken for granted under the banner of multiculturalism. Thus, multiculturalism does not acknowledge the Canadian national majority and has not led to a major redefinition of power institutions and social hierarchies.

According to Will Kymlicka in "Marketing Canadian Pluralism in the International Arena," the official constitutional enshrinement of multiculturalism, bilingualism, and human rights serves Canadian nationalism, advancing this model of diversity management as an example for the world to follow. The marketing of this new Canada obfuscates other features of Canadian history. First, racist immigration policies were adopted in the form of quotas, head taxes, and bans. Second, Canadian political elites share a conception of democracy that is suspicious of popular participation. Third, during the Second World War, Japanese, German, and Italian Canadians were interned in labour camps on suspicion of disloyalty. Fourth, there was a repeated use of emergency powers by the state to suspend civil liberties. Fifth, the struggle of women for socio-political recognition was long and hard, and its's still ongoing. Sixth, from the 1920s to the 1950s, the left-wing protest groups were repressed by the state. Seventh, the recognition of trade unionism is still precarious. Eighth, francophones and those who were neither British nor Protestant suffered discrimination and systemic racism. Finally, Indigenous peoples had their lands confiscated and were alienated, confined on reserves, and forced into assimilation into Canadian society.

Reconciliation between classes, ethnocultural groups, and nations should not mean forgetting a long history of struggles and injustices in favour of rallying and optimistic speech, since, for example, francophones still bear the burden of bilingualism in a continuing context of linguistic assimilation, and the treatment of the First Nations remains scandalous.[2] Recognition and compensation of past and ongoing injustices must involve not only a change of tone but also a profound transformation of the idea of Canada and of the country's power relations.

Since the interventionist and centralizing report issued by the Royal Commission on Dominion-Provincial Relations (1940), Canada, outside of Quebec, has constructed a new pan-Canadian nation, one that responds to social demands and identity needs while integrating national minorities. For the French minority, the choice is between assimilation and political struggle resulting in secession. The pan-Canadian identity was recently reasserted by Justin Trudeau in the "Statement by the Prime Minister of Canada on Canada Day" (2016): "Today, we celebrate the day, exactly 149 years ago, when the people of this great land came together, and forged one nation, one country—Canada." This statement implies that Canada is not a multinational federation.

The recent invocation by the prime minister of a post-national Canadian identity[3] does not change our history; the promise of a universal identity by national majorities is also a call to assimilate national minorities.[4] This is the same assimilationist vision that awakened Aboriginal nationalism in the late 1960s, a time when Indigenous peoples became a political force seeking "nation to nation" relations, refusing to abide by either the official unitary history (one Canada, one nation) or the counter dualistic history (compact between two founding peoples) promoted by Quebec.[5]

Over time, nationalism in the territory of Quebec has had two progressive liberal moments (Patriotic Republicanism and the Quiet Revolution) that have sought to redefine the political regime and its links with the Crown (British, yesterday, and Canadian, today). These have been followed by major defeats (military, then, and constitutional, now) that led to a closure of the political horizon and a cultural conservative withdrawal, as an escape road for preservation.

Rejecting the conservative nationalism of the "survivance" ideology, the progressive neo-nationalism of the Quiet Revolution sought political modernization and social progress. It responded to Canadian nation-building and to a global context of decolonization. The reform focused first on improving the socio-economic situation of white francophones. The Royal Commission on Bilingualism and Biculturalism, launched by Prime Minister Lester B. Pearson in 1963, revealed that this group suffered systematic socio-economic discrimination across Canada and especially in Quebec. They were the "water bearers" of Anglo-Protestant capital who were required to speak the "civilized" language of their masters.

The Quiet Revolution laid the groundwork for pluralism. National belonging was no longer officially defined through race and religion, but rather through language. Quebec governments also secularized the education system and, in so doing, encouraged the integration of immigrants into French schools. In 1978, the Parti Québécois (PQ) government launched an intercultural policy that recognized the Quebec nation and, concomitantly, respected the cultural diversity of immigrant communities on their path to integration into francophone Quebec society.[6]

And yet, the progressive and pluralist momentum emerging in the wake of the Quiet Revolution was stalled by the failed sovereignty referendums of 1980 and 1995. Quebec political elites (from both the Liberal and PQ parties) were denied by Quebecers (who twice said no to independence), by the federal government (which refused asymmetrical federalism), and by Canadians outside Quebec (for whom provincial equality means uniformity). What became clear is that Canadian nationalism, which follows its own centralizing evolution, cannot accommodate Quebec's claims without undermining itself. Although there has been a decline in support for independence, an emerging majority is identifying itself as Quebecers first (or exclusively), and two-thirds of the population are dissatisfied with the status quo solution for Quebec.[7]

This constitutional stalemate is compounded by the toxic effects of neo-liberal globalization fed on the rise of cultural conservatism. Neo-liberal economics, which have been important in Quebec since 1996, serve the aims of both the PQ (demonstrating that independence is financially viable) and the provincial Liberals (developing the economy by attracting foreign investors). The rise of a conservative nationalism—combining liberal institutions and traditional values—in both Quebec and Canada at large acts to reject so-called divisive issues like ethnocultural diversity, feminism, social contests. This anxious nationalism perceives multiple threats to "Quebec identity" and is obsessed by the decline of the "Quebec national subject," as if this entity could be frozen in time and reproduce in isolation by "assimilating" all foreign elements. Yet, this conservative nationalism runs contrary to the idea that the national majority must evolve under the influence of first-generation Quebecers.

For the conservative fringe of Quebec nationalism, the "national community" seems to include only "native-born French people." But any project that speaks only to white francophones is out of touch with modern Quebec. This narrow view of Quebec society also condemns one of the vehicles of the Quiet Revolution, the PQ, to political insignificance because of the growing cultural and ethnic diversity of the province, and the youth's lack of interest for identity and sovereignty and their focus on social and environmental issues. The PQ, incapable of reaching all conservative nationalist voters, now finds itself at odds with its own progressive and pluralistic wing. Losing votes to the independentist left (Option Nationale and Québec Solidaire) and the autonomist right (Coalition Avenir Québec), the PQ is weakened, seeking above all to regain power and unable to retake the initiative on the constitutional front.

Understanding the deadlock and the danger of reviving the nationalist flame, the Parti libéral du Québec (PLQ) has for twenty years avoided the constitutional minefield, arguing that the "fruit is not ripe." Instead, the party has lauded its administrative agreements with the central government, although these have not altered power relations between Quebec and Canada. Just as the PQ has not sought to mobilize citizens around independence since 1995, the PLQ has not promoted the federal idea in Quebec, contrary to its old days under the leadership of the likes of Robert Bourassa. Quebec nationalism is thus returning to a sterile defensive and powerless position, caught between the impossibility of asymmetrical federalism in the Canadian framework and an apparently unattainable independence.

Yet, for Canada outside Quebec, the patriation events of 1982 were moments of national renewal, completing Canada's independence from Britain, sacralizing its modern identity, and, for many, promising a path away from historical injustices. Canada, outside Quebec, now seeks a more functional and integrated social and economic union in which members of the national minorities are asked to blend. Quebec and this pan-Canadian nationalism thus follow parallel and irreconcilable trajectories.

With the inevitable generational renewal of Quebec nationalism, one possible outcome is the emergence of a pluralist movement that will mobilize a strong popular base to back a more progressive society project, while also giving Quebec a more favourable position in a constitutional renegotiation with the rest of Canada. To be viable, renegotiation must take into account the reciprocal aspirations of Quebec and the rest of Canada. This means the continued development of a French, plural-ist, and progressive society alongside the pursuit of a pan-Canadian nation-building project, or in the words of Samuel Laselva, to reconcile "the will to live together and the will to live apart." The only position that can accommodate both national projects and simultaneously maintain a political link between Quebec and the rest of Canada is a confedera-tion: a union of sovereign states that chooses to act together on crucial issues by delegating some general powers (defence, currency) to a cen-tral government, while retaining their local powers (education, health). This general central government would play a role of coordination and support for the member states but remain subordinate to the sover-eign states from which it was born. Canada, then, as a multination that emerged out of compromise in 1867, would attain its vision of a collec-tive society that is, at once, both progressive and pluralist.

Hard of Herring

Tony Pitcher, Mimi Lam, Matthias Kaiser,
April (SGaana Jaad) White, and Evgeny Pakhomov

OVER THE PAST 150 years, herring—an iconic small, silvery fish—has had a profound influence on the ecology, economy, and culture of Canada's Pacific coast. British Columbia Coastal First Nations celebrate the crucial ecosystem role of these "silver darlings," which provide sustenance for many marine mammals, predatory fish, and seabirds, and—through their eggs at spawning time—even terrestrial species such as wolves, raccoons, and bears. This awareness of an integrated ecosystem is displayed in much First Nations art, including the work of one of us, Haida artist April (SGaana Jaad) White. Collaborating with our scientific team, she produced a series of hand-pulled serigraphs ("Herring People") depicting the interconnectedness of herring with beings in all of the natural realms—undersea, earth, and sky. The artwork shown in Figure 1 features herring and the humpback whale. It's one of eight images of a silvery herring cloaking and nurturing other important species in the ecosystem: humpback whale, dolphin/porpoise, dogfish/shark, sea lion, chinook salmon, eagle, and male and female humans.

Despite the importance of these silver darlings, a dysfunction in governance of both the cultural and the ecological aspects of herring fisheries in western Canada has led to conflict in its management. As we reflect on the 150th anniversary of Canadian Confederation and look forward to the future, we envisage a path toward improved fishery

FIGURE 1. Two artistic representations of the ecological role of herring, used in interviews and community consultations in Haida Gwaii concerning values related to herring fisheries: upper panel: "Hunger Games" © by Haida artist April (SG̲aana Jaad) White, representing the interconnected food web of orca, chinook salmon, and herring (including a red herring); lower panel: "Herring People: Humpback Whale," one of a set of eight serigraph images depicting the interconnectedness of herring with its predators from the undersea, earth, and sky. © *Haida artist April (SG̲aana Jaad) White.*

management that could enhance the value of herring to First Nations, to the fishing industry, and for the marine ecosystem, so that this "little fish that could" may once again recover to support the many animals and people who depend upon it.

Traditionally, and still today, many west coast First Nations—such as the Haida, Heiltsuk, and Nuu-chah-nulth—welcome herring to provide the first fresh food after winter. In early spring, the fish gather in huge inshore shoals to spawn on kelp, an important traditional source of First Nations' food. Kelp fronds or hemlock branches are placed in "ponds" in the water, and ripe herring are herded to spawn upon them. This Aboriginal technique represents one of the few non-lethal fishing methods around the world; the spawned eggs on kelp fronds are collected, leaving the adult fish unharmed to return and spawn another year. This herring spawn on kelp, known as "k'aaw" in the Haida language, was eaten in spring village feasts in Haida Gwaii. Today, although some spawn on kelp is usually harvested, large Haida community events are rarely celebrated, given the depleted herring stocks of northern BC. Throughout the year, herring were traditionally caught with nets from shore and wooden rakes from canoes, and spread out on wooden racks to dry in the wind like salmon. These dried fish could be eaten when needed, thus sustaining the diets of First Nations during challenging seasons and years.

Commercial herring fisheries did not begin until 1888 and remained small for about twenty years, but soon thereafter came into conflict with Aboriginal uses (See Figure 2). The commercial fleets initially obtained large catches from semi-urban areas by setting seine nets from small steam-powered vessels. The herring were originally destined to be dry-salted or sometimes to become fertilizer, but they soon began serving additional small local markets for smoked ("kippers"), pickled ("roll mops"), and fresh herring in Canada's west coast cities. The 1930s saw the introduction of a European industrial technique of cooking the herring carcasses to produce refined oil and fishmeal, herring fishmeal production often sharing factory facilities (and ownership) with salmon canneries. In the 1950s, foreign trawler fleets, mostly Russian, also began fishing herring close to shore in BC, adding to increasingly serious overfishing by local Canadian purse seine fleets that were serving the large fishmeal plants. This massive fishing pressure precipitated a collapse of the herring stocks and led to a coastwide closure of the BC fishery by the federal government between 1968 and 1971.

During the closure, the herring population recovered enough to be opened to support a new lucrative commercial fishery for the eggs of spawning herring, which is still in operation today. The eggs were exported to a largely Japanese market that opened up in the wake of a collapse of the once massive Hokkaido herring stocks. In addition to

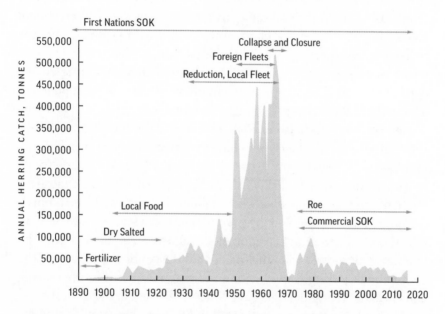

KEY TO PLOT LABELS
Fertilizer = herring caught to be used as fertilizer spread on agricultural fields
Dry Salted = salted preserved herring for consumption (local and export)
Local Food = fresh, smoked, and pickled herring
Reduction = herring caught by local fleets with carcasses cooked to produce fishmeal
Foreign Fleets = herring caught by foreign fleets, mostly Russian
Collapse and Closure = collapse of herring stocks and closure mandated by Canadian government
Roe = fishery for ripe herring eggs
Commercial SOK = spawn on kelp (SOK) and related products

FIGURE 2. The history of catches from the British Columbia commercial herring fishery, showing major changes in products and management.[1]

spawn on kelp, ripe eggs ("roe") are stripped from female herring immediately after they are caught at sea—either in specialized shaken gill
nets or, mainly, by highly mechanized purse seine boats. Both male and
female carcasses from this "roe fishery" are then discarded or sent for
fishmeal or export. Younger Japanese have not acquired the same taste
as the older generation, for whom this food was part of their culture.
Consequently, in recent years, roe prices have fallen, reducing some
of the pressure on Canada's herring stocks. Today, a local demand for
fresh herring as food has emerged largely from European and Asian
immigrants. The demand is only partially served by a small recreational
fishery and popular annual charity sales in early winter. Small amounts
of herring are also caught for bait to be used by the salmon and halibut
fisheries. The current herring fishery from depleted stocks is relatively
small, thus providing an opportune moment to gather local support for
a natural herring recovery and more sustainable fisheries management.

And yet, conflicts between First Nations and the commercial roe herring and spawn-on-kelp fisheries have persisted, and have even become
more intense. In 2014 and 2015, Fisheries and Oceans Canada (DFO)
reopened commercial herring fisheries in the north and the central BC
coast, despite the failure of stocks to rebuild and against the recommendations of First Nations and the government's own scientists. In the case
of Haida Gwaii, the Haida Nation filed and won an injunction from the
Supreme Court of Canada that mandated the continued closure of the
commercial herring fishery, citing the potential harm to the herring
and to Haida Aboriginal rights and title.[2] In the case of the central coast,
the Heiltsuk Nation mounted a well-publicized campaign of civil dis-
obedience that resulted in DFO cancelling the herring fishery opening.
The conflict is not over, but, in 2016, under a new federal government,
the Pacific herring fishery has remained closed until any recovery is
clearly measured, as per local First Nations preferences and scientific
recommendations.

At the heart of the herring conflict lies an absence of responsible fisheries governance in Canada, as measured against international social,
fiscal, and ecological criteria for sustainability. One issue is the lack of
equitable distribution of benefits from the fishery. The highly profitable
modern herring fleets have moved from an owner-driver model toward

corporate ownership, where ownership, procedures, fixed fish prices, and loans are effectively determined by the political and financial influence of just one processor. As a consequence, policy and regulation by the government fisheries agency has been "captured" by the large-scale fishery industry. A similar dysfunction in governance in the 1960s led to a failure to rein in the herring fleet serving the fishmeal plants, which almost destroyed the resource. BC herring populations were actually saved in 1968 after local small-scale herring fishermen (like Joe Bauer from Steveston, BC) voted to stop fishing because they were alarmed that stocks might be completely depleted within a matter of weeks. The federal government eventually responded to this by mandating a coastwide herring fishery closure. Failure to effectively reflect the constitutional public ownership of marine resources in Canadian fisheries policy has been accompanied by a tendency to privatize the resource through the introduction of rights-based quotas and market-driven licence holding. This pernicious process of privatization has effectively abrogated Canadian public trust in fisheries management.

So, in light of past regulatory failures, what hope might we place in the future?

First, values and ethics should be explicitly addressed in any discussions of how natural resources are managed for society, and the ultimate use of these resources should be a factor in any policy equation. All too easily, monetary values trump all other considerations. The cultural importance of Canada's west coast herring to the Haida First Nation was assessed in a series of interviews on Haida Gwaii led by Dr. Mimi Lam, revealing the primacy of two values: respect and responsibility. Incorporating these values into policy decisions is a new venture and challenges not only decision-makers but also scientists. New values-based methods and appraisal tools are needed. One such approach measures how people's values accord with management by asking them to place a set of cards representing their ranked values onto images of scenarios that represent alternative policy options for the fishery: for example, in Haida Gwaii, many preferred a scenario in which the roe herring fishery was closed, at least until stocks had almost fully recovered.[3]

Second, we need to employ the best science available to us. Like most fish, herring swim to their birthplace to spawn. Yet this "local" biology is not well reflected in Canada's herring fishery management, which is based on larger spatial scales, unlike in other countries with herring fisheries. Tagging herring, a tricky procedure for such delicate little fish, has been carried out since the 1930s. Evidence from tagging—and, more recently, from DNA sequencing and chemical diaries of the herrings' local environment written in their ear bones—now confirms that Pacific herring home to a general spawning area within a few kilometres. This new scientific understanding is critical, as it implies that fishing quotas should be set separately for each local stock. When this is not done, small local stocks that can be fished as part of a larger-scale quota can collapse, as they are not easily replaced by herring from elsewhere. The history of BC herring includes the extirpation of many of these small local stocks that never recovered from the massive collapse in the 1960s, resulting in a serious loss of traditional food for many BC First Nations.

Third, we need to address dysfunctional governance and regulatory issues. Among maritime nations, Canada is unique in that all marine waters within our two-hundred-nautical-mile Exclusive Economic Zone (EEZ) are controlled by the federal government. Canadian provinces have no inshore "territorial waters," unlike, for example, European countries, and American and Australian states, all of which have local jurisdiction over three, six, or twelve nautical miles from their coasts. If Canada were ever to adopt the world standard in this respect, fishery conflicts with First Nations, such as those surrounding our herring, might be resolved through co-management arrangements with provincial and regional governments. The implementation of this "subsidiarity principle" has the potential to be more responsive to local needs, as exemplified by improvements in the local collaborative management of forest resources in Haida Gwaii and inshore herring fisheries in Alaska. Ultimately, we must work toward a collaborative governance of living natural resources that is informed by both science and societal values.

Herring is a little fish that has reflected much of the 150-year maritime history of the people of western Canada. It is iconic of the holistic value our natural resources have in different aspects of our lives. Robust and culturally sensitive herring management programs are currently underway through the collaborative efforts of scientific researchers and the Haida and Heiltsuk Nations.[4] We are in the process of investigating how the local ecosystem and stakeholders interact with, and are impacted by, the herring fishery, with the aim of improving the management of this valuable fish.

Reconciliation between First Nations and the federal government is presently being played out in a hopeful fashion, trickling down into Canadian life and culture, and reflected in a vibrant art and an integrated understanding of how to promote healthy societies and natural systems. As the future unfolds, we should finally learn to respect, conserve, and use these "silver darlings" wisely, as an example of the kind of balanced social and ecological systems we aspire to.

Reclaiming the Tower of Babel

Linda Siegel, Judith Wiener,
and Esther Geva

UNLIKE THE BIBLICAL story of the Tower of Babel, Canadian multi-lingualism is neither a punishment nor a problem. Instead, we must celebrate and encourage the many languages and cultures that form the basis of our society.

The languages we speak are a key to our personal identity, our thinking, and our ability to express our thoughts to others. Geographical and historical circumstances have made multiculturalism and multilingualism two of the basic foundations of Canadian society, and a central part of our conception of what it means to be Canadian. The result is a country that prides itself on its linguistic diversity—although it is also a country that struggles to be true to that self-image at the same time. In particular, on the 150th anniversary of Canadian Confederation, we continue to strive to unite the three elements that weave a uniquely Canadian linguistic fabric: bilingualism, multiculturalism, and Indigenous languages and cultures.

Canada is officially a bilingual country. Our two official languages, English and French, reflect the European explorers and settlers who first arrived in this land in the seventeenth century. We are a land of linguistic islands that reflect these historical settlement patterns. In modern-day Canada, French is the predominant language spoken in Quebec and parts of New Brunswick, Nova Scotia, Ontario, Alberta, and Manitoba.

English is the predominant language in the rest of Canada, although there are small French-speaking pockets among this English concentration. The Indigenous languages of Canada, once spoken across this land, have been significantly diminished over the past century, although they are now showing hopeful signs of resurgence.

Making a nation bilingual is not an easy task. How do we teach children to become fluent in two languages, one of which is not spoken in their home, with no exposure until they first enter school? Ideally, all Canadian children learn both English and French at school, but, in practice, we have not achieved this goal. Most Canadian children do not become fully bilingual at school because they do not have the same amount of learning in each language. The majority of children in English-speaking Canada can speak only some French and, similarly, most children in French-speaking areas have limited English.

Canada's experience in this regard is unique—a story of some real successes and some disheartening failures. About fifty years ago, a group of English-speaking parents in Saint-Lambert, Quebec, were dissatisfied with their children's inadequate progress in French. With the collaboration of two professors from McGill University, Wallace Lambert and Richard Tucker, these Quebecers came up with the idea of French immersion. In this innovative method, children who know no French start learning it from the first day that they enter school. The teacher speaks only French to them, except in certain rare situations, and they learn all of their subjects in French. There are some variations to this French immersion model. In some cases, English and French are taught at the same time in a bilingual program. In other cases, French immersion starts later, usually in grade four or five, or some subjects may be taught in English in the later grades. Students who remain in the program acquire native-like facility to speak, read, and write in French. This achievement is remarkable: these students encounter French only at school. Their English-language learning tends not to suffer, and the children develop an excellent understanding of both languages. Lisa, five years old and in French immersion, is typical. She told her anglophone father when he attempted to speak French to her, "The words are right, but the pronunciation is wrong." Lisa needs to learn some diplomatic skills along with her language skills. But her language acquisition in bilingual education—easy and accurate—is testament to the success of the program.

Why start when the children are so young? The answers lie in the brain of a young child. Young children absorb language like sponges absorb water. The mysterious ability of the young child to learn languages is astounding to adults who struggle with the pronunciation and grammar of a foreign language. These adults wish for a chip that could be implanted in their brain that would then allow them to speak a foreign language without effort. Such chips are still the dream of science fiction writers.

Although the idea of immersion has become the model for language programs all over the world, the reality is more complicated. It can be difficult to find qualified teachers in areas of Canada where little or no French is spoken. Inadequate cultural resources outside the classroom, such as plays and movies, limit wider exposure to French for the students in anglophone Canada. And anglophone children for whom immersion French is a struggle are likely to switch into the mainstream English program, where their studies may be easier and in which better academic supports are available. There are parallel programs in Quebec where English immersion is the method of instruction for some francophone children.

In recent years, children of immigrants who speak another language at home are attending French immersion, with secondary instruction also in English. This is a real Canadian phenomenon—children who converse with their parents in the home language, and learn French and English at school! Another combination that reflects the Canadian reality is Chinese immersion—you may think that most of the children who attend Chinese immersion programs come from Chinese backgrounds, but this is not the case.

What about bilingualism for children not in immersion programs? It is true that children not in French immersion are encouraged to learn French. Unfortunately, too often French is offered too late and too little, not until upper-elementary-school grades, middle school, or even high school. Language learning is harder in these later years; we waste valuable time by not introducing French early. In addition, this approach sends the message that languages are not an important school subject;

many students drop it as soon as they can. French immersion works. It is a good solution for all children, but, without adequate support for this form of schooling, bilingualism will remain a lovely but impossible dream.

And what of Canada's other languages? When the English and French European settlers arrived, they found more than eighty Indigenous languages in the lands that are now Canada. Most of these languages did not traditionally have a writing system, and many are now dying or almost extinct, as a terrible legacy of the residential schools program and other racist Canadian policies toward Indigenous peoples. Apologies and financial compensation have begun, but they cannot really make up for the legacy of residential schools and for the disappearance of many Aboriginal languages.

The future may look brighter, however, for at least some Aboriginal languages. A variety of initiatives are underway to restore and strengthen this linguistic diversity. Although many languages are lost permanently, some may be restored and become living languages again. Indigenous Elders work in schools to teach Indigenous languages to children. For example, on the Huron reserve of Wendake, near Quebec City, people are learning their ancestral tongue, Wendat. On the west coast, Elders are teaching the younger generation a language called Hul'qumi'num, the Coast Salish language spoken by the Cowichan people in British Columbia. Books are being written in various Indigenous languages for children, and these efforts are being supported by a number of innovative digital platforms.

Canada's future as a multilingual country echoes our past as a land of many Indigenous languages. And, as immigration patterns in Canada shift, Canada is increasingly becoming a microcosm of global linguistic diversity. There are many children who speak neither of the two official languages. For example, in Vancouver and Toronto, schoolchildren from immigrant or refugee families may speak one of 150 different languages. This trend reflects the fact that Canada is a country built on immigration; other than the original Indigenous inhabitants, we are all immigrants. Investment in the linguistic capital of Canadian citizens thus reflects our commitment to Canada as a multicultural nation.

Nonetheless, this situation is a challenging one for the educational system. Traditionally, many educators have encouraged parents to speak only English or French to their children (in anglophone and francophone regions respectively), even if their parents have only a weak command of these languages. Research has shown, however, that this is not the best path to second-language acquisition. Rather, it is better for children's cognitive development if they hear language spoken fluently; parents should thus be encouraged to use their native language at home. Canadian schools provide ESL (English as a second language) or FSL (French as a second language) programs for newcomers. It is important to remember that it takes many years to acquire full language skills and that children will continue to develop their English- or French-language skills years after they stop attending these formal classes.

Canadian government policy and attitudes toward cultural diversity have led to the development of heritage language programs, in which children receive additional instruction in reading and writing in their first (neither English nor French) language. The lessons occur outside school hours, after school or on weekends. Heritage language programs are a distinctive feature of the Canadian educational system, and exist in both English- and French-speaking communities across Canada. These programs promote not only facility with the language but understanding of and pride in the culture of the children's ancestors. By cultivating linguistic diversity, such programs directly support multiculturalism in Canada, strengthening traditions across the vast cultural mosaic of this nation.

How do we build on successes and move beyond historical failures? Going forward, Canada as a nation needs to expand and refine its policies regarding language education. If we wish to make a truly English-French bilingual country, every school in Canada should incorporate at all levels of the curriculum at least an hour a day of training in either English or French, whichever is not the primary language of instruction. As part of this initiative, there needs to be adequate help for students struggling in English or French as their second official language.

And what of all of our other languages? How do we make room for this linguistic diversity under the umbrella of official bilingualism? Preserving and teaching Aboriginal languages are essential to the health and well-being of Indigenous individuals and their cultures. We thus need to devote resources to preserving records of Aboriginal languages and to develop teaching skills and resources for not just the survival but also the flourishing of these languages. And to continue to be a country where immigrants are welcome, we must be more open to the various (and growing number of) languages that are part of the Canadian cultural and linguistic landscape. We need to support heritage language programs and respond flexibly to world events and the languages of new immigrants and refugees.

Canadians are justifiably proud of the linguistic diversity that is a critical part of the country. But we can be better. We need to make Canada truly multilingual, where every person acquires proficiency in more than one language. Language is a fundamental part of identity, and our many languages are central to the identity of Canada as a nation. Bilingualism, Indigenous languages, and heritage languages are the threads that bind communities together, creating the conditions for a society in which diverse peoples can flourish. We have the opportunity in Canada to do something unique, to be a beacon to the world for how citizens can live together in a multilingual and multicultural community. Now, more than ever, the world needs the example that Canada can set.

North Vancouver, British Columbia, looking toward
Stanley Park in Vancouver | TERRY BEAUPRE

Airdrie, Alberta | NICHOLAS TAFFS

Victoria, British Columbia | MIKE LANE

MIKE LANE

Indigenous Land and Food

Dawn Morrison and Hannah Wittman

Food will be what brings the people together.
The late Secwepemc Elder WOLVERINE

The first time I went to a workshop at the BC Food Systems Network, I heard Brewster Kneen, one of Canada's founding leaders of the food security movement, talking about the exploitation of Haitian workers in the sugar fields, and the dangers of corporate control of the food system. The things he was saying sounded so similar to what I had heard Elders say about the social and environmental injustices that we, as Indigenous peoples, have experienced over the years.
DAWN MORRISON, Secwepemc, founder of the Working Group
on Indigenous Food Sovereignty (WGIFS)

I first met Dawn at a WGIFS meeting while enjoying my first taste of soapberry foam (Indian ice cream). As a settler who came to Canada as an "expert" in food systems, I realized my total lack of knowledge and understanding of this traditional food and of the relationships between Indigenous peoples and landscapes that created it.
HANNAH WITTMAN, Centre for Sustainable Food Systems,
University of British Columbia

WE GATHER AT BC Food Systems Network gatherings as Indigenous peoples, farmers, urban consumers, dieticians, and environmental advocates at a place of dialogue and intercultural learning. We have come to understand that Indigenous peoples and sustainable food systems advocates face similar realities around social and ecological injustice in the food system. There is a lot of common ground, but there are also huge disparities and historical injustices.

Canada has a reputation as a global breadbasket, but food insecurity and inequality have also been defining experiences for many peoples across the diverse territories where Canada has asserted dominion over the past 150 years. Today, one in eight Canadians face hunger on a regular basis, and food insecurity rates for Indigenous peoples are three times higher than the national average.[1] Extractive natural resource development, urbanization, mining, pipelines, climate change, and many forms of agriculture also threaten the forests, fields, and waterways where Indigenous hunting, fishing, farming, and gathering societies have persisted over thousands of years.

While Indigenous peoples have been cultivating Indigenous foods for thousands of years on a broad landscape scale, settler forms of agriculture on privatized plots of land have been much more recently introduced. Cultural hierarchies imposed by early settlers unjustly viewed and classified Indigenous hunters and gatherers as "savages and heathens" inferior to European settler agrarians. These cultural hierarchies led to a long legacy of social injustice through the establishment of the 1857 Gradual Civilization Act, the Gradual Enfranchisement Act of 1869, and the Indian Act of 1876, which continue to assert "control with no soul" over Indigenous land, water, and ways of life. The introduction of settler agriculture also led to large-scale land privatization that dispossessed Indigenous peoples; fragmented landscapes; decreased access to hunting, fishing, and gathering areas; and eroded complex systems of Indigenous bio-cultural heritage.

In this conversation, we aim to foster dialogue on how settler society can work in solidarity with Indigenous peoples to overcome social and environmental injustice in the land and food system. How can we understand the future role(s) for settler agriculture in a land where many Indigenous peoples have never surrendered or ceded traditional territories? How can we build a food system that acknowledges the ways that Indigenous peoples continue to assert sovereignty outside the techno-bureaucratic silos and sectors of the agri-food system that has made them invisible?

We call on all Canadians to advocate for adaptive policies and practices, and culturally appropriate institutional frameworks that nurture social and ecological resiliency. We honour the long legacy of political activism upheld by the late Secwepemc Elder Wolverine of Adams Lake and the late Chief Arthur Manuel of Neskonlith Secwepemc. They have demonstrated a lifetime dedication and commitment to fighting for Indigenous rights and title to the forests, fields, and waterways where Indigenous foods are hunted, fished, farmed, and gathered. In their footsteps, we traverse a series of cross-cultural "learning edges" where Indigenous food sovereignty meets sustainable food system research, actions, and policy proposals. This dialogue provides a framework for bringing deeper meaning and understanding of how Indigenous sovereignty could potentially coexist with settler society and the nation-state of Canada. We explore the guiding principles of Indigenous food sovereignty in Indigenous nations and communities to learn how communities are mobilizing in response to social and ecological crises imposed by 150 years of resource extraction and settler agriculture.

DAWN: The ninety-eight nations of Indigenous peoples and eleven major Aboriginal-language groups who occupy the vast territories over which Canada unjustly asserts dominion have adapted a highly localized abundance of Indigenous foods in our respective traditional territories. How can settler allies work in solidarity with Indigenous peoples as we heal from historical injustices and come to realize more fully the potential solutions we offer to address current socio-ecological crises?

I am coming to see myself more clearly in the rich context and true meaning of what it means to be Secwepemc, a name that translates to "the people of the land where the water flows from the highest mountains, through the rivers, on its way to the ocean." My reflections bring deeper understanding and appreciation of the way the water connects our complex system of Indigenous bio-cultural heritage. Similar to the way that water droplets reflect light to form a rainbow, my reflections shine a light on the Rainbow Nation (people of all colours), who are coming together within the rapidly expanding food sovereignty movement to chart a path toward a more just and sustainable food system.

Guided by the visionary roles that Wolverine and Arthur Manuel played in leading our people out of the dark and oppressive narrative of social injustice that continues to unfold, Indigenous food sovereignty provides a framework for reclaiming my Secwepemc identity and healing the trauma and stress associated with intergenerational impacts of Indian Residential School. It also provides a framework for the growing networks of Indigenous and sustainable agri-food system advocates who are coming to see themselves more fully in the narrative of the Rainbow Nation, in a similar spirit as South Africa, where the term was coined.

The narrative of Indigenous food sovereignty is most accurately reflected in a subsistence-giving economy, with hunting, fishing, farming, and gathering strategies applied at a broad landscape scale. For example, before the introduction of agriculture in Salish territory, the twenty-five Salish-speaking tribes shared sophisticated co-operative governance structures, and economies based on common languages, kinship ties, and reciprocal sharing and trading economies where wild salmon and water connect us all.

However, the term "food sovereignty" is also problematic, because the English language is unable to accurately translate an Indigenous worldview. The etymological underpinning of the term "sovereignty" implies "reigning over, or controlling" the food. This is contradictory to an Indigenous worldview, where we are not intended to control or reign over our food, the wild salmon, the animals, the land, water, etc. Rather, we are intended to work with natural systems. Working with and controlling are two different worldviews. But we use the term "food sovereignty" because it has gained a lot of recognition around the world and takes us more deeply into the underlying policy issues of why we don't have enough food.

Indigenous harvesting requires that we manage our time and seasonal harvesting calendar in a less mechanistic concept of time than what was instituted in the agrarian productionist paradigm by settlers. There are different strategies and protocols in the way we relate to our food. We do not think of it as a product or a "resource" to be exploited, nor do we call ourselves producers. The Indigenous food economy is based on subsistence and making sure everybody is fed before any food is bought, sold, or traded. In the present-day economic reality, we apply mixed economic strategies at an appropriate scale. There is diversity in the spectrum, where some communities maintain traditional trading and sharing economies, while others are more assimilated into the capitalist economy.

With sensitivity to these diverse socio-political realities, it is most appropriate for each tribe or community to describe, rather than define, for themselves how food sovereignty is being expressed. However, there are some commonly held principles in communities that I have visited over the years.

The first one is the sacredness of food as it is expressed in spiritual protocols that continue to be observed in relationship to the land, water, plants, animals, and people that provide our communities with food. We uphold our sacred responsibility to maintain our complex system of bio-cultural heritage as we are healing from past social and environmental injustices. We are in a constant process of regenerating and realizing ourselves more fully in these sacred relationships and responsibilities to the land and food system, where we are experiencing social and ecological crises.

The second principle guiding the way that food sovereignty is expressed is participatory action. Community food sovereignty cannot be achieved unless individuals, families, and communities are actively participating in Indigenous food-related practices on a day-to-day basis. Nobody else is going to give us our food sovereignty. We have to be out there hunting, fishing, farming, gathering, and preparing or preserving our own food on a day-to-day basis. Participatory action is a very important principle that has helped people understand how we must teach our children and get involved in ways that affirm our culture.

The third principle is self-determination, which is best described by our ability to resist the corporate control of the food system and respond to our own needs for Indigenous foods at the individual, community, or tribal level. On an international scale, self-determination is supported by conventions such as the United Nations Declaration on the Rights of

Indigenous Peoples (UNDRIP), and by extended circles of Indigenous peoples mobilizing around the world in transboundary co-operation under the banner of food sovereignty.

The fourth principle is related to policy. While our self-determination is grounded in our day-to-day practices, it is also affected by oppressive land and water policies imposed by the nation-state of Canada. Engaging with a colonial policy framework calls for moving away from the silos and sectors that characterize the techno-bureaucratic institutional framework for agricultural research and development. These approaches have fragmented the land and food system and dispossessed Indigenous peoples based on the notion of *terra nullius*. While there have been many laws and courts that have ruled in favour of Aboriginal title and rights, many policies and practices have yet to be formed and implemented to support Indigenous peoples in conducting our food-related research, action, and policy proposals for and by ourselves. Truth and Reconciliation—as it has been proclaimed by federal, provincial, and municipal governments—calls for redesigning of institutional frameworks, which can be more effectively defined by the scopes and scales of watersheds and sovereign Indigenous nations.

HANNAH: In working toward food sovereignty for Indigenous peoples, you've also been leading intercultural initiatives, relationships, and conversations within Food Secure Canada and the BC Food Systems Network for over a decade. What are some key lessons learned from that intercultural engagement?

DAWN: The system of apartheid and the reductionist approach of Western science has fragmented us and eroded our ability to appreciate the complexity and interconnectedness of our realities. As settler friends and allies are waking up to unfolding narratives of social and environmental injustice, there is a huge response to the recent proclamations of Truth and Reconciliation. Indigenous peoples are being asked to carry a heavy burden—we're on the front lines of many struggles right now, protecting water and land for future generations, and educating about reconciliation, while at the same time we are healing from historical trauma and living in disparity.

The edge effect is a phenomenon observed in the study of ecosystems, where you find the greatest diversity at the edge of two types of ecosystems. This also applies to social systems where diverse knowledges and experiences cross-fertilize within and across learning edges, where we increase our collective abilities to adapt to changes in climate, economy, and socio-political realities. Coming together across diverse knowledge systems and experiences has generated very rich learning on the edges that often comes with a lot of cross-cultural tension and discomfort. Just as with a young toddler learning to walk, there is a vulnerability and risk of falling and getting hurt. Opening ourselves up to vulnerability is necessary to deepen our understanding of how to build resiliency in the process of overcoming political imbalances. While Indigenous peoples are burdened to respond to overwhelming numbers of proposals for research and extractive development with little or no financial or technical support, more and more people of all creeds and cultures are coming together along the cross-cultural learning edges, seeking solutions to the social and ecological crises of our time.

HANNAH: How can Indigenous peoples and settlers work together in a new paradigm of resilient food systems? What are some examples of social and environmental initiatives that would support the principles of Indigenous food sovereignty?

DAWN: The late Secwepemc Elder Wolverine said, "Food will be what brings the people together." Wolverine's wisdom and words gave me direction when I was reconnecting to Secwepemc land and people. Food sovereignty was a way that I could grab on to my culture, to heal and reclaim my identity in a dignified way outside the techno-bureaucratic framework that caused the damage. I got involved with the BC Food Systems Network, where I learned about social and environmental issues being discussed by non-Indigenous peoples who are also concerned about the highly unsustainable path charted in the global food system. It resonated with what I heard my people say about the social and environmental injustices associated with colonization. I started asking, Where do Indigenous and settler peoples meet in the movement toward a more sustainable land and food system?

One of the most critical issues that connects people of all cultures is water. The Canadian court system has recognized Indigenous social and ceremonial relationships to wild salmon, yet the provincial Ministry of Agriculture and federal Department of Fisheries and Oceans continue to fail us by attempting to assert a reductionist Western scientific approach that is unable to understand the complex system of intertribal relationships and knowledge underpinning Indigenous water and fisheries governance. Indigenous peoples from within each of the twenty-seven nations in BC rely on wild salmon. It's our most important Indigenous food. They feed not just the people; they also feed the bears, the wolves, the eagles, and the trees. Wild salmon cycle huge amounts of nitrogen through ancient forests, fields, and waterways. The health of the food systems that connect us all is interdependent on the health and integrity of watersheds and abundance of wild salmon.

For example, the Mount Polley mining tailings pond breached in 2014 and spilled twenty-four million cubic metres of toxic sludge into Hazeltine Creek, a tributary of the Fraser River and home to one of the largest salmon runs in Secwepemcul'ecw (land of the Shuswap). But current provincial and federal environmental assessment processes are unable to assess the cultural and spiritual risks and cumulative impacts of mining spills, hydroelectric dams, and oil pipelines. Everybody's health and well-being is dependent on our collective ability to decrease reliance on high-energy inputs and dirty fossil fuels that are accelerating the rate of climate change, and other extractive industries such as mining that are contaminating waterways.

Water teaches us how to work in a co-operative transboundary approach to managing our relationships to one another, and to the land, plants, and animals that provide us with our food. For example, while there are still conflicts and imbalances with local ranchers and farmers who have settled in Indigenous territories in many areas, some Indigenous and sustainable food systems advocates are working together toward shared visions and goals of stopping the Site C Dam that threatens to flood valuable agricultural land and important Indigenous bio-cultural heritage areas. Some local ranchers and farmers are willing to work with Indigenous peoples for one of the first times in history.

In 2017, when Canadians reflect on 150 years of Confederation, many Indigenous communities continue to assert sovereignty of our inherent rights to land and water. We are forced to do this under duress, as many of our communities do not have water rights or clean drinking water, and our wild salmon habitat is threatened. This situation is a fourth-world reality, where Indigenous peoples live in third-world conditions in a first-world country like Canada. We can start to address these social and environmental injustices by going to the learning edges—to support Indigenous food sovereignty and social and ecological resiliency in the land and food system as a whole.

Privacy and Technology

Michael Vonn

CANADA'S 150TH BIRTHDAY occurs against a backdrop of fear and concern about global politics that has seen George Orwell's classic surveillance dystopia *1984* spring onto the bestseller list. There is renewed punch to security technologist Bruce Schneier's acerbically understated warning in *Secrets and Lies* that "it is poor civic hygiene to install technologies that could someday facilitate a police state."

There could hardly be more urgency to a discussion about privacy and surveillance and yet, for various reasons, privacy is astoundingly difficult to talk about. One reason for this is that the discussion seldom includes a critique of technology. Technology is treated as (politically and morally) neutral. From this dominant perspective, technological innovation is inevitable and threats to privacy are to be managed independent of thinking about technology. But, as the great Canadian intellectual Ursula Franklin explained decades ago, technology is not neutral. And it is Franklin's "real world of technology" framing that is required to address the privacy threats we face.

The threats are enormous. Even the lightest once-over of current challenges is apt to be stunning in all the wrong ways. People's capacity to take in the full picture is understandably limited, usually ending somewhere around the Snowden revelations, how your Facebook friends can be used to determine your credit rating, and nanotechnologies in pharmaceuticals reporting back to various motherships about the pills we've ingested. But this is only a "toe dip" into the ocean of current privacy and security issues.

Everything about this subject is overwhelming. While privacy advocates and concerned citizens have an array of tools that have sometimes secured privacy rights victories against amazing odds, it is hard to blame anyone for feeling that these are paltry defences against forces that command most of the money and power in the world. The Surveillance Society Clock is no longer at five minutes to midnight; it's well nigh on for 3 a.m. the next day.

So it's no surprise that privacy advocates are often asked how we manage to even get up in the morning. My response is to borrow a line from my colleague Professor Ian Kerr, who described himself in this context as "cautiously apocalyptic."

The critical questions at this juncture are twofold. What beyond current efforts is needed to address this overwhelming situation? And how do we both understand the magnitude of what we're up against and get out of bed in the morning?

Here are some preliminary thoughts about, first, the complex that we term "privacy," and, second, how thinking about technology is critical.

Privacy is a rather strange beast among the fundamental rights and freedoms. Having a much-contested definition and diffused within myriad issues, privacy rights often struggle for top billing. Privacy is decidedly a constitutional right, and yet, the word "privacy" does not appear in the Canadian Charter of Rights and Freedoms (the right is implicit in the sections on "search and seizure" and "security of the person"). Privacy is at the heart of so many issues, ranging from health care to policing, national security to democratic rights, that the right sometimes appears as a secondary, "and also" issue. Spying on journalists, for example, is an issue of freedom of the press, free expression, police accountability, and also privacy.

In addition to a constitutional right of privacy, Canada has statutory data protection rights. We have legislation that governs the private and public sectors, federally and provincially. These laws protect our personal information and give us access to government information, including information the government holds about us personally. These statutory rights to informational privacy align much closer to the European approach to informational privacy than to the US approach, which is sometimes known as "the Wild West of privacy."

But our statutory privacy rights are strange beasts, too. Canadian courts tell us that these laws are so important that they are quasi-constitutional. But, given that they can be as readily amended as any other ordinary statute, it's tempting to wonder if "quasi-constitutional" isn't a bit like "Miss Congeniality." It's a title, but not much goes with it.

And finally, the realm of privacy protection is insanely complicated by government secrecy and questions of how we can effectively make those institutions that operate in the shadows accountable. Indeed, several surveillance scandals erupted in the midst of the recent national security consultation on topics that included the radical expansion of powers under the Anti-terrorism Act, 2015 (known as Bill C-51). Perhaps the highest-profile example of this was the discovery that CSIS (Canada's security intelligence agency) had breached its duty of candour by failing to inform the courts of a decade-old illegal secret surveillance program. It is evident that we have only a very partial understanding of how extensively we are under surveillance.

Consequently, privacy as a cause has arguably not coalesced into a social movement. To discuss privacy today is invariably to discuss privacy-and-new-technologies (uttered in a single breath) and certainly Big Data (with capital letters). Yet, privacy as an issue pertains to almost all the technological architecture and governance systems of the modern world. At the moment, that reality is mostly paralysis-inducing. But what might transform it into fertile ground for a broader social movement is a real-world discussion about technology.

There is no one better for that job than Canada's own Ursula Franklin. Ursula Franklin was a scientist, teacher, and activist. In 1989, she delivered a Massey Lecture called "The Real World of Technology." Everyone needs to read it. Granted, a complex, deeply un-tweetable, nearly thirty-year-old Massey Lecture is an unlikely candidate for viral superstardom. But we urgently need Franklin's views on technology now, in part because they are not myopically topical. They are fundamental principles not mired in what tech-thinker Tim Wu calls "the sociology of the last five minutes."[1]

The starting point for Ursula Franklin is to understand technology as not just the latest e-gizmos, but as the house we live in; technology as practice. Computers are technology, and pens and paper are technology. Technology is the way-we-do-things-around-here. Its power is to reorder and restructure social relations and shape identity (we do it this way, they do it that way).

As Franklin explains, holistic technologies are mainly controlled by the "doer," and prescriptive technologies are externally controlled and designed for compliance and management of others. The Luddites, as both Ursula Franklin and David Noble, a historian of technology, were careful to point out, were not superstitiously afraid of technology in the way the term "Luddite" is now (mis)used. Rather, the Luddites objected to prescriptive technologies of control and understood clearly whose ox was gored by purported "advances."

It takes a feat of historical memory to recall how the first generation of Internet enthusiasts were truly and deeply Luddite in their desire to reassert control. Here is the opening of John Perry Barlow's 1996 "A Declaration of the Independence of Cyberspace":

> Government of the Industrial World, you weary giants of flesh and steel, I come from Cyberspace, the new home of Mind. On behalf of the future, I ask you of the past to leave us alone. You are not welcome among us. You have no sovereignty where we gather...[2]

Obviously, that did not go well. The "weary giants," governmental and corporate, weren't weary after all, and they didn't listen. But note how integral privacy is to the mission for independence and autonomy and identity. The top-billed "ask" for the authors of the declaration is the classic, late-nineteenth-century Samuel Warren and Louis Brandeis definition of privacy, "the right to be let alone."[3]

It is an eminently reasonable ask. But what about the other, opposing perspectives and needs, the endless public and private sector arguments that you (and your data) can't be let alone because of everything from national security to personalized service provision? How exactly do we decide what is or isn't a reasonable and allowable invasion of privacy? That, in my view, is the most fascinating aspect of working in privacy. You need to assess both the loss (in privacy) and the gain (in security, for example). And an implicit part of that analysis requires going beyond glossy brochure promises and everyday assumptions and finding out how things actually work. This is a far from simple task.

How, for example, do we stay safe in our communities? Should we "securitize" our homes and public buildings with gates and high fences and CCTV? Isn't it obvious that there will be a security gain from such practices? In fact, this is not a given: such measures can have the opposite effect. There is a fascinating study called "Fortress Britain" that looks at the UK's government-backed design policy called Secure by Design.[4] The study found that the new approach had the unintended consequence of changing social relations to the detriment of security. Ursula Franklin would not be surprised.

Privacy is a very unlikely entry point into the issues discussed in the "Fortress Britain" report. The majority of people aren't going to start in on such discussions by asking about the collection of personal information by CCTV. People are going to talk about their own sense of safety, about crime and the kinds of neighbourhoods they want to live in, what community means to them and whether they want their children's school to look like a prison. This is a conversation about technologies: how we do what we do and what that means for who we are.

Most people care about those things very much.

Like most people care about fundamental fairness. We have time-honoured technologies for trying to ensure fairness. If a decision about us is made by government, we are supposed to be able to challenge the decision, understand the basis of the decision, and correct misinformation that was relevant to the decision. But big-data analytics in decision-making challenges every aspect of what we ordinarily call "fairness" and due process. In big-data analytics, decisions are made about us based on our data from vast, diverse sources that have no apparent relevance, which we cannot challenge or correct, nor can we understand the basis for the assessment (in fact, if the analytics are based on machine-learning, literally no one can understand the basis of the assessment).

One of the key purposes of surveillance is social sorting,[5] but, as these kinds of automated, big-data analytical processes increase their effects on our daily lives, I don't expect most people to talk about it using the language of privacy and surveillance. I expect most people to use different language, about fairness and discrimination, a sense of insecurity and loss of responsiveness. But it all leads back to the central question: Is this the right technology?

And almost assuredly the biggest potential push-back in relation to new, privacy-invasive technologies is the one the Luddites would have understood the most viscerally: these technologies replace people. I commend Australia's Department of Immigration and Border Protection on its candour in its recently announced proposal for the world's first "contactless" system for flight arrivals. Passengers won't need to show their passports; they will be processed by machines doing biometric recognition of their faces, irises, and/or fingerprints. The department's goal, frankly stated: "No human involvement."[6]

There is the economic situation—unemployment, precarious employment, the growing disparities in affluence and economic security that analysts tell us were the leading factors in "Brexit" and the last US election. And there is the rapid advancement of privacy-invasive, people-replacing technologies. It seems inevitable that we will have to ask ourselves whether these are the right technologies for us. Almost certainly "privacy" will not be at the top of the menu of the concerns that will be expressed on this front. But it is an inevitable part of the mix.

Privacy is connected in one way or another to almost all important questions about how we believe we should treat one another. But the current language and approach to privacy too often misses the mark and has no meaningful place for non-specialists. Privacy advocacy is critically important and yet increasingly doomed if we continue to operate in the framework that refuses to critique technology or even understand technology in the way that Franklin explained.

It's not about data. It's about the house we want to live in.

Museums and Culture

Anthony Alan Shelton

THE CREATIVE ARTS can simply be defined as materializations that express our thoughts and creativity, define our history and identity, and provide manifestations of the anguish and grandeur of our humanity. "Art flashes" and the cultures they embody become irrefutable expressions of the myriad ways societies humanize and express variants of common identity across time and geography. We preserve, share, and pass on this precarious yet essential legacy through our all-too-fragile museums, galleries, and libraries, and through archives, ceremonies, and digital media. Far from being an ornament or instrument, the arts are an essential part of our holistic well-being and communal connectivity. Without them, there lies alienation, despair, mundanity, and ignorance. The arts, in all their forms and with all their necessary anguish and contradictions, are expressions of the human spirit, which must be promoted and supported as an essential and inalienable part of our identity and citizenship throughout Canada.

Within our country, there is a striking contrast between First Nations, who value the arts as essential to the health and well-being of their communities, and other sectors of Canadian society, who too often regard them as a costly investment or, at best, a pleasurable indulgence. In these non-Aboriginal "Second Nations," the instrumental value of the arts is invoked too often to secure sponsorship, in place of more honest abstract and holistic justifications.

Art museums, when seen as parliaments of that heightened consciousness, provide us the forums through which the nation is visualized, disputed, and arbitrated. Yet, when gauged against these lofty ideals, the provision for Canadian arts, outside Quebec and Ontario, fall far short of their calling. Since the 1930s, federal policy on culture and arts developed as an instrument to prevent Canadian culture from being absorbed or abnegated by the mass entertainment industries of the US. This approach has worked to protect Canadian "cultural sovereignty," but in so doing its culture becomes a commodity itself, a branded niche product, sometimes lacking the glamour of the American industry, though happily avoiding superficiality and glib values.

Cultural institutions, not unsurprisingly, predated policy. As in most countries, a Canadian national museum (est. 1841), national archive (est. 1872), and national gallery (est. 1880) were established with close attention to industrial and mercantile calculations. Only later with the 1929 Aird Commission and subsequent 1951 Royal Commission (co-chaired by Vincent Massey and Georges-Henri Lévesque) did the interventionist and regulatory role of government in the arts become enshrined in legislative philosophy. Building on the achievements of the Aird Commission—the establishment of the National Film Board (1939) and a public broadcasting corporation (1936)—the Massey/Lévesque Commission recommended weaning the arts off foreign funding bodies and expanding Canadian government provision to heritage and the fine arts. These two commissions furnished the blueprint for a highly respected and influential postwar national arts policy that established the infrastructure through which arts and museums are currently funded and regulated in Canada. This approach to the manufacture and dissemination of national culture, though successful by many metrics, did not necessarily focus on innovation, creativity, or the mobilization of cultural pluralism. Rather, it promoted the fortification of an insular, vague, historical sensibility often driven by virtuous faith in historical exceptionalism, progress, and moral improvement. For all their undoubted merit, the Aird and Massey/Lévesque reports were reactionary. They were more concerned with "fostering national spirit and interpreting national citizenship" than with serving the multicultural, internationally networked nation that Canada became, and which admittedly they could hardly have imagined.

A second expansion of the museum sector occurred between 1960 and 1969 as part of the 1967 centennial celebrations. Provincial museums, including the Manitoba Museum (1965), the Glenbow Museum (1966), and the Museum of Vancouver (1967), moved into new buildings or expanded existing facilities; the National Museum of Science and Technology (now the Canada Science and Technology Museum) and the National Library of Canada were founded, and, in Charlottetown, the innovative Confederation Centre of the Arts, was opened in 1964 with funding from the federal government and ten provinces. In 1968, the National Museums Act established an integrated management structure that embraced, under a single Crown corporation, the National Gallery, the National Museum of Man (now the Canadian Museum of History), the National Museum of Science and Technology, and the National Museum of Natural Sciences (now the Canadian Museum of Nature). The National Museum Policy followed four years later, in 1972. Devised by Gérard Pelletier, André Fortier, and Kenneth Heard, the 1972 National Museum Act took a holistic approach to incorporating local, municipal, provincial, and national museums within a singular network designed to facilitate more effective planning and to ensure the circulation of artistic and cultural materials across Canada. In 1990, a task force recommended the abolition of the single Crown corporation, leading to the establishment of the four national museums as autonomous corporations, expanded in 2008 and 2010 to include the newly envisaged Canadian Museum of Human Rights in Manitoba and the Canadian Museum of Immigration in Halifax. The 1990 act envisaged the national museums as "a source of inspiration, research, learning, and entertainment that belongs to all Canadians," providing a "service that is essential to Canadian culture and available to all." The act required the national museums to promote "the heritage of Canada" and contribute "to the collective memory and sense of identity of all Canadians."

Unfortunately, the 1990 Museum Act also ended the federal government's commitment to an integrated national museum policy. Cuts to federal and provincial budgets in the 1990s increased the need for municipal intervention, with municipal contributions increasing to a quarter of total arts funding by 1998. Between 2008 and 2011, under Stephen Harper's Conservative government, the Department of

Canadian Heritage suffered an approximately 30 percent reduction in its budget, which resulted in funding cuts to the National Gallery, the Canadian Museum of History, and the Canada Science and Technology Museum of between 5 and 10 percent. Even more drastically, the Canadian Museum of Nature was forced to absorb a 50 percent reduction in its budget. While funding for Canadian Heritage was partly restored in 2012, and increased again in 2016 by the Trudeau Liberal government, the system of Canadian arts funding remains dependent on three levels of government support, each with its own shifting priorities. This funding structure promotes unequal access to arts and heritage, and constrains long-term and integrated planning between institutions.

Looking forward, a more integrated approach to Canadian cultural policy and planning is urgently required. Policy needs to be refocused on creating effective institutions to incubate, develop, and mobilize creative ideas and expressions from Canada's vast patchwork of communities strewn across its expansive territory. Policy needs to promote Canada as a multicultural, multilinguistic, and intellectually exciting crossroads of world cultures, a vast studio/factory where different cultural expressions are valued, stimulated, and brought together to create startlingly novel and previously unimagined cultural forms. Canada's cultural policy should not only revive the principles of the 1972 act but redeploy them to imagine a common and inclusive future.

In a country as vast as Canada, our geography can be a significant barrier to inclusivity and access to the country's stored arts and heritage. Unlike museums in much smaller European countries, Canada's national museums have established no substantial satellites outside Ottawa to share collections and address the country's imbalanced cultural integration. In fact, instead of providing the leadership envisaged in the 1990 act, Canada's national museums have become seemingly more dedicated to storing than to circulating the nation's arts and heritage.

The continued concentration of art institutions and collections in the east ignores the aspirations of the rapidly expanding population of western Canada, which now has one-third of our country's total inhabitants. According to the 2016 census, the population growth of Ontario and Quebec was below the 5 percent national average, while all the western provinces far outstripped their eastern counterparts. While Canada is far from culturally integrated along its east-west axis, arts provision is massively more imbalanced between the south and north of the country. With 90 percent of Canada's population living within a hundred miles of the US border, cultural resources are overwhelmingly concentrated in the country's southern cities. Provincial museums mandated to provide outreach are ill-funded, and the cost structures and distance of northern communities create difficulties in networking culture. Take British Columbia, for example. This province possesses a strong network of Indigenous museums and cultural centres, yet collections are concentrated in the south, while expert knowledge holders and source communities are, to a large degree, in the north. Collections and interpreters need to circulate between these polarities so heritage and expertise can be reunited for the benefit of all. Despite their increasing utilization and impact, new technologies in circulating culture cannot break personal solitude in the way that live arts and programs can.

Twenty-seven years without a national museum policy has left much of Canada stripped of meaningful federal arts funding and dependent on provincial, territorial, municipal, and private agencies and foundations. How then, in the next fifty years before our bicentenary, can Canada become the arts and ideas factory that we aspire to be? We can begin to answer this by reviewing what we have lost. Gérard Pelletier, André Fortier, and Kenneth Heard's 1972 National Museum Policy was inspired. Under the five themes of democratization, decentralization, pluralism, federal/provincial co-operation, and internationalization, it created a vision for Canada as a whole. Matched by generous financial support, it proposed that "the movement of objects, collections, and exhibits be increased and expanded throughout Canada for the benefit of more people." Its predominant goal was similar to that which is urgently needed today. Its objective was "to better distribute those cultural resources which are obtainable through Canadian museums, both national and regional, to the end that the greatest number of Canadians be exposed to our national heritage." We do not need to dismantle our national institutions, but we do need, in a cost-effective way, to restructure their relations to provincial and community museums and resource centres. We need to integrate, consolidate, and radically reform the basis and organization of their federal, provincial, and municipal funding, and develop constructive and transformative ways for local provincial and national museums to work together.

Canada has much work to do in achieving reconciliation between Inuit, Metis, First and Second Nations; in reshaping its identity; in building sustainable, healthy communities; and in devising a socio-economic development path that is less dependent on resource extraction. As an integral part of this work, we must turn our attention to the challenge of forging a new cultural contract between the three tiers of Canadian government. We need urgently to culturally integrate our country and to better recognize the largely untapped creativity that lies outside the major urban areas located along our southern border. The time for a top-down approach to cultural provision has passed. Radical and impassioned reform, and revisioning of the funding, organization, and purposes of arts institutions should be part of a national debate that embraces federal, provincial, and territorial governments, as well as local communities. Working together, museologists, scholars, artists, and communities can harness the ability of the arts to heal, strengthen, unite, and ignite intellect and creativity in a new twenty-first-century Canada.

The Future in the Past

**South Asian Canadian Histories
Association (Naveen Girn, Anne Murphy,
Raghavendra Rao K.V., Milan Singh,
and Paneet Singh)**

In the beginning, there was nothing.

Well, technically, there was one week. One week of histories that resonated with me. And even then, it was only one day for Chinese head tax, one day for Japanese internment, and one day for the Komagata Maru.

There was Hockey Night in Canada, *the railroad, and "two" official languages—at every step, the grand narratives of the country did not embrace me. Who were they speaking to? What was the impact? What was the intent? These stories demarcated where I—and my history—should belong.*

There had to be more. We had to exist somewhere, and in more varied ways than they packaged us. That's what inspired the desire to see, hear, read, make visible, and provide a platform for stories of people who looked like me.

WE CANNOT LOOK forward from Canada's 150 mark without embracing the difficult formations of our present, and their relevance for our collective futures. Prime Minister Justin Trudeau's recent apology for Canada's refusal of entry to most of the South Asian passengers aboard the ship *Komagata Maru* in 1914 (delivered in Parliament on May 18, 2016) reminds us that the story of Canada is not only a story of triumph, as so many national stories aspire to be. It is also a story of betrayal and trauma, as well as one of recognition, responsibility, and healing. What happened to the passengers on the *Komagata Maru* was not an isolated event relevant simply to a singular, homogenous community. Instead, it represents a trauma that must be shared. In calling attention to such aspects of Canada's history, we invite Canadians to embrace the complexity of our nation's story and the dynamic exchange of past with the present and future that must inform its narration.

From Pasts to Present

History is just as much about erasure as it is about presence. It represents a form of agency—the ability to tell and retell our stories as a way to imagine and reimagine a collective future.

The *Komagata Maru* arrived in Vancouver's Burrard Inlet carrying 376 British Indian passengers on May 23, 1914 (Figure 1). The refusal of entry to most of the passengers reflected a broad movement against Asian immigration and the desire for a singularly white Canada, impacting

FIGURE 1: The *Komagata Maru* and its passengers. *Canadian Photo Company, 1914. Vancouver Public Library, Accession no. 136.*

not only South Asians but also Japanese and Chinese immigrants. It reflected and reinforced racialized understandings of the Canadian nation that already had—and would continue to have—devastating consequences for the Indigenous people of this land. This was a time, we must never forget, when European immigration was encouraged and freely enabled as national policy.

The 2014 observance of the centenary of the arrival and departure of the *Komagata Maru* allowed for a collective revisiting of its history in British Columbia. Historical investigation continues to be central to our understanding of the story of the *Komagata Maru* and its significance. This is one form of engagement with this past, and it is one that must always be prioritized. Along such lines, 2014 saw the development of an important online resource bringing together archival and textual sources on the history of *Komagata Maru* (http://komagatamarujourney. ca). These now broadly available materials are crucial for our understanding of the *Komagata Maru*, as is the innovative and important film *Continuous Journey* by Ali Kazimi (2004).

The creative arts provide another form of engagement. It was in the spirit of reflection and re-examination that the project *Performing the Komagata Maru: Theatre and the Work of Memory* was created in 2013–14, exploring how this past has been imagined by Canadians over time. This project featured parts of three plays about the *Komagata Maru* and its passengers: Sadhu Binning and Sukhwant Hundal's *Samuṇḍarī Sher nāl Ṭakkar* (*Battle with the Sea Lion*, in Punjabi, 1989); Sharon Pollock's *The Komagata Maru Incident* (in English, 1976); and Ajmer Rode's *Kāmāgātā Mārū* (in Punjabi, 1979). Through the staging of these three plays in conversation, we see how the representation of the *Komagata Maru* has evolved over time, reflecting diverse ideas about Canada and the world. Here, in Figure 2, we see a female character common to one of the Punjabi plays and the English play, played by Jasleen Kaur, speak defiantly to the audience, indignant at the treatment the passengers on the ship received.

Such creative engagement with the *Komagata Maru* illustrates how the performing and expressive arts augment and enhance traditional historical archives, and how progressive interventions in the story of the *Komagata Maru* may enable a *particular kind of future* that allows forms

FIGURE 2: Final scene of *Performing the* Komagata Maru, as performed by students in the Department of Theatre and Film at UBC, and members of the Rangmanch Punjabi Theatre group. *Photo courtesy of Ali Kazimi (York University).*

of inclusion that were disallowed in the past. This rumination on the past and its performance in the present thus link to a vision for the future.

This was also the spirit of Paneet Singh's recent contribution to the re-experience of the stories of the *Komagata Maru*, not as a scholarly investigation of history *as past* but as a living spectre of the past in the present. Singh's *The Undocumented Trial of William C. Hopkinson* was inspired by the urban legend of "Charlie the Ghost"—the spirit of Immigration Inspector William C. Hopkinson, which is rumoured to roam the halls of the Vancouver Art Gallery. The inspector was shot dead in the building when it served as a courthouse. Hopkinson had helped orchestrate the exclusion of the passengers on the *Komagata Maru*, targeting members of Vancouver's small and fragile South Asian community by hiring some members to conduct surveillance on others, and using threats of violence and deportation to force compliance. The man who admitted freely to killing Hopkinson, Mewa Singh, acted to stop him from continuing to wreak havoc on the community. Mewa Singh was tried and sentenced to hanging in the same building where the murder occurred. Staging the play where the original events took place allowed the exploration of ideas of belonging and *invasive* presence. During the staging of the trial—where Hopkinson and Mewa Singh meet (Figure 3)—the character of Hopkinson reads aloud the written statement of Mewa Singh, in which Singh detailed Hopkinson's abuse of his power as an agent of the state. This simultaneously articulated Mewa Singh's perspective, and—delivered by Hopkinson—acted to mute his voice. This is not only a story about the past: we are only slowly giving space to marginalized stories, and deeply ingrained narratives continue to dominate.

FIGURE 3: Scene from *The Undocumented Trial of William C. Hopkinson*. Photo courtesy of Pardeep Singh Photography.

When I look at images from the time of the Komagata Maru, *I see empty spaces and absent people and objects. I see images of the past but also the present. Both act as kinds of archival photographs, absent presences. To commemorate these absences is to look also at what will be in the future.*

Raghavendra Rao K.V.'s set of paintings (Figures 4 and 5) represents a parallel attempt to reimagine the gap between past and present. These small acrylic-on-canvas paintings and two larger images in acrylic on tarpaulin are an effort to bring together processes, surfaces, and imageries not always seen together. Tarpaulin, so often used on ships, serves as a metaphor for migration—life on the move. The surface for the small paintings is canvas, coarse and richly layered with paint. The main figures in the paintings are small and centrally placed, frozen in a kind of formal pose, with intentionality, reminiscent of miniature paintings from the Mughal period in India. Yet, the medium is acrylic, and the images are not of kings and elites but of Sikh labourers in North America in the early twentieth century. We think we know such images, things we'd find in archives and libraries, in ethnographic collections: unnamed men, facing the camera, silent and serious, but obviously recently toiling in the fields or in mills. Here, however, they stand out in a different way: they are monumental, perhaps even regal. Singular. All attention is on them, attractive but unsettling; they look out at the viewer as if asking a question. They demand that we answer them, to account for ourselves and for them. The splash of red in some of the images suggests the violence of this accounting.

FIGURES 4 AND 5: Paintings in acrylic on canvas and ink stain on tarpaulin, by Raghavendra Rao K.V.: "Visions of a Living Past," exhibited in Bangalore, Karnataka, India, in February 2014; and at Surrey Art Gallery, BC, "Ruptures in Arrival: Art in the Wake of the *Komagata Maru*," April 12–June 15, 2014. *Images courtesy of Raghavendra Rao K.V.*

Through art, we see the histories, legacies, and responsibilities that we carry in new, creative terms. This brings the past into the creative and living present, and into the future, collapsing space and time, cutting across geographies.

Here is another, perhaps more "vernacular," telling of the *Komagata Maru* incident:

FIGURE 6: "Emoji Maru: An Illustrated History of the *Komagata Maru* Episode." *Courtesy of Paneet Singh. Icons provided by EmojiOne.*

Remembering a Present Future

What would the story of Canada be if the marginalized, and the people who are included as tokens—men and women who are allowed to tell only one story but who have many more to tell—were placed at its centre? That story might not create new national icons or new grand narratives of origin and destination. Instead, it would provide *space*: space for modest stories of survival, arrival, and struggle. This kind of story might recognize the intrinsic beauty of the Partial, the Hesitant, and the Incomplete— histories that have at times been obscured in the grand national story.

What might it mean, to let this story—these stories—be told and heard? To let the values that direct our story be engagement, trust, sharing, dialogue, reconciliation, accessibility, openness? Prime Minister Justin Trudeau has spoken of Canada as a "post-national" state, without a core identity. Instead, what we share is what we *choose* to aspire to.

> *I often think about my own family's experience of migration. I wonder about my great-grandfather's voyage on the* Clyde *in 1897, to Fiji. Was it similar to that of the passengers on the* Komagata Maru *in 1914, to Vancouver? My mother still has his colonial emigration papers, which documented that he was "fit" to travel. Baba travelled with his mother, passenger number 472.*

Stories of migration interweave and flow together: different kinds of arrivals and departures, lands lost and found, lands seized without consent and fought for. We hear of the risks passengers took—and take, today—in hopes of changing their futures, and the futures of generations to come. Stories of indentured and racialized labour—from lumber mills to gold mines, from canneries to sugar cane fields—and the impact of this on families—these are stories of resistance to Empire and of revolution; of divided territories, partitions, and borders.

Most of all, these are histories and stories untold. They are connected to our present and form a part of our future. In this way, they are parallel and connected to the processes of Truth and Reconciliation in Canada: a past that must be owned in our present, refracted through the particular and the personal.

> *Forgetting, for me, was never an option. The history that has been lived through generations now lives through me. I understand and appreciate that*

as I grow and change, so does my understanding of history, and so does my storytelling. In this way, the history I carry stays current and relevant. While the essence of the stories I tell doesn't change, my perspective and relationship to them evolve.

The ability to see our world in different ways is a part of the past that can create a new kind of future. We can see this in the Second Avenue Gurdwara or Sikh temple, built at the beginning of the twentieth century in Vancouver (but no longer in existence). It was built to be a Sikh Gurdwara but designed in a vernacular Canadian style (Figure 7). We can see in this an effort to own a Canadian identity. At the same time, this place asserted its difference, as Canadian, through the placement of a prominent image of Guru Nanak, the founder of the Sikh tradition, high above its entrance. This is an aesthetics of both commonality and rebellion. To build at such a crossroads is to negotiate an emergent form of being. If we look for this now, we see that it was already here.

FIGURE 7: Entrance to the Khalsa Diwan Society (Sikh Temple). *Don Coltman and Steffens Colmer, March 1945. City of Vancouver Archives CVA 586-3632.*

It is said that we should learn from the mistakes of the past. There is truth to this, but there is also more to learn. The future—both the future we want and that we do not—is the product of our present. It is always in the making, within the trials and triumphs of our lives now. If we do not understand this, we fail to understand the ways our actions both create our world and *cannot* create it: we are constrained by the past decisions and actions that constitute us. At the same time, we act to make things possible. To consider Canada's past, then, is to consider its future. If we choose a path over the next 150 years that is as mindful of the past, we can find a future that was always with us.

Reimagining Aging

Joanie Sims-Gould, Heather McKay,
Anne Martin-Matthews, Deborah O'Connor,
Laura Hurd Clarke, Alison Phinney, and
Christiane Hoppmann

THE INCREASINGLY LARGE proportion of older adults, in Canada and internationally, is an unprecedented societal achievement. Human life expectancy has almost doubled over the past century, and Canada is now among a host of "greying nations" whose older citizens may live twenty to thirty years past the traditional retirement age of sixty-five. With more people living longer, Canadian society today provides novel opportunities for connection across different age and social groups. What will this new world of unprecedented co-longevity of generations be like? Europe and Japan, both demographically much older than Canada, provide limited insight, for their societies are far less ethnoculturally diverse than ours. Canadians—aging and aged—are still negotiating this new terrain.

Much has been made of the challenges population aging poses for Canadians. For many, living longer is accompanied by increased chronic disease and need for care. This is perceived as placing increased demands on our health and social care systems. While these concerns are, in part, related to structural aspects in our health care system, they also rest on a false perception of older people as necessarily frail, dependent, and an economic burden. Ellen Gee, a leading Canadian demographer, notes that the characterization of population aging as a "global public health and economic catastrophe" with "ruinous impacts for society" contributes to this apocalyptic view. Consumer culture further plays upon these fears by marketing myriad products and practices designed to help us avoid the consequences of aging, at any cost. In this discourse, old age is positioned as something we need fear, resist, and even "cure."

We believe that these ageist narratives can and should be challenged. We suggest an approach that rethinks aging, to embrace notions of agency and social citizenship, and co-longevity of generations. In doing so, we advocate for a comprehensive view of aging, one that fosters an inclusive and just society for all Canadians, now and into the future. The challenges are real, but so too are the opportunities.

To begin, we must first seek to alter current views of aging as a "crisis," which reinforce images of aging and later life predominantly in terms of health status. These notions are based on a dichotomous view of independence and dependence: independence is recognized as good and dependence as something to be avoided. This has implications for societal interpretations of aging where independence connotes worth and value, while dependence does the opposite. The predominant perspective internalizes ageist views that constrain the potential, both real and imagined, of older adults in our society. Importantly, this way of thinking also perpetuates doomsday imagery of a pending crisis in Canada's health care system unless we can all age "successfully"—in other words, deny aging as a process. Such ageist perspectives position Canadian society as an uncaring, non-relational community of individuals, a view that many would argue is harmful. Interdependence is a foundational attribute of a relational society, where giving and receiving are recognized as fundamental.

To reconceptualize aging we must respond to it as both a challenge and an opportunity. This requires that we reconsider our own assumptions and values about life and society in general. Within this context, Indigenous knowledge of Canada's founding peoples, particularly as they value aging and Elders, offers a way forward. As we move through the Truth and Reconciliation process, there is an opportunity to better understand and embrace the importance of intergenerational relations. Many challenges of later life involve its proximity to the end of life. While the search for a "fix" will inevitably continue, Canada has already taken important steps to recognize agency in decision-making surrounding end of life, with an increasing focus on questions of quality of life in older citizens. This process teaches us important lessons about human connection, well-being, and caring.

A reconceptualization of aging recognizes its fundamental variability, complexity, and diversity. People grow up and grow old with different emotional, social, mental, and physical realities: some with vigour, others with disease and disability; some with economic security, others in poverty; some with support, others with none—and all points in between. Aging is not a disease to be cured. Rather, it is part of a life continuum that requires a shift to celebrate and reconcile new realities, as individuals and as a society. There is more heterogeneity in later life than during earlier life stages. Later life and old age are about possibility and diversity.

As our society ages, our families and personal communities are also changing. This creates new opportunities to "know" one another across generations. It was not uncommon a hundred years ago for a family to span twenty-five years from the birth of a first child to the birth of a last child. Lower life expectancies often meant that children did not know their grandparents; grandparents rarely knew adult grandchildren. As noted by Chris Phillipson, today, families are typically smaller, yes, but with the "increasing length of our days" we have the entirely novel phenomenon of increased "co-longevity of different generations." This provides unique opportunities for multi-generational families to share information and resources, and to create new living environments. For Canada, these opportunities intersect with high levels of migration and immigration, and the globalized nature of ties across families and personal networks. Assistance and support across generations, from older people to younger people, is an essential feature of family life for many. This is particularly true given the increasing casualization of labour with more part-time and casual employment (as opposed to full-time and permanent), women's engagement in the labour force, and issues of work-family balance that challenge younger generations. Our ability and willingness to offer and receive support contribute to a reconceptualization of family in later life.

As the Canadian population ages, individuals and families recreate family life and "do aging" in new ways. However, societal institutions, policies, and services have not kept pace. Matilda Riley and other scholars have described this "mismatch between lives and structures" as a "structural lag" that is evident in many aspects of Canadian society. Retirement policies are built on assumptions of workers remaining with one employer during their working lives; work arrangements rarely accommodate needs of family members as carers, particularly for their parents. Later life is assumed to be a time for preoccupation with leisure pursuits (or conversely, survivorship). However, older people themselves rewrite later life as a time for continuing labour force engagement, volunteer work, provision of intra- and intergenerational support, education, and "encore" careers.

Structural lag is perhaps nowhere more prominent than in Canada's overburdened health care system. Hospitals are filled with older people awaiting space in more appropriate environments and living situations. Residential care facilities (nursing homes) have lengthy wait lists, sometimes upward of two years. Home care has been systematically cut across Canada despite recognition that it is a cost-saving mechanism and the preferred option to support the medical and non-medical needs of older people. Structural lag is further reflected in health services delivery models that fail to recognize the multi-faceted, and often complex, array of issues facing people in deep old age and near the end of their lives. Fee-for-service and "single problem" modes of delivery are prime examples. The Canada Health Act makes no provision for home and community care, and neo-liberal political agendas assume that families are available (and willing) to care for their aging relatives. We also devalue the labour of those who provide paid and unpaid care to our most vulnerable older adults. In the absence of environments and structures needed to support an aging population, we slowly erode older people's agency.

Two Canadian health economists, Dodge and Millar, portend that by 2030 health care expenditures will account for about 80 percent of program spending in our provinces. Costs are driven by the need to treat largely preventable diseases. Recent evidence from several economic case studies of preventive strategies underscores their importance (and economic imperative). Despite this, governments invest a relatively meagre amount in upstream (preventive) solutions—even where there is evidence to support their effectiveness. Canada can and must do more to promote health and prevent disease in our older citizens, shifting from a reactionary health system geared presently to treat acute illnesses to one that focuses on prevention.

Matilda Riley and others predict that as we move to a more age-integrated society, age will lose its power to constrain people's entry, exit, and performance in such basic social institutions as education, work, and retirement. As Canada celebrates its 150th birthday, and anticipates the future, policies of age integration are thus needed to reduce "structural lag," so that the dynamism of human aging no longer outpaces the dynamism of structural change.

The future holds promise. Communities continue to retrofit and build towns and cities to enhance the participation and active engagement of older people. Design features include enhanced walkability of local environments, transportation hubs, improved pedestrian crosswalks with longer crossing times, and the presence of benches and green spaces. With community redesign, the commonly held notion of "aging in place" shifts to that of older Canadians "aging in the right place." Innovations in provision of care support older people in living in their homes in a manner that they choose. Fewer older people are admitted to hospital. New strategies respond to a growing desire for meaningful social connections. We embrace aging as something more than a physical process; the strength, power, and experience of older people finds a place within our schools, communities, and workplaces. We embrace the social citizenship and agency of older people. Instead of searching for a "fix," we first and foremost accept that we grow old. We adapt our communities, structures, systems, and policies to support an aging population—adaptations that benefit everyone. Just as Canada took a leadership role in promoting the World Health Organization's "Age-Friendly Cities" initiative, so too can we now promote the recognition that an age-friendly society is, indeed, a society for all ages.

This blue-sky vision is beginning to emerge but requires a revolution of sorts. We must all challenge or fundamentally rethink our hidden ageist assumptions. We cannot continue to react within a set of structures designed for a different time and a different population. We must very purposefully close the structural lag and overcome some thorny issues. It is time to reconceive, redesign, and reimagine existing structures and systems. We would be better as a society if we looked upon aging as an opportunity, not a burden.

Partnerships for Conservation

Peter Arcese, Amanda Rodewald, Richard Schuster,
Oscar Venter, and Joseph Bennett

CANADA IS IN the enviable position of having vast expanses of wild lands still relatively unaffected by the direct impacts of human development. While these remote landscapes make critical contributions to human well-being by providing clean water, air, and productive habitats for thousands of species, they contribute surprisingly little to the protection of our most threatened species and ecosystems. Indeed, of the roughly six hundred species now at risk of disappearing from Canada, most rely on human-dominated ecosystems that hug our southern border. Protecting these species and ecosystems is one of the greatest challenges facing Canada on the 150th anniversary of Confederation.

Many species besides humans are attracted to landscapes with rich soils and mild climates. But unlike any other species, humans rapidly alter these landscapes in support of agriculture or infrastructure. Transitioning to life in human-dominated landscapes is a losing battle for many species. Habitat loss and fragmentation reduce the size and extent of most native plant and animal populations, particularly those sensitive to pollutants or invasive pests, or those that rely on other declining species, such as pollinators. Consequently, a growing number of native species in Canada's productive southern fringe are at risk of extinction.

A closer look at these southern ecosystems reveals a particularly tragic story. The eastern Mixedwood Plains, southern Prairies and

Coastal Douglas-fir forest and Bunchgrass ecosystems of southern BC host most of Canada's threatened species. These biodiversity hotspots have been reduced in size to less than a tenth of their historic extent, while our human footprint within these areas continues to expand. Agriculture and urbanization, in particular, remain key threats to most endangered species in Canada. And, sadly, chances are we haven't seen the worst of it. It takes time for habitat loss to cause endangerment. Thus, the more than six hundred species now at risk of extinction in Canada almost certainly represent the tip of an extinction iceberg. With so little habitat remaining, and extinction looming, the number of conflicts between conservation and economic development seems likely to grow.

Canada is not alone in this predicament. Habitat conversion and species endangerment are intimately linked worldwide. But solutions are also emerging as we develop tools to manage land conversion, retain native habitat, restore degraded sites, and by doing so, stem extinction. Canada has already begun to lead in this challenge and has made a bold commitment to conservation by joining 194 other signatories to the Convention on Biological Diversity (CBD). This global framework was established to prevent extinctions by expanding protected areas to cover 17 percent of terrestrial and freshwater ecosystems.

In a country where roughly 90 percent of the land mass is publicly owned, allocating land to meet CBD conservation targets might seem straightforward. And, indeed, we have already made some progress by roughly doubling the amount of protected land from 5.6 percent to 10.6 percent of Canada's area since 1995. However, remarkably little protection has occurred in the human-dominated landscapes that need it most. As a result, protected areas in Canada and many other nations are smaller and rarer in regions with many species at risk than in regions with few endangered species. Such disparities are due in part to a preponderance of private land in southern Canada, which makes acquisition especially challenging. Addressing such challenges thus requires innovative approaches that can deliver area-based conservation plans that are affordable, efficient, and supported by Canadians.

Fortunately, novel approaches to conservation in human-dominated ecosystems are encouraged by the language of the CBD, which allows for "other effective area-based conservation" measures in addition to the expansion of protected areas. Although such approaches are still being refined, several exciting examples now illustrate that species and ecosystem protection can be achieved by incentivizing conservation on private land, prioritizing stewardship actions, and investing in projects most likely to maximize returns on conservation investments.

In a country such as Canada, with its immense public land base, providing incentives to private landowners to maintain rare species and ecosystems may seem misplaced. However, consider for a moment that land values in human-dominated landscapes reflect, in part, the financial rewards of converting native habitat to human uses. By comparison, owners of intact or recovering habitat often forgo potential economic returns—for example, by conserving forest habitat instead of harvesting mature trees. But by doing so, owners of relatively "natural" ecological landscapes also represent repositories of natural capital that pay dividends on and beyond property boundaries via the species supported and ecosystem services rendered. Such services include water and air purification, pollination, carbon sequestration and storage, and many intangible, aesthetic values. At large landscape scales, these values represent an enormous stream of public benefits that are rarely rewarded. In contrast, the degradation of these services has the potential to accelerate species extinction in Canada. These ideas suggest that quantifying ecosystem services and biodiversity values, and identifying mechanisms to conserve and restore them, could represent a powerful approach to meeting our conservation targets.

Although economic incentives to conserve rare species and ecosystems may be unfamiliar to many Canadians, subsidies to agriculture and industry are well-known. Agricultural subsidies in Canada totaled $6–$8 billion per year from 1986 to 2011, accounting for up to 14 percent of gross farm receipts. By comparison, subsidies, or tax credits for private land conservation, remain in their infancy, are largely owner-initiated, and offer comparatively modest financial rewards. In British Columbia, for example, owners of agricultural land can receive an 85 percent reduction in annual property taxes by demonstrating $3,000 annually in gross sales of agricultural products. In comparison, the Natural Area Protection Tax Exemption Program (NAPTEP) offers a 65 percent reduction to landowners willing to establish conservation covenants to restrict development on their ecologically sensitive lands. Despite this inherent bias toward practices that may threaten biological conservation, some landowners have used agricultural incentives to reduce the costs of sustainable agriculture activities that support conservation. For example, North America's second-largest private landowner (Ted Turner) pursues this mixed strategy on two million acres of ranchland managed, according to the company's mission statement, "in an economically sustainable and ecologically sensitive manner." Such examples suggest that strategic, forward-looking incentives have great potential to facilitate biological conservation and to return enormous public benefit via the tangible and intangible services generated on conserved lands.

Recent research demonstrates that strategic incentives also have the potential to greatly reduce the public costs of meeting Canada's national and international targets for biological conservation. For example, the Coastal Douglas-fir Conservation Partnership (CDFCP) recently prioritized approximately 200,000 land parcels based on biodiversity values and estimated the cost of acquiring enough high-priority parcels to protect 17 percent of this critically imperilled ecosystem. The estimated cost of land acquisition exceeded that of any single conservation project as yet undertaken in Canada. By comparison, eliminating property tax on priority parcels amounted to 1 to 2 percent of their total assessed value. Moreover, stable tax revenues to government were maintained by slightly shifting the tax burden to less biodiverse parcels. This shift represented an annual tax increase of about $2 per year on a $100,000 parcel, a nominal increase compared with the 3 percent property tax hike imposed on property assessments in BC's Lower Mainland in 2017. "Tax shifting" could become even more attractive if governments targeted biodiverse parcels with the potential to offset conservation costs. For example, at $12 per tonne, the value of forest carbon in the priority parcels identified by the CDFCP was worth $20–$40 million. This amount suggests a significant investment potential via carbon offsets.

The feasibility of incentivized approaches to conservation rises as governments demonstrate leadership in the creation of market-based tools to achieve positive environmental outcomes. Despite initial public skepticism on carbon markets, Prime Minister Trudeau's 2016 Communiqué of Canada's First Ministers asserted that "pricing carbon pollution is an efficient way to reduce GHG emissions, drive innovation, and encourage people and businesses to pollute less." Carried into action, these kinds of initiatives could transform conservation in Canada, demonstrate global leadership in economic and environmental sustainability, and provide enormous tangible and intangible benefits to Canadians.

Although voluntary covenants and ecological gifts of land already exist as mechanisms for Canadians to donate ecologically valuable land in exchange for tax benefits, existing evidence suggests that we require more flexible and creative approaches to meet our national and international targets. Moreover, in the absence of strategic, area-based plans, there is a real danger that voluntary programs will lead to a patchwork of conserved lands that fail to substantively enhance conservation at landscape levels, or to maximize conservation returns on invested public funds. As a result, critical research is now underway to test additional market-based incentives for private land conservation, including the solicitation of bids for habitat protection. In such "reverse auctions," conservation organizations or the government offers payments to landowners for specific, costed conservation projects. By creating competition among landowners for limited conservation funds, reverse auctions reveal the market value for given conservation actions and increase the likelihood of maximizing biodiversity returns.

One particularly innovative example, led by The Nature Conservancy, California Rice Commission, and Cornell Lab of Ornithology, is now underway to protect habitat for migratory and wintering birds in California's Sacramento Valley. The BirdReturns Project pays farmers to flood rice fields two to three months longer than they normally would, thereby supporting hundreds of thousands of ducks and geese, and a third of all shorebirds migrating through the Pacific Coast Flyway. By soliciting bids to create specific habitat types at key times, this program pays market prices to provide high-priority habitat in an area where less than 5 percent of historic wetlands remain.

Other rapidly emerging "conservation finance" markets for ecosystem services are catching the eye of investors motivated both by a potential for returns and by positive conservation outcomes. The Natural Resources Investment Center has developed projects to conserve natural resources while simultaneously building infrastructure to enhance water conservation and resilience. In Canada, "green" loans delivered working capital to Iisaak Forest Resources, a First Nations–owned company, to revise and implement sustainable forest management. In Australia and California, conservation banks are being piloted wherein area-based conservation projects are verified by a central body and offered for sale by landowners.

Relative to many other countries, Canada remains an oasis of wild places and has reasserted its global leadership in conservation by signing the CBD. However, our current predicament suggests that bold and innovative ideas are still needed to overcome the many challenges that could prevent us from reaching those conservation targets. Since 1970, Canada has experienced some of the most dramatic wildlife declines recorded globally, losing half of all migratory birds in the boreal forest (more than three billion individuals) and some of the world's largest mammal herds on Earth. With more than six hundred species already identified as at risk of extinction, and indications that five times that number could be threatened with extinction within decades, we should anticipate an accelerating extinction crisis in the absence of immediate action to conserve our most imperilled regions.

Conserving Canada's biological legacy requires looking beyond land protection on public lands to embrace the fact that species and the ecosystems they rely on must be conserved in the places that most Canadians live—our productive plains, valleys, prairies, and coastal forests. To do so, we must find win-win outcomes that recruit private landowners in conservation. Strategically applied tax shifting and reverse auctions for key ecosystem services and habitats represent potentially powerful economic tools to incentivize species and ecosystem conservation to meet or exceed Canada's national and international goals. Developing the policies to enable such mechanisms will require the vision, fortitude, and action that Canadians regularly bring to the international stage as leaders in business, equity, and environment. As we mark the 150th anniversary of Canadian Confederation, we must create a blueprint to meet the letter and the spirit of our international commitments to biological conservation. Doing so will help to ensure that our precious ecological heritage remains a defining aspect of our country in the future.

Victoria, British Columbia | MIKE LANE

Whitehorse, Yukon Territory | STEPHANIE XU

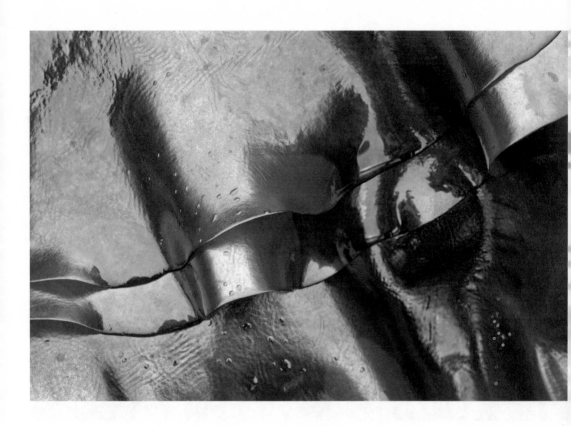

above: JUNE SZASZ

facing: MIKE LANE

Hunger and Poverty

Elaine Power

CANADA, WE ARE so often told, is among the world's richest countries, with a high standard of living enjoyed by the majority of our population. To many, this is something to celebrate as we mark the 150th anniversary of Canadian Confederation. Yet, there is a darker side to this story. In reality, a surprising number of people living in Canada struggle to meet even basic needs. Take food, for example. Along with shelter and clothing, there is nothing as critical to sustain life. For many Canadians (about 12 percent of households, and more than four million people), food insecurity—inadequate or unreliable access to food—is a real presence in daily life.

Without enough money for food, food-insecure Canadians may cut portion sizes; buy cheap, filling food instead of costlier, healthier items; or simply skip meals and go hungry. This includes the parents of one in six children, who do whatever they can to ensure that their children don't go hungry. The stress of living in a food-insecure household takes a toll. Children who grow up in food-insecure households are more likely to have asthma, behavioural issues, and depression. In adolescence and early adulthood, they are more likely to contemplate suicide. Experiences of food insecurity are also associated with a variety of adult health problems, including back pain, diabetes, and various mental health issues. These impacts have significant and direct implications for Canadian health care costs, especially for people who experience severe food insecurity. And, in a country where most people have so much, struggling to get adequate food results in social isolation, marginalization, and despair.

Not having enough to eat is a symptom of poverty; we cannot talk about hunger without talking about poverty. Over 60 percent of all food-insecure households in Canada are working poor, highlighting the inadequacy of low-waged work to cover the costs of basic needs. Canadians who are more likely to be poor are also more likely to be food-insecure. These include households headed by single mothers, African-Canadian families, people living on social assistance, and those with children under eighteen. As well, rates of food insecurity among Indigenous peoples are much higher than for non-Indigenous Canadians. For off-reserve Indigenous people, rates of food insecurity are more than double the national average. In some remote First Nations communities, the majority of the population is affected. The problem is particularly acute in Canada's remote northern settlements, where logistical considerations greatly increase prices for the market foods that make up an increasingly large portion of northern people's diets. Nunavut has the dubious distinction of having the highest rate of food insecurity of any Indigenous population in a developed country, with 60 percent of households affected. Seven out of ten Inuit preschool children live in food-insecure households.

How have we come to separate food insecurity from its primary cause, poverty? And how is it possible, in a country so wealthy, that food charity is the dominant collective response to such a widespread and serious problem?

The answer can be traced back more than three decades. Since the fiscal restraint and social spending cutbacks of the 1980s, there has been no systematic, comprehensive federal or provincial policy response to either poverty or hunger in Canada. Canadians now respond to food insecurity with food charity—that is, with food banks. While their existence signals the generosity of Canadians unwilling to see their neighbours go hungry, food banks are a grossly inadequate response. The overwhelming majority of those affected by food insecurity never visit a food bank. And even those who do visit food banks remain food-insecure. Charity is unable to solve a problem caused by systemic poverty and deprivation. Charity is no response to injustice.

Resort to charity as a response to poverty is consistent with a shift in the broader political discourse toward neo-liberalism that began in the late 1970s. Neo-liberalism has delegitimized government action to support citizens' health and well-being, and it has elevated the free market as the solution for all social problems. An important plank of neo-liberalism is tax cuts, especially for the wealthy. These cuts strangle the ability of government to protect the welfare state and implement much-needed public health and social programs. The consequences include job losses, precarious part-time work, and increased economic insecurity and instability for millions of Canadians. At the same time, welfare state programs that once reduced hardship resulting from job losses and economic insecurity have been decimated. In place of government policies and programs that ensure adequate income security, voluntary organizations, such as food banks, must do what they can to support communities.

Canada's first food bank opened in 1981 during a deep economic recession, when unemployment rates rose steeply. The idea of food banks was imported from the United States, after the founder of the world's first food bank, John van Hengel of Arizona, paid a visit to Edmonton. Within four years, there were almost a hundred food banks in cities across Canada, and the idea of food charity as the best policy response to poverty took root. There are now more than seven hundred food banks and three thousand charitable food programs across Canada, in every province and territory.

Although the provision of food as the dominant response to poverty is relatively new to Canada, it has a long history in the United States. During the Great Depression of the 1930s, America was faced with the paradox of high rates of unemployment, poverty, and hunger amid huge quantities of food, from oranges to milk to hogs. The crisis of overproduction in US agriculture began in the 1920s but became more acute with falling demand during the 1930s. As demand fell, prices plummeted, and farmers responded by producing even more. The US federal government intervened to support farmers, propping up prices by buying up some commodities, such as wheat, and paying farmers to destroy other crops.

The public were outraged at the "wickedness" of destroying perfectly edible food while so many Americans could not meet basic needs. While the government delayed action to alleviate unemployment and hunger, the framing of the problem shifted subtly. The central issue changed from hunger to food waste, which could be remedied by distributing the excess to those who were hungry. The Roosevelt administration set up the Federal Surplus Relief Corporation (FSRC) to purchase and distribute a variety of surplus agricultural products. The plan was widely hailed because it supported both farmers and unemployed workers, while relieving the distress felt by better-off Americans about wasted food. The actions of the FSRC supported the notion that providing food was the appropriate public policy solution to hunger, rather than policies aimed at ensuring adequate income so that hungry people could buy their own groceries. This idea rooted itself deeply in US consciousness and remains present today. Even in the late 1960s and early 1970s, when the solution to hunger was reframed using the language of the civil rights movement, the problem was seen as the failure of government to ensure citizens' right to food through access to food assistance programs.

The policy tale in Canada is different, even though rates of unemployment, poverty, and hunger were comparable to those in the US during similar time periods. The economic collapse of the Great Depression affected Canada almost as severely as it did the United States. During the worst years, approximately 20 percent of the labour force was unemployed, and another 15 to 20 percent of Canadians depended on public relief. Many others could have benefited from relief but were too proud to apply. In response to the crisis, Prime Minister R.B. Bennett declared that he wouldn't let anyone starve and set up ad hoc emergency grants to the provinces in 1935 to help the unemployed. The experiences of the Great Depression led directly to the introduction of Unemployment Insurance in 1940, and the family allowance (or "baby bonus") in 1945, Canada's first universal social security program, which gave income directly to families to spend. This approach was distinct from that taken by the US; the Canadian focus was on income support, not food distribution.

Similarly, in the late 1960s and early 1970s, when poverty and hunger were once again in the spotlight, Canadian activists and policymakers embraced a different approach to that of the United States.

The 1971 *Report of the Special Senate Committee on Poverty in Canada* suggested that the national poverty rate during the 1960s was approximately 20 percent. The committee declared poverty our "national shame" and made special note of poor nutrition as a "critical" factor in poverty, with poor nutrition linked to poor health and mental apathy. In recommending a guaranteed annual income (GAI), the committee cited the director general of the Medical Services Branch of the Department of National Health and Welfare, who argued that funds used to treat poverty-related diseases might be better spent on alleviating poverty. In response, the federal government took steps to do just that, by setting up a GAI experiment in Dauphin, Manitoba, tripling the baby bonus, and creating a child tax credit.

It was in the 1980s that Canadians began thinking about food insecurity in ways that aligned more closely with long-standing US policies: food charity, rather than poverty reduction, became the policy solution to hunger. In turning to food provision as a solution, Canadians stopped treating the problem as an issue of poverty. Food banks were set up as an "emergency" response to a perceived "crisis" in the economic system, and at least some food bank founders expected that food banks would close once the economic emergency disappeared. As late as 1991, food banks in Toronto were still debating when and how they might close.

As food banks have expanded and spread across Canada, they have also become more complex, co-opted by interests other than simple provision of food to the hungry. They now also provide easy opportunities for corporate marketing, disguised as social responsibility and philanthropy, and for ordinary citizens to "do something" about hunger. Although the national organization of food banks, Food Banks Canada, and some of the largest food banks in the country have called for public policies to address poverty, such as a GAI and affordable housing, the idea that Canadian food banks might one day close has become unthinkable. Too much is now vested in handling hunger in this way. Given this present-day reality, how do we move forward?

The influential American economist Milton Friedman, whose ideas underpin neo-liberalism, has a theory about change that was popularized in Naomi Klein's book *The Shock Doctrine*. Friedman argues that "only a crisis—actual or perceived—produces real change. When that crisis occurs, the actions that are taken depend on the ideas that are lying around." What ideas do we want "lying around" about tackling poverty-induced hunger when the next crisis inevitably strikes? Over nearly the past century, we have accumulated a number of "solutions" to hunger and poverty, including ideas about food charity, food waste, and the right to food. But among these ideas, there is one that holds the most promise and that is the most consistent with historical Canadian tradition. This is the idea of an adequate, universal guaranteed annual income or basic income guarantee—a policy that would eliminate poverty and complement other essential health and social programs.

A basic income guarantee could be the Canadian Medicare of the twenty-first century, a program to be proud of, and, like publicly funded universal health care, something we will one day not be able to imagine living without. As part of a progressive renewal of our social safety net, an adequate and effective universal basic income would eliminate poverty and, thus, also food insecurity. It would give us a renewed sense of community, one that manifests a kinder, more compassionate, just, and healthy society. It will give us a society that tackles hunger from the appropriate angle: poverty eradication. Then, and only then, will food banks finally close.

Soft Matter

Joseph Dahmen

FROM COD, BEAVER, and timber to petrochemicals and minerals, Canada owes much of its wealth to natural resources. The rich natural wealth that lured early Europeans to this land set in motion more than four hundred years of resource extraction that continues at massive scales today. The natural resource sector of the Canadian economy accounted for 10 percent of GDP and 4 percent of jobs in 2015.

Although it is a major source of prosperity, the resource base of our economy comes at a cost. Canada's ecological footprint is among the top ten largest in the world, and our per capita carbon emissions are the fourth highest on the planet. Addressing climate change and protecting our natural resources are national priorities, linked to both our health and our economic well-being. At the 150th anniversary of Confederation, we must shift our focus from the absolute limits of extraction to the creation of more just and equitable relationships with the natural systems from which we draw our wealth.

It may come as a surprise that 40 percent of all resources are used in buildings. Those same buildings consume 40 percent of all energy produced, more than either industry or transportation. Reducing the energy required to heat and illuminate buildings is a major focus of efforts, such as Vancouver's "greenest city" initiative, to diminish the environmental impacts of buildings. Targeting operating impacts makes sense in the short term, because significant reductions can be achieved relatively painlessly though improved design and efficiency measures in new buildings.

But operating impacts are only a part of the story. To this must be added the "embodied" impacts, which include all of the upstream environmental impacts related to producing materials for the construction industry. These include carbon dioxide and other emissions from harvesting and processing raw materials, as well as from manufacturing and actual construction—from cement kilns and logging equipment to cranes and everything in between. These embodied impacts can be roughly equivalent to those associated with operating a contemporary building over a fifty-year period. As building operations become even more efficient over the coming decades, the embodied impacts of materials will account for an even larger share of the overall environmental footprint of buildings. This shift requires that we refocus our efforts on reducing the environmental impact of architectural materials themselves.

Consider two seemingly innocuous materials used in large volume by the Canadian construction industry: concrete and polystyrene foam. Although they are at opposite ends of the spectrum in terms of strength and function, these two materials play a central role in architecture. Concrete is a mix of cement, gravel, sand, and water. Fifteen cement plants in five provinces across Canada produce thirteen million tonnes of cement annually, with a total value of more than $1.6 billion, according to the Cement Association of Canada. So, what's the problem? Manufacturing cement requires burning raw limestone in kilns heated by fossil fuels. The chemical reaction, and the fuels required to sustain it, effectively transfers carbon dioxide from geological formations (limestone and fossil hydrocarbons) into the atmosphere. Cement production in Canada is as efficient as anywhere in the world, but it still emits approximately ten million tons of carbon dioxide into the atmosphere annually (about 1.4 percent of Canada's total greenhouse gas emissions). The United Nations Environment Programme reports that global cement production is responsible for 7 to 8 percent of human carbon dioxide emissions.

Polystyrene foam insulation is no less essential than concrete to contemporary architecture. Although polystyrene foam is effective at reducing building heat loss in the extreme Canadian climate, the manufacture of it requires chemical compounds called hydrochlorofluorocarbons

(HCFCs) that are destructive to the ozone layer. In addition to HCFCs, the blowing agents used to expand the foam are greenhouse gases with over one thousand times the potency of carbon dioxide. Polystyrene also contains styrene and benzene, which are suspected carcinogens and neurotoxins. A study by the Danish Environmental Protection Agency concludes that the total environmental impact of polystyrene is second only to aluminum among architectural materials. The irony is that polystyrene foams are used primarily as insulation to reduce energy consumption in buildings. Two steps forward, one step back.

How did we arrive at this disassociation between architectural materials and their environmental impacts? The Confederation of Canada is roughly coincident with the advent of architectural Modernism. In contrast to earlier architectural movements, the International Style, the hallmark of the Modern Movement, enlisted technology to free buildings from local and regional concerns. Emerging global supply chains enabled architects to specify construction materials irrespective of location, while temperature control systems compensated for designs that disregarded local climates. Two well-regarded projects by the architect Ludwig Mies van der Rohe provide a prime example. Toronto-Dominion Centre, completed in downtown Toronto in 1969, the year of Mies's death, could be considered the apogee of the International Style in Canada. The functionalist beauty of this uncompromising collection of towers is undeniable, perhaps matched only by its astronomical energy use. Similarly, Mies's Seagram Building in New York (completed about a decade before the TD Centre) was rated the most significant building of the millennium by architecture critic Herbert Muschamp in 1999. It was also rated the worst-performing building in Manhattan by the New York State energy audit of 2012. We can admire these projects as striking relics from a different era, but to continue working this way in the contemporary context of climate change would be madness. If the last 150 years were the result of increasing disassociation from place and climate, the next 150 years must be characterized by the use of technology to reconnect with and augment, rather than replace, natural systems.

Reframing the challenge of architectural materials benefits from a look back at history. For thousands of years before the arrival of Europeans, Indigenous inhabitants of North America managed local and regional ecosystems so that desired species, including themselves, could flourish. In the Pacific Northwest, First Nations developed methods of harvesting timber from living trees without destroying them. Human interaction with the environment was not a question of limiting damage but rather of engaging in positive exchanges with local and regional eco-systems. The earliest buildings erected by Europeans in the New World were also constructed of wood. The clearing in a forest to construct a building could provide the material for the building, with the remain-der supplied by thinning the forest immediately adjacent. The simplicity and site-specificity of these early schemes, well-suited to a population dispersed across a vast landscape, was short-lived. Industrial logging eventually produced clear-cuts visible from space. When we fly over the patchwork of timber concessions on Vancouver Island today, the dis-continuous forest below suggests nothing so much as the mangy coat of a sick animal. A return to our earlier history, when human inhabitation was by necessity connected to local and regional ecologies by sensitive feedback loops, can provide valuable inspiration for rethinking our rela-tionship to materials.

Fortunately, new approaches now make it possible to reforge the links between natural and constructed environments in novel ways. The key innovation has been the use of data-driven computation meth-ods to represent the complexity and heterogeneity in natural materials. These computations methods, which are similar to those already used in weather prediction and other common applications, allow us to embrace the complexity of natural materials, supporting more nuanced relation-ships with existing ecologies. We could call this a shift toward a "soft" interrelationship of matter and information, both in the sense of the software used to process the data and in the potential to foster more supple relationships with the natural world. Applying these new-found "soft approaches" enables us to augment natural resources by creating architectural materials from local environments. These locally sourced materials are capable of delivering high performance with a fraction of the environmental impacts associated with current approaches.

Consider some examples.

Soil is complex, consisting of different minerals, particle sizes, and qualities. Natural clays, in particular, can be difficult to characterize, and the complex interrelationships of the different ingredients can lead to previously unpredictable behaviours. Faced with these challenges, engineers traditionally opted to limit concrete to a small number of highly processed ingredients, ensuring the most consistent and homogeneous product possible. Technology and energy are used to eliminate heterogeneity in the material, producing a more uniform building product with predictable and well-characterized properties. This energy-intensive, one-size-fits-all approach produces a homogeneous material that provides predictable performance at the expense of the environment.

There is, however, a softer approach. The natural clays that we currently wash away during concrete production can be activated to produce geopolymers that mimic the function of cement. Blocks made with these activated clay soils can attain the same strength and durability as conventional concrete blocks, with a fraction of the environmental impact. In many cases, the soils used to provide these binding agents can be taken directly from foundation excavations, eliminating high transport costs and the associated fossil fuel consumption. Compared with the established energy-intensive method of producing concrete, this process resembles something closer to the process of biomineralization, in which the human body synthesizes bone by absorbing minerals from its immediate environment. And, similar to bones in a body, the structural geopolymer blocks can be produced at a range of strengths depending on their intended use.

Similar efforts are underway to marshal biotechnology to provide sustainable alternatives to the polystyrene foams that currently insulate buildings. One method produces lightweight insulation materials from a blend of mushroom roots, called mycelium, and cellulose, which can be sawdust or chopped cornstalks, typical by-products of forestry and agriculture. The product is grown rather than manufactured. The sawdust is sterilized to remove competing micro-organisms and mixed with mushroom spores. A short incubation period, in which a tangle of mushroom roots grow throughout in the damp sawdust, produces a bio-composite material that can be moulded into a wide range of shapes. The moulding process, which lasts only a few days, requires no toxic chemicals or additional energy, and produces materials that are comparable to polystyrene in terms of both strength and insulating properties. Applying a small amount of heat at the end of the process ends the mushroom life cycle, ensuring that the final product is stable for use in buildings. And, unlike polystyrene foams, the materials produced are fully biodegradable, making them environmentally sustainable at all stages of their life cycle. In natural systems, mushrooms play a critical role in recycling carbon and nutrients in soils. It may be possible, in the future, to use mushrooms in a similar recycling role in buildings. Research is underway to create biological pathways that enable mycelium bio-composites to lie dormant while they serve as insulation in buildings but become active when buildings are demolished, helping to break down other building materials. These processes draw on soft systems to produce materials that are tightly integrated with local ecosystems.

A global paradigm shift in our approach to materials holds the potential to mobilize the built fabric as a carbon capture and storage infrastructure. If architectural materials can be synthesized from atmospheric carbon, the built fabric itself could be shifted from a leading contributor to climate change, to a potential mitigating factor. Canada is currently a world leader in geological carbon capture of carbon in underground formations, owing in part to large government and private sector investments ($4.5 billion in 2015 alone, according to a fact sheet published by Natural Resources Canada). It is tempting to ask what might be achieved with similar investments in soft architectural approaches to support truly sustainable built environments. A soft revolution in architectural materials would represent a twentyfold increase in investment combating climate change, while creating a responsive architecture that strengthens connections with natural and hybrid environments.

Eighty percent of Canadians now live in cities, and the urban population of Canada is increasing at a rate double that of rural areas. What materials will we use to build the Canadian cities and towns of tomorrow? Soft approaches to materials and environments offer a greater degree of responsiveness at local and regional scales, serving multiple needs simultaneously. They offer architects new avenues for expressing regional variation and responding to local climates. A shift from the limits of extraction to a humane regenerative built fabric will strengthen meaningful connections to the natural world, enabling the buildings of tomorrow and their inhabitants to engage as productive participants in complex ecosystems.

Audacity in International Engagement

Marc-André Blanchard

THE WORLD LOOKS to Canada as the "gold standard" of nations on so many issues, and our potential to make a difference on the global stage is therefore significant. As we look to the future, we need to focus our efforts and resources on contributing to solutions to real and urgent problems faced by the world, thereby ensuring our continued international relevance. In a time when more nations than ever before compete for influence, and when countries have a choice of partners, Canada needs to approach the world more proactively than in the past. This is a time for innovation and audacity.

Of course, our relationship with the United States remains our most important priority. It deserves our utmost attention. But we also need to develop and deepen relationships with a range of other countries. Thus, our relationships with Mexico, our important North American Free Trade Agreement (NAFTA) partner, with the countries of the European Union and with North Atlantic Treaty Organization (NATO), Japan, Israel, and the like are also critical. To be effective in these partnerships, we must build deep relationships with countries like China, but also with Bangladesh, Brazil, Egypt, Ethiopia, India, Indonesia, Nigeria, Senegal, Singapore, South Africa, and South Korea, to name a few. It does not mean we will agree with each of these countries on everything, but, on issues where we have an alignment of interests, we should engage and do things together. Working together brings trust, and trust is key to having influence. This matters because Canada is more relevant to the world when we have a breadth of influence located in strong relationships with a diverse range of countries, including the least-developed countries, the small-island developing countries, and emerging nations in the Caribbean, Latin America, and Africa.

I am hopeful that Canada can enhance the difference we make in the world for four reasons. First, the priorities we promote and defend, the values we embody as a country, and our reputation as honest brokers enhance our ability to act internationally. When anxiety is so prevalent in so many parts of the world, Canada has a unique and reassuring story to tell. Our experience with diversity and multiculturalism is particularly important. Our ongoing efforts to eradicate discrimination, to advocate for the equality of women and girls, to tackle climate change, and to strengthen and expand the middle class are extremely important. We can share these experiences—our successes and our challenges—and we can help fashion a global move forward on important issues of equality, diversity, and sustainability.

Second, trust is at the core of our engagement; and trust matters. Many colleagues at the United Nations have taken the image of Prime Minister Trudeau greeting Syrian refugees at the airport as a symbol of Canada's leadership role in welcoming those in need. The world saw more than words; it saw a gesture, concrete action. This enhances trust. Another anecdote highlighting the perceived trust of Canada involves a recent experience I had in Addis Ababa with Defence Minister Harjit Sajjan, the Honourable Louise Arbour, and General Roméo Dallaire, when we met with a high-ranking UN representative in Africa. The UN representative observed, "We are so glad to see that 'Canada is back' on the international stage . . . It gives us so much *hope*." When I asked why, he pointed to the fact that Canada is *trusted*. And, he added, "because of your history, your culture, your bilingualism, your diversity, your current leadership, your friends, and the people you can get around the table, you make things happen."

The third reason to be hopeful is that our domestic "fundamentals" are healthy. Economically, we have the best growth since the Great Recession in the G7 countries, with a gross domestic product

(GDP) of 12 percent higher than it was before the 2007 recession. We have the lowest net debt-to-GDP ratio in the G7 at 26 percent. *Forbes* and *Bloomberg* report that Canada is considered the best place for doing business among the G20 nations. We have over 60 percent of global GDP covered by free trade agreements such as NAFTA and CETA (Comprehensive Economic and Trade Agreement), and by bilateral agreements with countries such as Peru, Chile, and Korea. These economic fundamentals allow us to have a voice internationally that resonates across many issues.

The fourth reason to be hopeful about Canada's engagement in the world is that the global agenda is tailor-made for Canada. Economic growth, security, migration, and climate change are four of the world's biggest issues. None of these issues can be solved by one nation. None of these issues can be solved bilaterally. These issues must be dealt with in multilateral forums like the UN, and Canada is effective in these sorts of arenas. The global priorities are our priorities, and the promise for resolution draws on the kinds of leadership Canada exemplifies.

Some might consider the UN to be an institution that is ineffective or removed from Canadians' daily lives. It is, indeed, true that the UN is imperfect. It needs reform in order to better represent the world of 2017. But it has had real successes over more than seventy years of existence. For example, since 1948, the UN has helped end conflicts and foster reconciliation through peacekeeping operations in dozens of countries, including Cambodia, El Salvador, Guatemala, Mozambique, Namibia, and Tajikistan. There are currently sixteen peacekeeping operations around the world, carried out by 125,000 men and women from 120 countries, working for peace and security. In 1990, there were three electoral democracies in all of Sub-Saharan Africa; today, there are twenty-one such democracies, and the UN played a big role in making that happen. Liberia, Sierra Leone, and Côte d'Ivoire all experienced civil wars in the 1990s and early 2000s. The UN worked with regional actors to broker peace agreements, deployed thousands of peacekeepers to assist in stabilizing the countries, helped bring the architects of the conflicts to justice, disarmed and demobilized thousands of combatants, monitored elections and assisted in building institutions, provided life-saving aid and services, and helped refugees and displaced populations to return and rebuild their homes. Now all three countries are democracies, and the final UN missions are winding down.

South Korea is another success of the UN. Today, we see this country as an economic superpower. Of course, the South Koreans are the ones who made this happen, but the country got its modern start thanks to the UN. At the time of the 1954 armistice, the country was poorer than any African nation, with its people facing widespread starvation. The UN fed the population and built an education system from the rubble. Ban Ki-moon, the former UN secretary-general, has said that he, like millions of other South Koreans, was a child of the UN.

Countless other children from across the globe have also benefited from the efforts of UN organizations. Since 1951, more than sixty million refugees (including many children) fleeing persecution, violence, and war have received aid from the Office of the UN High Commissioner for Refugees (UNHCR). Since 1990, the annual number of children who die before their fifth birthday has been cut by more than half, from 12.7 million to 5.9 million in 2015. In 2015 alone, UNICEF provided 270 million children with vitamin supplements.

Beyond these very tangible examples, the UN has also created and maintained a truly unique space for countries of the world to come together to discuss global issues and resolve their differences. It is not always successful, of course, but it is an absolutely essential forum. Where else can one spend the morning discussing the challenges of climate change with representatives from small-island developing states, the afternoon with a coalition of member states looking to improve the humanitarian situation in Syria, and the evening developing strategies to ensure that the world can respond to the current refugee crises we face? International diplomacy is about relationships, and it is at the UN that Canada can build effective relationships with all member states, improving mutual understanding, enhancing trust, and working together toward making the world better.

The UN is important for the world, but it is also important for Canada. Through multilateralism, Canada can play an active role internationally. We can contribute to resolving key global challenges by convening, engaging, and collaborating with others. We can create coalitions of like-minded partners based on our objectives. It is through these relationships and by being an active member of this international community that we ensure our own economic and security interests.

In my discussions with heads of states in Africa, all mention that the youth bulge is the biggest threat to security. In some countries, close to 70 percent of the population is under thirty years old; 50 percent of these youths are unemployed, and many are driven to desperation in search of economic livelihood. What are heads of state asking for? Opportunities for their citizens. Economic development in fields such as infrastructure, renewables, and agri-food is seen as essential. In addition, "FinTech," the rapidly growing sector of financial technology and innovation for delivery of financial services, is a high priority in many nations. Canada is champion of and expert in these areas, providing us with a tremendous opportunity to support the sustainable growth and development of other nations, while also enhancing our own economic growth. We can make an important contribution to skills development and creating new economic opportunities for youth, here and globally.

To succeed in creating economic growth globally and in our own country, we need peace and security. When people ask why we should care about the economic development of Africa, the answer is quite simple: we care because we are responsible and generous partners engaged in the world. Equally, we care because Canada's international support for security, economic development, and social well-being is also support for economic and social well-being for ourselves and our children. Our contribution to further develop a global middle class will enhance the prosperity and well-being of our own Canadian middle class. Our trade relationships and investment flows also need to expand to new cultures and economies around the world, reflecting novel ways of looking at social and economic security. This expansion is necessary to create new economic relationships that respect the multipolarity of the world, while also providing solutions to real and urgent problems, and opportunities for Canadians.

To succeed in this hyper-competitive world, we need to work with other countries to ensure Canada's prosperity and continued relevance. The door has been opened, and many parts of the world are expecting Canadians to come in. It is now up to each of us to go and make a difference. We need to be ambitious, innovative, and audacious. We need to engage differently than we have ever done: it is about innovative partnerships and new coalitions. It is about new ways to look at risks and returns on our investments. It is about leveraging the entire Canadian society: non-governmental organizations, academia, the private sector, our pension funds, and governments, engaged together domestically and abroad.

In this sense, the UN will continue to be a key forum and a growing platform. According to the 2017 Edelman Trust Barometer, the UN is the most trusted convening forum addressing international issues. Canada should contribute to enhancing and leveraging this UN role. The prime minister did so in the fall of 2016 by co-chairing the Leaders' Summit on Refugees. We currently do so through our leadership with Jamaica on supporting private sector financing of SDG implementation. This is also why Canada is running for a seat on the UN Security Council in 2020. Running for the Security Council is not an end in itself; rather, it is one more tool available for Canada to help support other nations, bolster the effectiveness of the UN, and bring concrete solutions to the world's most pressing needs. Our membership in the UN calls us to look outward to the world. And we must do so with confidence in what Canada has to offer on the international stage and with courage to grasp the leadership opportunities the world is eager to see us embrace.

Arctic Archipelago

Robie Macdonald and
Mark Mallory

ACCORDING TO LEGEND and the scattered evidence left by the earliest peoples, Canada's northern archipelago was discovered and crossed long ago. The first transit of the Northwest Passage was from west to east by foot. Prehistoric cultures, superbly adapted to life on the ice, achieved this voyage over generations. Thousands of years ago, these peoples made their home the labyrinth of inland seas and channels, from the Beaufort Sea to Baffin Bay, from the North American mainland to the northern tip of Ellesmere Island. Perhaps because of a friendlier sea during the Medieval Warm Period, about a thousand years ago, a second crossing of the Northwest Passage occurred, also from west to east (the Thule Migration). The Inuit, who had invented kayaks and umiaqs, were a sea people proficient at hunting marine mammals. Thus it was that the first "navigation" of the Northwest Passage was also achieved long ago by peoples who viewed the archipelago as a seaway leading from Alaska to the far shores of Greenland. The very idea of a Canada was still centuries away.

Enter the historical era. In school, we learned of the epic struggles during the past few hundred years by European explorers like Frobisher and Franklin to discover a Northwest Passage and its eventual crossing during the search for Franklin. It is the heroism of these explorers that is celebrated in Stan Rogers's iconic "Northwest Passage," arguably an unofficial national anthem of Canada. Especially resonant with many Canadians today is the last Franklin Expedition (1845). The resting places of his ships, the *Erebus* and *Terror*, have only just been found where the sea ice discarded them 170 years ago, a scant two decades before Canadian Confederation.

Lesser-known stories are the extraordinary explorations over land that came before Franklin's Northwest Passage expedition. In 1770–72, Samuel Hearne and his Cree and Chipewyan guides crossed Canada's vast Arctic landscape to the Kugluktuk (Coppermine) River estuary, and in 1819–22, Franklin and his men followed Hearne's travels to map the nearby Arctic coastline. They barely survived that expedition, eating their boots on the way south. In 1833–35, George Back descended the Thlewechodyeth River (known also as the Big Fish or Back River) to its estuary at Tariunnuaq Bay. These travels, which fixed the location of two important estuaries of the southern archipelago, likely led Franklin to make his final, fateful choice of the route that ended in disaster. By the time of Canada's Confederation, the Northwest Passage was known to link the Atlantic and Pacific Oceans, thanks to the extraordinary efforts of Hudson's Bay Company man John Rae, who, like the very first explorers, completed the journey by foot. The first historical crossing of the passage by a ship awaited Amundsen's *Gjoa* (twenty-one metres, forty-five tonnes) in 1902–06, going against the ancestral flow and passing through east to west.

Scientific exploration has been a latecomer to Northwest Passage waterways. Interest in the archipelago's waterways began in about 1900 and continued with little governmental vision and no vigour until 1958, when Fred Roots's creation of a Polar Continental Shelf Program provided a practical means to expand scientific study in Canada's Arctic. By the time of our centennial in 1967, there were but a handful of oceanographic studies, and many major wildlife aggregation sites remained unknown to science. The discovery of contamination of northern food by industrial chemicals in the late 1960s, followed by the launch of ArcticNet in 2003, and International Polar Year 2007–08, changed everything. Unlike the early explorations, the post-centennial surge in scientific effort has been vigorously led by Canadians using Canadian ships and facilities. But like all earlier stages of exploration, the most recent science has also been defined by climate change. Today, focus seldom shifts far from the alarming demise of summer sea ice in the Arctic during the past twenty years. The vulnerability of the archipelago's inhabitants—both human and wildlife—to climate change is now accepted as urgent.

But where is this change leading? Permafrost is thawing; ponds are drying out; small glaciers are dwindling; rivers are changing their flow patterns; snow cover is declining; river, lake, and landfast ice are melting earlier; weather patterns are becoming harder to predict; sea ice is disappearing; and coastlines are becoming more vulnerable to erosion by waves and storm surges. The Arctic is not what it used to be: in contrast to the epic battle with the ice that Franklin's expedition lost 170 years ago, we now see sailboats jostle in early summer to attempt the Northwest Passage. In the last decade, ninety-one have succeeded. In 2016, the *Crystal Serenity*, a luxury cruise ship that offers fitness classes, restaurants, and pools for its eleven hundred passengers, took less than a month to cross the Northwest Passage from Alaska to New York. The modern Sedna Epic Expedition, fittingly named after the Inuit Goddess of the Sea, has ten women snorkelling through the Northwest Passage. And this is just the tip of the proverbial iceberg.

Today, at the 150th anniversary of Canadian Confederation, climate change looms large over the coming century. The contamination of country food by industrial chemicals like PCB and mercury remains on the science radar, but focus has shifted dramatically to climate. Why? On one hand, marine scientists worry about changes to food-web structure and function. What's going to happen when ice melts, when pests and parasites ride in with ballast waters, when new species invade a friendlier Arctic, when resident species are pushed out? On the other hand, Inuit have a practicality framed by living on the land. What's going to happen when food no longer arrives in the usual places at the usual times? Will the people be able to travel to those places to gather food when ice melts earlier and land thaws? Will southerners start fishing in the north? Will their increasing traffic pollute it with chemicals and noise?

For many Inuit, the sea ice is their highway; the water is their life. Like the Polynesians and the Norse, they are a marine people. Take, for example, the voyage of shaman Qitdlarssuaq, who crossed Lancaster

Sound by dogsled to reach Devon Island in the early 1850s, and met Captain Inglefield, who was searching for John Franklin. Inglefield told the shaman of the Inughuit (Polar Eskimos) of northwest Greenland. In 1859, Qitdlarssuaq and his followers initiated a seven hundred kilometres migration from Devon Island to Greenland to meet the Inughuit and rekindle lost traditions, including the building of kayaks and fashioning of bows and arrows. He and his followers reached northwest Greenland a few years before our Confederation.

Such a migration is almost unthinkable now. Safety of the routes long used by the Inuit to travel to hunting and fishing areas has become a major concern. Many stories are now told of Elders and hunters who have been injured or who have perished while travelling "safe" routes across lakes and the sea between communities or to hunting areas. Climate change already threatens subsistence hunting, which means the loss of less expensive, nutritious food, to be replaced by less nutritious items shipped up from the south at great cost. Sea-ice decline will thus worsen the existing food security crisis in many northern communities.

Inuit know that climate change has arrived in the Arctic. Elders can no longer predict the weather or the ice as they once did, because everything is more variable. Scientists know that climate change is more rapid and more extensive in the Arctic than just about everywhere else. Research has sought connections between change in sea-ice cover and the Arctic's food webs, in an effort to project what the future holds for resources that support the livelihoods of northern communities. Large-scale, ship-based research programs have examined the chemistry, biology, and oceanography of important locations like the North Water Polynya, Lancaster Sound, and the southern Beaufort Sea, and these efforts have provided a wealth of new information on Canada's Arctic seas.

Like the early explorers, marine researchers have begun to work their way through the myriad passageways of the Northwest Passage. Continued decline of the sea ice within these passages will promote international shipping, ecotourism, fishing, and resource extraction, all of which bring opportunity and environmental risk to the region. The conflicting claims—by Canada that these waters are internal, by other countries that these are international seaways—brings urgency to the resolution of sovereignty, duties of stewardship, and rights of the inhabitants.

Moving forward from our 150th year as Canada, where should we focus our exploration? What should be the priority of science in our northern waters? To date, one area has been woefully neglected—the shorelines, shallow bays, and estuaries of the Canadian Arctic Archipelago. The archipelago is a coastline ocean holding a global record of 160,000 kilometres of shore. The archipelago's labyrinth of estuaries and shallows too numerous to count is of central importance to wildlife like fish, birds, and whales. These animals migrate to selected estuaries and reproduce within them. Cliffs provide important habitat for bird colonies. These are the Northwest Passage's nurseries and refuges.

It is widely recognized that estuaries are important for biological resources in every ocean, but we have little understanding of how these thousands of small estuaries in the Arctic will be affected by rapid and relentless change in the foreseeable future. Small estuaries have long been valued by Native cultures for their assured, widely distributed supply of food (Arctic char, whitefish) and their favoured location for migratory animals like belugas and birds. Estuaries are also the first places to open up in early summer, because the sea ice is melted by heat brought in from the south as warm river water. Small Arctic estuaries are also stunningly beautiful and therefore attract ecotourism (Macdonald image, p. 272). These estuaries are in the vanguard of change simply because they are at the crossroads of land and ocean. Changes on land affect what the rivers supply to the estuaries; changes in sea ice affect what the sea does with it. Changes in both affect how northerners access and use estuaries.

Why would we want to study small estuaries at a time when far bigger concerns like disappearing sea ice across the Arctic Ocean and thawing permafrost across Canada's North are grabbing headlines? Because it is here that change is going to affect people the most. From the open sea, ice loss and sea-level rise lead to seabed destruction, coastal flooding, and coastal erosion. From the land, the demise of permafrost, the loss of ponds, and change in vegetation lead to altered quantities and qualities of river water, with as yet unknown effects on estuarine biology. To maintain vigilance here would seem to be an obvious duty.

Looking over the long history of exploration from the earliest peoples to the latest science, we arrive at a place where past experience of Canada's Arctic Archipelago may be inadequate to the task of adapting to an uncertain future. Human exploration has always been driven by need and curiosity. The earliest explorations were motivated by the need to find new sources of food, new places to live, new routes of travel to access food or other communities and, perhaps, to respond to pressures or opportunities brought by climate change. Later explorations sought new routes of trade with distant countries, new resources. But now the most urgent need is to adapt to change. Here, science and Inuit interests may become aligned in developing a deeper understanding of the coastal boundaries in Canada's archipelago and how best to preserve their value for the people who have long depended on them.

Digital Storytelling and Reconciliation

**Jan Hare, Ron Darvin, Liam Doherty, Margaret Early,
Margot Filipenko, Bonny Norton, Darshan Soni,
and Espen Stranger-Johannessen**

IN HIS ADDRESS to the United Nations in September 2016, Prime Minister Justin Trudeau presented a vision of Canada as a country committed to diversity rather than division, collaboration rather than conflict. He focused in particular on the role education plays in providing the next generation with the tools needed to be successful citizens and active contributors to the global economy. A critical component of this endeavour is the important work of maintaining and developing the linguistic capital of our nation, with particular emphasis on Indigenous, immigrant, and refugee communities, which have struggled for legitimacy in our society. Our diverse linguistic landscape leads us to commemorate a very complex history as we celebrate the 150th anniversary of Canadian Confederation.

We speak different languages, and a compelling way to share our personal histories is through our stories. The work of Canada's Truth and Reconciliation Commission (TRC) demonstrates the power of stories to engage all Canadians in what defines and challenges us as a nation. Indigenous storytelling and ways of knowing can play an important part in reimagining a multilingual Canada in the twenty-first century. The critical work of reconciliation started by the TRC will allow us to forge a multicultural, multilingual Canada, in which reconciliation is meaningful and inclusive, and where Indigenous priorities are powerful in our nation-building agenda.

As we seek to reimagine a multilingual nation, language and literacy educators are keenly aware that the digital revolution has dramatically transformed how we interact with one another, how we represent ourselves, and how we speak, write, and tell stories. Digital tools have enabled the genesis of a broader range of vocabularies, genres, and styles. Languages are documented and shared in creative ways, with the goals of preserving those that are endangered and promoting a greater awareness of how multiple languages coexist. Through texting and chatting on social media, we have begun to speak by writing. In doing so, our voices create change that underscores the goals of reconciliation.

Moving across online and offline spaces with greater fluidity, Canadian youth are able to engage with an even wider set of people, cultural histories, and languages. In the digital era, the multilingualism that is emblematic of the rich diversity of our country continues to grow and find dynamic spaces in which languages thrive and reshape each other. This growth not only affirms the value of these languages but also asserts how Canadians of different cultural backgrounds—whether Indigenous, immigrant, or refugee—all hold a legitimate place in our vision of the future. In digital media, these stories can take shape through words, images, voices, and gestures, heightening their contributions. Publishing and production companies no longer have a monopoly to decide whose stories are shared and whose voices get to be heard in the grand narrative of our nation.

The dramatic increase in technological innovations has not benefited all Canadians equally, however. In particular, there are Canadian children and youth (potentially at risk in our reimagined future) who do not have equitable access to and use of digital technology. Children living in low-income families or in homes with limited access to digital technology are vulnerable. While we work toward building greater digital infrastructure and integrating technology into schools, we need to be aware of who is reaping the benefits of this digital future and who remains on the margins.

A related challenge stems from our nation's colonial history, which has created a different set of educational, social, and economic realities for Indigenous peoples as compared to their non-Indigenous counterparts. By harnessing the power of the digital, youth from a range of backgrounds have the opportunity to assert a legitimate place in this narrative and to claim their right to speak. The ongoing challenge for educators, communities, and policy-makers is thus to understand the extent to which digital innovations can promote a multilingual Canada in the era of reconciliation.

Before reimagining the future, we must fully understand the present. Officially a bilingual country, Canada is increasingly, in practice, linguistically diverse. In the 2011 Census of Population, 20 percent of the population reported a mother tongue other than English or French, and more than 200,000 people regularly speak an Aboriginal language at home. The Multiliteracies Project, based at UBC and the University of Toronto, was one of the first national Canadian initiatives to recognize that the linguistic and cultural diversity of schools is a source of great strength to our nation. This collaboration resulted in exciting innovations, including the creation of multimodal dual-language digital stories, digital sister-class projects, and the use of the students' home languages to facilitate content and language learning, in both first and second languages.

Indigenous communities are also embracing digital storytelling as a means to revitalize their cultures and languages. These technologies have brought new approaches to language and literacy learning with opportunities for expressing contemporary Indigenous identities for children and youth. For example, the Young Lives Research Lab at the University of Prince Edward Island has engaged Indigenous youth in digital storytelling projects to communicate and share their experiences of mental health well-being (katetilleczek.ca). These young people took part in their own community-based research to creatively represent cultural events, practices, and realities that shape their lives, studies that have implications for enhancing youth-related programs and policies.

The link between new technology and ancestral knowledge is also supported by emerging mobile applications, virtual games, and online tools developed by or in partnership with First Nations communities. An early online initiative by the South Slave Divisional Education Council in the Northwest Territories has made a dictionary and audiovisual stories and resources available in Dene languages such as Chipewyan and Slavey, as well as Cree (ssdec.nt.ca/ablang). In British Columbia,

First Voices archives and provides new technologies that allow First Nations communities to document and learn their languages, helping to ensure their survival (fpcc.ca/language/FirstVoices). Simon Fraser University's First Nations Languages Centre has launched a digital app consisting of eighteen episodes of a story built around a significant Secwepemc cultural character, whose powers allow viewers to learn language and cultural traditions tied to the land, ecology, and social relations (sfu.ca/fnlc.html). In Alberta, Little Cree Books has published the first freely available online collection of stories in an Indigenous language to be released under an open licence in Canada (littlecreebooks.com). In the north, a special Inuit-language keyboard enables Inuit speakers to type using Roman orthography and have their messages conveyed in syllabics, while Apple's app store offers language applications in Cree and Ojibway for hand-held devices. These exciting developments point the way forward to a more inclusive future shaped by multilingual contributions.

Building on these initiatives, and in the spirit of the TRC, we must seek to create productive communities for younger multilingual learners in the multilingual Canada we envisage. Although one in five Canadians speaks a language other than English and French as their mother tongue, fluency in other languages drops sharply by the third generation. This intergenerational loss of language not only is a personal loss for individuals and families but also represents a great loss for Canada as a multilingual nation. First-language maintenance is associated with many benefits, including better academic performance, enhanced identity, and improved ability in English and French. Although many teachers recognize the importance of bi- and multilingualism for their students, a lack of available resources too often compromises support efforts.

In seeking a path forward for a multilingual Canada, we can seek inspiration from a number of exciting innovations over the past decade. For example, UBC's Storybooks Canada is a powerful interactive website that makes stories from Saide's African Storybook initiative available in refugee and immigrant languages of Canada, such as Arabic, Punjabi, and Mandarin, in addition to English and French (storybookscanada. ca). Powerful tools on this website help beginning readers and language learners make connections between speech and text, and between their home and official languages. A related project at UBC is actively pursuing applications to support the learning of Indigenous languages, and is making stories from Little Cree Books available in a variety of accessible formats in both Canadian Aboriginal syllabics and standard Roman orthography, as well as developing language-learning tools and resources from the open-licensed texts (global-asp.github.io/lcb). Another promising digital initiative for Canadian schoolchildren is SFU's Scribjab, a multilingual tool available as a mobile phone app that enables children to create and illustrate their own stories in English, French, and other languages, including Indigenous languages (scribjab.com). This program creates a space for children to communicate their stories and to increase appreciation of their own multilingual resources. With such digital tools, young Canadians will have a better chance of becoming and staying multilingual in future generations.

Notwithstanding the exciting digital developments in Canadian language and literacy education, we need to ensure that teachers are adequately trained in twenty-first-century pedagogies. Teacher education programs are experimenting with innovative educational strategies that weave inquiry and critical thinking together to address real-world problems. Currently trending is the massive open online course (MOOC) "Reconciliation Through Indigenous Education," developed by the Faculty of Education at UBC to assist educators with the goal of acknowledging Indigenous histories and languages in Canada, and promoting reconciliation. This course draws on Indigenous knowledge keepers, educators, and resources to create learning environments that strengthen Indigenous-settler relations. The MOOC contributes to the revisioning of this relationship by creating a community of diverse learners through its interactive and accessible structure.

Although there are intersections in the histories and realities of Indigenous, immigrant, and refugee people that contribute to patterns of marginalization in this country, the 150th anniversary of Canadian Confederation reminds us that we must create a new national legacy that includes Indigenous stories and perspectives, attending to the urgent priorities of Indigenous language and cultural revitalization and maintenance. We must also celebrate and foster the full range of immigrant and refugee languages in Canada. Indigenous, immigrant, and refugee youth need opportunities to learn from each other's experiences, to engage productively with difference, and to build coalitions to advance reconciliation. In our efforts to build a stronger nation in the digital age, the challenge for educators is to harness insights from the TRC to ensure that the stories of Canadian children and youth are those of diversity rather than division, collaboration rather than conflict. It is a vision for a twenty-first-century Canada that honours and celebrates the linguistic contributions of all our storytellers.

Quebec and Confederation

Philip Resnick

OVER THE PAST 150 years, multiple national identities have coexisted, sometimes uneasily, within the Canadian Federation. Unlike countries such as Germany, the Netherlands, Poland, and Japan, Canada did not evolve as a single nation-state, where notions of "nation" and "state" coincide. Rather, over its relatively short history, Canada has existed as a "plurinational" state made up of multiple national communities, with unique, though sometimes overlapping, cultural and historical identities. The Québécois constitute one of Canada's national communities, Aboriginal peoples constitute a constellation of micro-national communities scattered across the country, and what is sometimes referred to as "English Canada" makes up the single largest national community within the federation. As has been made plain by the Truth and Reconciliation Commission (TRC), the relationship between the French and English settler nations and the First Nations has long been troubled by systematic discrimination and lack of respect for the original inhabitants of this country. However, in the case of the relationship between English and French Canada, our history shows that accommodation and compromise have been key elements in overcoming what might otherwise have proven mortal threats to the survival of our country.

At the time of Confederation, a majority of French Canadians (as they were called until the 1960s) saw themselves as constituting a distinct linguistic and cultural community. What ultimately made union

with the English-speaking provinces acceptable to French Canadians
was the degree of autonomy that the province of Quebec would secure
over areas of jurisdiction directly relevant to their cultural and societal
concerns. Canada's first prime minister, John A. Macdonald, would have
preferred a more centralized union, but it was the French-Canadian
presence in what was to become Quebec that made this impossible.

A key part of the Canadian federal equation has involved reconciling English-speaking Canada's desire for shared national policies with
the desire of Quebec governments for significant autonomy. During the
two world wars, the difference in national sentiment between English
and French Canadians had the potential to tear the country apart. Conscription was imposed in the First World War over bitter opposition in
Quebec. A plebiscite on the question of conscription in 1942, in the middle of the Second World War, revealed the depth of division between
the eight English-speaking provinces of the time, which voted overwhelmingly in favour of conscription, and Quebec, which voted almost
as strongly against. It took considerable equivocation and skill by Prime
Minister Mackenzie King, including postponing conscription almost
until the war's end, to avert a full-scale crisis.

In the post–World War II era, Quebec governments have often
refused to participate in federal initiatives or have sought to fund parallel
programs of their own. This resulted in Quebec establishing its own con-
tributory pension plan in the 1960s, when the other nine provinces were
perfectly happy to participate in the newly created Canada Pension Plan.
A decade later, the Cullen-Couture accord of the 1970s gave Quebec
considerable autonomy in the selection of immigrants coming to Quebec, and financial help toward their settlement and integration. In 1999,
when the federal government and the other nine provinces entered into
the Social Union Framework Agreement, to cover a range of programs
involving child benefits and disability, Quebec did not sign on. Rather
the Quebec government challenged Ottawa's use of its spending power
in domains of provincial responsibility. Quebec did, however, participate
in the negotiations and received funding that was equivalent to that of
the other provinces.

Language is another area where Quebec governments have been
able to wield their power effectively. The most striking example of this

is Bill 101, the Charter of the French Language, passed in 1977, the first year of Parti Québécois government. This legislation affirmed the role of French as Quebec's official language and its central place in the Quebec economy and public sphere. Simultaneously, the legislation placed tight restrictions on access to English-language schools. All this took place when federal policy, through the Official Languages Act and subsequently through the Canadian Charter of Rights and Freedoms, was moving Canada toward a form of official bilingualism at the federal level. Some sections of Bill 101 were struck down by the Supreme Court of Canada, and the provisions regarding the language used on signs were ultimately amended by a Quebec Liberal government in the early 1990s to permit for a limited use of other languages alongside French. However, Bill 101 has remained by and large in force, providing considerable comfort to francophones, who are conscious of the French language's minority position, not only within Canada but on the North American continent.

One must also highlight the emergence of a sovereigntist party, the Parti Québécois, which formed majority provincial governments in 1976, 1981, 1994, and 1998, and a short-lived minority one in 2012. Its federal counterpart, the Bloc Québécois, won a majority of Quebec's House of Commons seats in six consecutive federal elections, until its eclipse following the 2011 election. There are no political parallels to this in Canada's other nine provinces. And there are few states in the world where parties advocating the breakup of the country have been able to operate through democratic norms and procedures.

But it has not been all win-win for Quebec. One can point to Quebec's failure to block constitutional patriation in 1982, and to the impact of the Charter, which has considerably strengthened the power of the judiciary and the culture of individual as opposed to collective rights. Nor was the Quebec government successful in winning recognition for Quebec's status as a distinct society through the aborted constitutional initiatives of the late 1980s and early 1990s. More telling still was the failure of the two Quebec referenda—the first on sovereignty-association in 1980, the second on sovereignty-partnership in 1995—to win majority support. The second referendum was decided by less than sixty thousand votes, less than 1.2 percent of the total ballots cast.

Following the second sovereignty referendum, the Supreme Court of Canada, in a unanimous 1998 ruling, held that Quebec governments did not have a unilateral right to secession. The court also held that if secession were to be a viable option, any future referendum would have to reflect a clear majority on a clear question. And certain fundamental principles involving federalism, democracy, constitutional procedures, and minority rights would need to be respected. The federal government promptly passed the Clarity Act in 2000, obliging Parliament to respond to referendum results only if the referendum question was deemed to be "clear" and the results reflected the "clear expression of will by a clear majority." The Quebec government responded with its own law emphasizing the principle of self-determination. However, in the decade and a half that has since elapsed, the question of Quebec sovereignty has been relegated to the back burner, so the angst that gripped the Canada-Quebec relationship for much of the post-1960 period has dissipated for the moment.

Where Quebec's impact on the federal system is concerned, one might note a greater responsiveness on the part of recent Canadian governments to Quebec concerns. For example, the Official Languages Act and the Charter provide for a much more extensive use of French as one of Canada's two official languages than is true of the Constitution Act, 1867. In the run-up to the Iraq War of 2003, vehement opposition in Quebec to Canadian involvement, when English-Canadian opinion was much more evenly split, helped to tip the balance in the direction of Canada's staying out. The Harper government provided additional funding to Quebec (and a number of other provinces) as a result of vigorous Quebec concerns about an ongoing fiscal deficit of federal transfer payments. And, in a resolution passed by the House of Commons in November 2006, the Québécois were recognized as constituting a nation within a united Canada.

In thinking about the future, it is important to distinguish between institutional arrangements, especially constitutionally prescribed ones, and tacit societal acknowledgement of Canada's multiple national identities. One of the paradoxes of trying to reconcile the interests of majority and minority nationalities is that their points of view are so very different. Majority nationalities, for all their diverging regional loyalties, tend to identify with the national imperatives associated with the central government, though their members may well differ about specific policy proposals. Minority nationalities are quite conscious of their position within the larger state and are determined to ensure that matters vital to them remain primarily under their own control. Majority nationalities prefer symmetry in the operation of a federal system—equal treatment for each of the constituent units. Minority nationalities prefer asymmetry, on the grounds that they constitute a distinctive national community with substantially different concerns from the majority. Reconciling these opposing views is not an easy proposition. Incorporating the views of Aboriginal peoples into the Canada-Quebec debate (as in the 1995 question of whether the Cree and other peoples of northern Quebec would remain part of Canada in the event of Quebec secession) underlines just how complicated plurinational relationships can be.

The main reason for the failure of the Meech Lake and Charlottetown accords of the late 1980s and early 1990s was that many in English Canada saw recognition of Quebec's distinct society status as potentially undermining minority rights within Quebec and the sense of a shared national community within Canada. Conversely, a majority of Quebec francophones saw in such recognition the minimum price that needed to be paid if Quebec was to be a willing participant in the major constitutional aggiornamento that had taken place over its government's opposition in 1982.

For minority nationalities, the central government is not the sole national government. The bottom line for these nationalists is the preservation of the distinctiveness of the minority nationality. For those who are not secessionists or sovereigntists, this can be best achieved by maximizing the autonomy of minority-controlled institutions within the larger ensemble. The logic that comes into play here is ultimately confederal, since it presses for something closer to a one-on-one relationship between the members of the minority nationality and the majority. But this runs counter to the reality that majority nationalities, by dint of their numbers, are invariably in a better position to get their way within the larger federal state than minority nationalities are. Hence, a centralizing logic is more likely to win out against a massively decentralizing one, a federal over a more overtly confederal approach.

Where Quebec is concerned, de facto forms of asymmetry already exist in the Canadian federation, and there is no reason one may not see more of the same in the future. Yet, there are palpable limits even here in just how much by way of special powers Quebec could acquire while MPs and federal government ministers from that province continued to make decisions in some of the same policy areas for the rest of the country.

Symbolism can be one way of tackling the question of multiple identities within plurinational states. The 2006 House of Commons resolution recognizing the Québécois as constituting a nation within a united Canada was an adept formula in that it left a lot of things unresolved. It recognized Quebec's distinctiveness, even more tellingly than the failed Meech Lake and Charlottetown accords, but did so without the constitutional entrenchment that had triggered so much of the opposition two decades before. It left open the question of who exactly the Québécois were—all residents of Quebec? French Canadians in particular? It avoided equating the national identity of the Québécois with any political claims by the Quebec government to be this national identity's exclusive embodiment. It accomplished this by presupposing that acknowledgement of the Québécois' national character was perfectly compatible with Canadian unity—something that hardline proponents of a single Canada from sea to sea to sea on the one hand, and proponents of Quebec sovereignty on the other, would have reasons to reject.

Quebec has acquired a voice within the Canadian delegation to UNESCO, on the grounds that the province has unique cultural concerns that need to be addressed at the international level. But here again there are limits to how far a non-sovereign national community can hope to go by way of acquiring international recognition in continental or global institutions limited to sovereign states. There has also been talk among sovereigntists in Quebec about establishing a form of Quebec citizenship, even without achieving independence. This, too, could quickly become a bone of contention, since citizenship is something normally associated with sovereign states—not sub-state nationalities.

Ever since the creation of the Canadian federation in 1867, pragmatism and a willingness to compromise—both on the English-Canadian and French-Canadian sides—have generally characterized

English-French relations, for all the periodic turbulence. Is there any reason to believe this will dramatically change in the near future? I rather think not. Does it mean there will ever be a complete meeting of minds between Québécois and other Canadians or, for that matter, between First Nations and other Canadians or Québécois? I also think not.

The ethos of plurinational and multilingual states rests on the need to live together despite at times seemingly insurmountable differences among their constituent peoples. This is quite a different rationale from the one that drives nationalist sentiment in traditional nation-states with a homogeneous concept of nationality. The plurinational rationale rests on overcoming the friend-enemy distinction, the reduction of the political to a single all-encompassing good, on learning the art of living together with civility, if not with excessive intimacy, despite linguistic and cultural differences. Ambiguity is built into the very logic of plurinational federations, and Canada will continue to dwell under its sway well beyond 2017. But the survival of our country over the past 150 years, when many other plurinational states have succumbed, is itself something of a miracle for which we can give thanks.

The Next Energy Transition

Walter Mérida

IN NOVEMBER 2016, the supermoon overlooking the market at Jemaa el-Fna provided an extraordinary backdrop for the twenty-second Conference of the Parties (COP 22) in Marrakech, Morocco. The crowd walking through the dark streets and passing enticing food carts included scientists, activists, heads of state, and executives from multinational energy companies. The moonrise was inspirational, but it was also a stark reminder of planetary fragility under a changing climate—across the Atlantic, the full moon coincided with tidal flooding in Florida and an unprecedented election in the US.

As we prepare to celebrate the 150th anniversary of Canadian Confederation, our country is well-positioned to become a global leader in climate solutions, building on increasing international momentum. We find ourselves at a pivotal moment, and the decisions and actions we take today will reverberate well beyond our own borders.

Despite recent geopolitical changes, the world is gravitating toward consensus on climate change. More significantly, the focus on the measurement and regulation of greenhouse gas (GHG) emissions is shifting to new risk-assessment metrics, financing instruments, and investment opportunities in a low-carbon economy. At the COP 21 in Paris, many countries, including Canada, championed an agreement to keep global warming below 2°C. The agreement has been ratified by more than 130 countries, and it is a political breakthrough. Equally significant global developments include the growth in the green bond market and a Green Climate Fund designed to mobilize $100 billion per year for adaptation and mitigation strategies. Other initiatives include the Breakthrough Energy Coalition, which aims to invest billions of dollars in energy technologies. Mission Innovation is an alliance between twenty-three countries (including Canada) planning to increase public investment in climate solutions up to $30 billion per year by 2021. National initiatives in Norway and Ireland are partially or fully divesting from coal, oil, and gas. Other long-term investors (pension funds, insurance companies, and sovereign wealth funds) may be able to deploy their assets (tens of trillions of dollars) to renewable energy projects and climate change solutions.

A robust financial infrastructure may be one of the most valuable Canadian assets, providing sophisticated investment services to aid the transition to sustainable energy systems. The Canadian banking system is still considered one of the best in the world; banks employ hundreds of thousands of people domestically and abroad, and no Canadian bank went through bankruptcy or required government assistance during the recent financial crisis. The Canadian financial system must capitalize on its robustness and reputation to embrace new funding approaches to climate change mitigation. The energy sector is the largest source of Canadian GHG emissions, and a significant portion of the investments should thus be devoted to de-carbonizing our energy system. Despite being a well-documented trend over the last few centuries, de-carbonization has only recently become a guiding principle for regional and national energy policies.

Canada's fragmented climate policies are coalescing into a national framework, but nationwide targets and regional measures have not incorporated the limits of current technologies. Canada has committed to GHG emissions reductions of 17 percent by 2020 and 30 percent by 2030 (compared with 2005 levels), but there is a gap between these targets and what can be achieved. In 2014, Environment Canada estimated that this gap will reach 116 million tonnes of CO_2-equivalent emissions per year by 2020, and it will more than double by 2030. These gaps between emissions reduction targets and achievable outcomes represent significant challenges but also an opportunity to transform Canada from a resource economy into a knowledge and innovation economy. Our history shows that we have the capacity to drive such large-scale transitions.

At present, and likely for the foreseeable future, Canada is and will remain dependent on the extraction of fossil fuels. However, oil and gas represent only the most recent stages in energy system evolution. In the last few centuries, Canada and the rest of the world underwent major transitions, from firewood to coal, to oil and natural gas. These transitions were accompanied by a progressive and systematic de-carbonization, and they occurred well before air pollution or climate change became global concerns. In all cases, the adoption drivers were innovation, quality, elegance, and convenience—not scarcity. When oil replaced coal, the coal supply was still plentiful, and natural gas is displacing oil ahead of the anticipated oil peak—we did not abandon the Stone Age due to a sudden scarcity of stones. For Canadians, it may be instructive to ask not why we must move away from fossil fuels, but why these fuels are so pervasive in the first place.

Fossil sources dominate because they can provide goods and services in both electrical and chemical domains. Electrical services encompass many things we now take for granted, including communications, entertainment, refrigeration, illumination, and social networking. These services can be provided without moving large amounts of material, or by powering devices that are tethered (with or without wires) to electricity and communications grids. In contrast, the chemical domain relies on products derived from hydrocarbons. Some well-known examples include transportation services, lubricants, cosmetics, plastics, and medicines. Fossil sources enable the manufacture of liquid fuels and other critical products. It took the planet tens of millions of years (and massive extinction events) to accumulate these valuable resources. To continue burning them to produce electricity may seem ludicrous to future generations. Canada can use its fossil fuels to drive economic transformation. But first it must cross the chasm between the electrical and chemical domains—a crossing that remains challenging for renewable energy.

Renewable energy sources are sparse and intermittent, and with a few exceptions (e.g., biofuels), they can generate only electricity. We cannot store electricity in large quantities, and with the exception of nuclear-powered ships, we cannot store enough electricity to power long-range travel. More importantly, the conversion of any energy source into electricity is trivial—virtually child's play. In contrast, it is much more difficult to convert electricity into chemicals or fuels. This asymmetry is one of the defining deficiencies of our current energy system. And one that must be addressed by new energy architectures.

The future energy system will be characterized by the convergence of integrated and connected energy services, with the same technology providing two or more services. For instance, fuel cell vehicles of the (near) future will be able to power a home for several days. And the same infrastructure will have multiple uses. Parkades, for example, may be able to store renewable energy by charging large numbers of electric vehicles. The same raw material (trees) will become the feedstock for two or more process streams, say bio-refineries, pulp mills, and gasification plants.

Energy convergence will also incorporate seamless and bidirectional conversion of electricity into fuels, products, and services. The simplest example is the hydrogen-electricity pair. Hydrogen is the only chemical fuel that can be produced (in large quantities) from electricity and water. Conversely, fuel cells use hydrogen to generate electricity across many scales and with zero emissions at the point of use. These electrochemical technologies may provide hydrogen refuelling and power-to-gas energy storage, while also helping to stabilize electrical distribution grids. The combined services (and revenue streams) may unlock business models for emerging technologies that struggle to grow beyond subsidized demonstration programs. Other examples, including synthetic fuels and bio-products, are now being explored. The availability of abundant hydrocarbons and low-carbon electricity thus represents a Canadian advantage.

According to the Canadian Hydropower Association, Canada is the third-largest producer of hydro power in the world, with this renewable source supplying approximately 60 percent of its domestic electricity demand. Under a changing climate, water resources may be stressed, but Canada's low electricity rates and the magnitude of undeveloped potential—more than twice the installed capacity—still represent globally competitive advantages. Moreover, the availability of large-scale generation and distribution grids (at times managed by a single Crown corporation) provides platforms across many scales (from communities to continents) to develop technologies and businesses for cities and mega-regions.

Beyond its leadership in hydro power, there is historical precedent for Canadian leadership in the global energy sector. Take, for example, the case of nuclear power. In 1941, George Laurence designed one of the first reactors at the National Research Council in Ottawa. By 1947, researchers at the Chalk River Laboratory ran the world's most powerful reactor, and Atomic Energy Canada Limited (AECL) was created in 1952. Shortly after, AECL, Ontario Hydro, and General Electric developed the CANada Deuterium Uranium (CANDU) reactor. By 1972, the first CANDU plant had been exported to India. Currently, the Bruce Power facility in Ontario is the largest operating nuclear plant in the world, and Canada is the second-largest producer of uranium—an energy source for nuclear reactors worldwide. Not many countries can mine the mineral, manufacture nuclear fuel, design reactors, and operate power plants safely and reliably.

Canada's nuclear sector has also triggered innovations in science and medicine. We lead the world in the production of medical radioisotopes for cancer treatment, neutron imaging in manufacturing, and cobalt-60 food sterilization. Research in nuclear energy has produced three Nobel prizes and employed tens of thousands of people. The nuclear sector is, undeniably, a major aspect of the Canadian economy, despite public-perception challenges associated with waste management, safety, and proliferation. Canada has all the ingredients to reproduce such innovations and become a leader in a low-carbon future.

Canada has been a pioneer of several enabling technologies for the twenty-first century. It hosts some of the leading companies developing artificial intelligence, fuel cells, bio-products, connected and zero-emission vehicles, electrolysis, carbon-capture devices, synthetic fuels, nuclear fusion, and quantum computing. Four of the world's top-twenty-five innovation hubs are centred in Toronto, Vancouver, Montreal, and Waterloo. One of them (along the Cascadia corridor) has been identified under the Pacific Coast Collaborative as a critical link to Washington, Oregon, and California. This corridor has a large population and a sizable economy, an established immigration culture, one of the best airports in the world, the three largest ports on the continental West Coast, leading higher-education institutions, a time zone compatible with three financial centres (London, New York, and Hong Kong), and global brand recognition as the birthplace of Boeing, Google, and carbon taxes. Along this corridor, vehicles, roads, and buildings can become active assets in an interconnected energy system compatible with new business models.

Under energy convergence, car electrification, car-share programs, and autonomous vehicles will improve urban air quality and render ownership models obsolete. New business and insurance models will emerge ("Your condo comes with a pool of shared vehicles in the garage"). Consumer behaviour and the nature of incentives will also change ("Yes, Dad, I know I am sixteen, but I don't need a driver's licence"). High-occupancy-vehicle lanes may become recharging lanes for electric cars. As cities merge into mega-regions, an operating system for transportation and other integrated services (a City OS) may be required. The coupling of smart electricity grids with oil and gas networks (among Canada's most valuable assets) will disrupt the business models for utilities.

Applying Canadian leadership in artificial intelligence and information technology will be critical in tackling concrete energy challenges (autonomous driving, data-centre power control, real-time energy and emissions trading, etc.), and may also enable breakthroughs in other areas (personalized medicine, forensic detection of insider trading, high-resolution climate modelling, etc.). Such innovation can permeate important sectors of the Canadian economy: compared with autonomous driving in downtown Toronto (in the winter), the automation of mining operations and grain delivery to the coast is relatively simple.

Finally, Canada must capitalize on its people. Canadian researchers generate 4 percent of the world's scientific publications and almost 5 percent of the most-cited papers. Our research apparatus has been effective in early-stage discovery and basic research, but the innovation infrastructure has failed to produce world-leading ventures systematically. Public and private priorities are misaligned: according to government sources, the public investment in research and development (R & D) ranks ninth out of thirty-four countries in the Organisation for Economic

Co-operation and Development (OECD), but the corresponding business expenditure in R & D ranks twenty-second on the same list.[1] Other barriers include the lack of domestic and scalable investment structures, and the difficulty in harnessing coordinated expertise in the social and natural sciences. The need for ethics, psychology, and political science in technology road maps has never been more critical.

If we capitalize on these challenges and opportunities, the next supermoon may witness our country leading the next transition in energy system evolution—a transition that is truly compatible with Canadian values for the next 150 years.

November 2034 is just around the corner.

Immigrant Nation

David Ley

IN RESPONSE TO the recent dispiriting turn to populism, nationalism, and protectionism in Western electoral politics, *The Economist*, an international magazine oriented to liberal economics, included columns in its October 29, 2016, issue with such stirring titles as "Liberty Moves North" and "The Last Liberals." These were reports on Canada, highlighting, as the magazine's optimistic reporter put it, "why Canada is still at ease with openness." A few months earlier, Bono, U2's lead singer, repeated an observation made by then-president Barack Obama to the Canadian Parliament that "the world needs more Canada."

The evidence for renewed internationalism does indeed appear to be decisive as Canada enters its 150th year. In an age of growing protectionism and nativism, Canada recently signed a free trade agreement with the European Union and accepted more than thirty-five thousand refugees from Syria. Among Canadian towns, villages, and cities, 350 had donned the mantle of "welcoming communities," with goodwill modelled by the private sponsors of Syrian newcomers.

Such cosmopolitan actions might be expected to flow from a broader reservoir of tolerance and goodwill. Indeed, opinion polls on immigration and integration invariably show relatively high levels of support for immigration and ethnic diversity in this country. In international surveys of Organisation for Economic Co-operation and Development (OECD) countries, Canadian responses to immigration are invariably the most positive; indeed, some years Canada is the only nation with a majority of respondents endorsing immigration. Polls by the German Marshall Fund (2011) and by Environics Analytics over a period of years repeat this affirmation. In the Marshall Fund poll, less than 15 percent of Canadians stated there were too many immigrants, the lowest figure in any of the countries polled, while an Environics survey the same year continued to show majority support of close to 60 percent for the current level of immigration. With such popular endorsement, it is no surprise that immigration is embedded deeply in Canadian economic, social, and population policy.

It has not always been so, and some critics argue that old acrimonies have not yet been resolved. Two political parties in recent elections—the federal Conservatives in 2015 and the provincial Parti Québécois in 2014—resorted to disparaging innuendoes and prejudicial policies about cultural diversity in an attempt to shore up a putatively intolerant core vote. Both parties lost badly on election day. Of course, Canadian tolerance rarely faces the same demanding tests as counterparts in Europe or the United States. The absence of a land border with refugee-sending countries, and the separation afforded by broad oceans, insulate Canada from the immediate pressures of large numbers of asylum-seekers.

Canada has always been a nation of immigrants. The profile of annual arrivals over the past 150 years has been shaped by the vicissitudes of national policy and global events. Particularly notable was the surge in numbers immediately before 1914, when in the course of only three years (1911–13) over 1.1 million new Canadians landed, adding, in 1912 and again in 1913, over 5 percent to the national population. These are extraordinary numbers that have never since been repeated. Post-1945 landings followed the crests and troughs of the economic cycle until around 1990, when a bold decision was made to hold immigration numbers at around 250,000 regardless of the state of the business cycle. That figure was raised to 300,000 for 2016 and 2017.

For the first hundred years after Canadian Confederation, immigration consolidated a European settler society with transplanted British institutions and largely separate British and French cultural and linguistic domains. Implicitly and, for many, explicitly, the task of immigration was to reproduce a white Canadian society that was a cultural outpost of Europe. Aspiring non-white migrants from elsewhere were defined as an out-group by this ideology, leading to public policy and everyday relations that were racist in intent and in effect. Most offensive were the increasingly punitive head taxes directed against Chinese immigrants, urged by activists in British Columbia and first introduced in 1885, culminating (as in the United States) in virtual exclusion through the terms of the 1923 Chinese Immigration Act. This highly racist legislation was not repealed until 1945. More covert and discretionary immigration measures checked the arrival of migrants from India and Japan.

The cultural—indeed civilizational—superiority felt by Euro-Canadians that had been deployed in the dispossession of Aboriginal lands was repeated against Asian migrants, leading to such sorry episodes as the *Komagata Maru* incident in 1914, when a crowded ship carrying several hundred male Sikhs from the Punjab was refused entry at Vancouver Harbour. In 1907, and following an earlier riot in 1887, mobs rampaged through Vancouver's Chinatown and Japantown, destroying property and randomly beating residents. Such actions, the outcome of racism and fears of cheap labour undercutting local wages, were not unique. The 1907 outburst in Vancouver was a copycat event from a riot in Bellingham a few days earlier, both of them triggered by the local "Asiatic Exclusion League." In a more liberal and multicultural present, Canada's leaders have acknowledged these profound injustices. In 2006, Prime Minister Harper apologized for the head tax, and the province of British Columbia made its own apology in 2014 for 160 racist and discriminatory statutes in force until 1947. In 2016, Prime Minister Trudeau offered national contrition in Parliament to Canada's South Asian community for the *Komagata Maru* incident.

Canada's current immigration framework was assembled in the 1960s. In an era of greater liberalism, geographical preference for immigrants from Europe and the United States was ended, and the points system was introduced, allowing entry to any qualified candidates. By the 1970s, the three streams of current immigration policy were in place: admission was possible through the points system for economic migrants (the independent or economic class), through family sponsorship (the family class), and through need for protection (the humanitarian class). While there have been numerous changes to these entry streams over the years—including new subcategories for live-in caregivers and business immigrants—these three principal legs of admission for immigrants and refugees have prevailed. These new immigration policies reflected the political realities of the Canadian federal system, with Quebec managing its own admissions and other provinces exercising variable autonomy over parts of their admission and settlement programs. While adding complexity to the execution of national policy, this arrangement does allow some sensitivity to regional interests.

The termination of European preference in immigrant admission had substantial consequences for the national origins of new arrivals, leading to greater cultural diversity in the nation, most notably in the larger cities. This increase in diversity was anticipated by the official declaration of multiculturalism in 1971. In the 1960s, 80 percent of immigrants to Canada originated in Europe or the United States, led by the United Kingdom. Fifty years later, this share had fallen to 15 percent, with substantial growth in particular among Asian-origin landings. In the past decade, India, the Philippines, and China have been the top-ranking sources of immigrants, and Asia has contributed 50 percent of all new arrivals. Despite these changes, some critics claim that visa discrimination persists against non-Caucasian applicants. However, a recent study of Canadian visa offices in various countries showed high overall acceptance rates of processed files, with no tendency to penalize non-European source areas.

Preference for immigrants in the economic stream remains a significant reality, and target admissions numbers for the economic class have risen steadily; as a share of new arrivals, they have grown from less than 40 percent in the 1980s to over 60 percent since 2010, with concomitant decreases for the family and humanitarian classes. Landing through the points system, with its credit for educational standing, new arrivals to Canada declare higher levels of education than the native-born. Moreover, the children of certain immigrant groups have the highest level of achievement of all Canadians. Two-thirds of the children of Chinese and Indian immigrant parents hold a university degree, compared with less than 30 percent of children of Canadian-born parents. This is a remarkable premium the Canadian nation has gained through immigration.

The reality of life for many highly skilled immigrants to Canada is often not as rosy as one might expect. Despite their substantial human capital, many new immigrants are not doing well in the labour market. Successive national census results show disproportionately higher poverty among recently arrived immigrants in metropolitan areas, and by 2001, immigrant status had become a leading predictor of urban poverty. The enigma of "non-performing" human capital among immigrants is attributed in part to the failure of Canadian employers to recognize foreign professional accreditation or the value of overseas degrees. This is aggravated in some instances by discriminatory hiring practices. The cost is borne by the immigrant, but the loss is shared by the nation, with estimates of billions of dollars of economic talent that are unrealized each year in the labour market.

The Business Immigration Program (BIP) offers a related case of policy failure and was terminated in 2014, leaving only an insignificant boutique program. The BIP became important from the late 1980s as a vehicle for wealthy entrepreneurs to fast-track their way to permanent residence through successful participation in the Canadian economy. But, once again, reality failed to live up to expectations. Detailed census and tax-filer data showed systematic underperformance within this cohort, with many of these would-be entrepreneurs (living mainly in Vancouver and Toronto) declaring the lowest incomes of all visa streams, including multiply disadvantaged refugees. Business immigrants were living from the fruits of their overseas enterprises and failing to develop vibrant businesses in Canada. The split allegiance of immigrant entrepreneurs between their origin and destination countries is a distinctive feature of the relatively new phenomenon of transnational migration, where migrants practise serial movement across national borders, with only conditional loyalties to any one nation-state. Transnationalism undercuts the premise of permanent residence upon which settler societies have been established.

But the state, too, can play a similar game, enforcing transnational status with limited citizenship rights upon temporary migrants who might themselves prefer permanent status. The numbers of temporary migrants have risen substantially, and annual arrivals of short-term workers, students, refugee claimants, and others now exceed the annual admission total of permanent residents. Temporary migration weakens the sense of belonging and identity that comes with full citizenship rights and that define successful immigrant integration.

Some critics see a further challenge to immigrant integration in the geographical concentration of recent immigrants in large cities, seeking both labour opportunities but also co-ethnic neighbourhoods to ease their adjustment. In this century, 60 to 70 percent of new immigrants have settled in Canada's three largest cities, increasingly in suburban locations. Their numbers have led to significant ethnic concentrations in "ethnoburbs" like Markham and Brampton, outside Toronto, and Richmond and Surrey, in suburban Vancouver. Such ethnic enclaves, sometimes falsely attributed to the identity politics of multiculturalism, are said by critics to impede integration, sustain cultural separateness, and even provide conditions where hostile attitudes may be incubated.

In Europe, such residential segregation is seen as a liability, if not a danger. But segregation has always been a feature of the immigration of large numbers of co-ethnic settlers to cities. Characteristically, such segregation has been a temporary feature, as newcomers, following the early years of adjustment, strive for districts with better opportunities: higher-quality housing, better schools, and more lucrative jobs. The ethnic neighbourhood as a temporary feature in the urban landscape may thus be considered as a case of what has been called "good segregation." However, significant negative consequences can arise if such ethnic segregation is enforced, involuntary, and long-lasting.

Such anxieties have not limited the appetite for immigration among most Canadians and their government in the nation's 150th year. Indeed, immigration is typically seen as a solution to many of the social policy problems in the country. A declining birth rate? Immigration will fix it! A need for new demographic energy in declining areas? Immigration will fix it! A shrinking workforce? Immigration will fix it! The necessity for a new generation of taxpayers? Immigration will fix it! In Canada at 150, immigration is seemingly a resource that keeps on giving.

Coquitlam, British Columbia | TINA-LOUISE HARRIS

NICHOLAS TAFFS

JUNE SZASZ

Victoria, British Columbia | COLUMBE LANE

Claiming the
21st Century

David Carment and Joe Landry

THE 150TH ANNIVERSARY of Canadian Confederation unfolds at a time when our nation faces significant uncertainty about its place in the world. Prime Minister Wilfrid Laurier's brave prediction of Canadian leadership in the twentieth century was not realized. Yet, with the right mix of audacity and strategy, Canada may well become the international political and economic extrovert that Laurier foretold: a home for those from troubled places around the world, a land of opportunity, investment, innovation, prosperity, and equality. But, although Canada's place on the international stage has changed for the better since 1867, it is not clear how we will maintain this trajectory without embracing fundamentally new approaches. Should we fully embrace continentalism and throw ourselves upon the tender mercies of unpredictable US power and influence, or seek out new partners and boldly go where no prime minister has dared take us before?

Canada's economic prosperity is challenged on a number of fronts—for example, by internal barriers to trade and rising global protectionism. Our southern neighbour's obsession with security detracts from our own leaders' capacity to achieve economic growth through immigration and trade. Domestic considerations have also had a major effect on Canada's own trade policy. Relative to our American neighbours, Canada's public does not have as strong a visceral reaction against large-scale international trade deals—for instance, the Trans-Pacific Partnership (TPP) and the Canada-European Union Comprehensive Economic and Trade Agreement (CETA). And yet a great deal of criticism (from all sides of the political spectrum) has nonetheless been levelled at the Canadian government for its pursuit of such agreements, including CETA, which promises to open twenty-eight European countries to Canadian goods and services.

From the left, we hear primarily of environmental and labour-rights concerns, along with worries over undue power for corporations in investor-state dispute settlement mechanisms. From the right (and sometimes from the left), we hear of wage stagnation and the loss of manufacturing and natural resource industry jobs. Both sides worry about the detrimental effects of rising inequality, which may be exacerbated by such trade agreements if low-skilled jobs are exported overseas. Opposition voices have been effective in making themselves heard, especially in the case of the now-defunct TPP.

With Donald Trump's recent election as US president, Canada finds itself in an interesting position. The new president is proving to be both disruptive and catalyzing—implicitly cajoling Canada's leaders to reluctantly and hesitantly embrace change. Trump makes us uncomfortable because of the stark choices we must make in reacting to his policies. Consider, for example, the subject of trade. A renegotiation of NAFTA is inevitable. That is not necessarily a bad thing if it means that Canada strengthens its economic relations with the US (though this will likely come at the expense of a weakened relationship with Mexico). The Trump administration has also negated the TPP, a deal that would have provided access to 40 percent of the global economy by expanding Canada's trade into the Asia-Pacific.

The collapse of the TPP is especially problematic for a country that is slowly coming to grips with shifting migration patterns that deeply influence its trading relations. While we are historically dependent on trade with the US and Europe, our increasingly multicultural population and its well-organized diaspora communities hold the key to the future prosperity of Canada. The pluralistic nature of our society means that Canada's leaders must understand that multiple communities in this country shape our political, economic, and social priorities. By the same token, Canada's leaders must also appreciate that favouring some groups over others can invite invidious comparison, promote exclusiveness, and generate ethnic identities at the expense of civic nationalism. Therefore, looking beyond the US means thinking of Canada as a "diaspora nation," a country increasingly influenced by global issues, as seismic shifts in world politics pull the country in different directions. The unipolar moment of American pre-eminence—and the predictability that entailed—has given way to a more dynamic multipolar system.

To add more uncertainty to the mix, Prime Minister Justin Trudeau's ambitious multilateral agenda faces unprecedented challenges from a southern neighbour that clearly prefers to negotiate bilaterally to better exploit American leverage over weaker partners. Traditionally, Canada has preferred to deal with American influence through a multilateral agenda, with its emphasis on the establishment and enforcement of collective rules guiding state behaviour. To be sure, defence and border security co-operation between Canada and the US is deeply bilateral. But on collective global issues such as climate change, failed and fragile states, and the global economy, Canada has generally favoured more multilateral approaches.

And yet, unlike countries such as Norway and Sweden, Canada is not a natural multilateral player. It has to work hard to support a multilateral agenda. It is through multilateralism and membership in various organizations that Canada has typically addressed questions of peace and security through the rule of law (as a member of the UN, NATO, and the Organization for Security and Co-operation in Europe, for example), and economic prosperity and competitiveness in trade and investment (as part of the World Trade Organization and NAFTA, for example), as well as national unity and Canadian sovereignty (as a member of the Commonwealth and La Francophonie). In the golden era of Canadian diplomacy, the determined efforts by Prime Ministers Lester B. Pearson and Pierre Trudeau were to offset American influence through multilateralism. Trudeau had his "third option," whereas Pearson favoured a strengthened United Nations and increasing contributions to NATO. But this era was not without rancour and discord between Canada and the US, especially when Canada chose to not support the war in Vietnam. Under Trudeau the younger, Canada thus finds itself revisiting that well-worn challenge. Resisting American dominance, under the banner of multilateral engagement, risks friction between the two countries.

In reality, Canada's foreign policy has always been driven by two views of the world, both carefully balanced with ebbs and flows over Canada's 150 years. The first path pursues deepening integration within the North American context to the point, perhaps, where Canada and the US embrace a common security and economic community. The second path looks beyond continentalism. If Canada's changing demography and sources of economic prosperity portend future policy choices, then surely there is merit in looking beyond North America. And the pull of this second path is fuelled by more than domestic considerations.

There are systemic transformations afoot driving the need to look beyond the US. By the mid-twenty-first century, it is estimated that Asia, led by China, along with Brazil and South Africa, will have a combined GNP larger than the G8.[1] The rise of the Asia-Pacific as an economic powerhouse is driving a dramatic shift in the global power balance. While neither China nor India will eclipse the United States as the globe's premier power in the foreseeable future, the postwar hegemony of the American economic order is clearly waning.

Simply put, relations with the United States cannot be the sole focus of Canada's foreign policy. Equally central are our own concerns around the establishment of peace and security through the rule of law, ensuring economic prosperity and competitiveness through trade and investment, and enhancing national unity and Canadian sovereignty. But the challenges facing Canadian governments as they pursue these objectives have changed as new global power balances and orders have emerged. For example, in 1947, Prime Minister Louis St. Laurent ushered in critical thinking on how Canada should engage with the world. Like his predecessor, Mackenzie King, St. Laurent believed Canada needed to uphold and defend the core values of freedom and liberty in the face of rising tyranny. In contrast, more recent Liberal and Conservative governments have grappled with the problems of a post–Cold War world confronted by failed and failing states, terrorism, and economic uncertainty.

For St. Laurent and, after him, Prime Ministers Diefenbaker, Pearson, Trudeau (the elder), and Mulroney, international organizations such as the United Nations, the Commonwealth, and NATO were central to achieving Canada's foreign-policy objectives. These commitments have, for better or worse, lingered on as key tools in the Canadian diplomatic arsenal. But even as their significance has evolved in a new global reality, we have hung on to our comforting, though somewhat outdated, notions of these international organizations. For example, while Canadians have high regard for UN peacekeeping missions, the reality is that Canada's most significant contributions since Jean Chrétien came to power in 1994 have been NATO-led deployments. These operations have focused on the use of force targeting intrastate conflict during complex humanitarian emergencies resulting from massive refugee flows, terrorism, and failed states.

Under Prime Ministers Paul Martin and Stephen Harper, the Canadian government spent billions of tax dollars on rebuilding failed states like Afghanistan and Haiti, working with G8 countries on African governance and poverty, and pushing through domestic legislation to strengthen the doctrine of the Responsibility to Protect (R2P) accepted by the UN in 2005. Since then, successive Liberal and Conservative governments have stood by while the R2P doctrine has glaringly failed, first in Darfur and then again in Libya and Syria. More recently, the International Criminal Court (ICC), which Canada helped develop, is under sharp criticism from a variety of corners, including the African Union, Russia, and the US. It is not hard to imagine the court weakening, if not fading away completely, in the coming decades.

At the same time, the world is witnessing a decline in the coherence and effectiveness of multilateral organizations. The pursuit of bilateral free-trade arrangements is but one example of a potential weakening in the World Trade Organization structure. Other recent examples include the UK "Brexit" vote, with its implications for EU integrity, and a perceived deterioration of the UN system, undermined by constant abuse by regional and global powers. Canada's current leaders remain at a loss on how to develop a coherent strategy to kick-start multilateral renewal.

Consider, for example, the challenges that Canada must confront on Arctic sovereignty and its stewardship of the northern environment under climate change. Though the Arctic has been a primary concern for Canada's prime ministers from Diefenbaker through to Harper, there are thorny problems up for consideration. These include our relationship with the US (with whom we share space but have different legal perspectives on Artic sovereignty), Russia (a rival but also a member of the Arctic Council), and China (whose desire for transit of goods through the northern passages places new demands on our infrastructure, our climate, and the people of the North).

Canada's strongest resource in weathering these challenges will undoubtedly be its peoples. A robust civil society has always been Canada's hallmark, notwithstanding some dark chapters in our history, as recently highlighted by the Truth and Reconciliation Commission of Canada. During the last half of the twentieth century, our country saw a significant increase in the number of individuals joining together through collective action, working to affect positive societal change. That said, there have been better times for civil society in Canada. We are fresh from the Harper years, when many prominent activist groups lost government funding and when government policies served to muzzle dissenting voices. These measures took a toll on the viability and efficacy of internationally oriented NGOs and other civil society organizations working abroad in zones of conflict. In the short time Prime Minister Trudeau has been in power, some of those restrictions have been relaxed, though it remains to be seen whether the federal government will again be open to the type of scrutiny, public debate, and engagement that is needed for effective, accountable, and transparent government. Canada can hardly project its core values abroad if it fails to uphold them at home. Whether it is the calamitous state of its relations with Indigenous peoples or the absence of civil society in the development of a foreign-policy agenda, these concerns weigh heavily as we engage with countries whose shortcomings on these matters are self-evident.

Beyond issues of Canada's democracy, civil society, and social justice, this country's momentous demographic shifts cannot be ignored. With more than 20 percent of the Canadian population having been born overseas (the figure is closer to 40 percent in large metropolitan centres), the country will continue to identify as, and reflect in reality, a true ethnic mosaic. As of now, Canadians do a reasonably good job of integrating newcomers, with robust social services, including language and employment training, aiding immigrant populations in adapting to the "Canadian" way of life. This strength has allowed Canada to proudly call itself a nation of immigrants, while managing to avoid (at least some of) the more insidious problems seen in Europe and the United States, where ghettoization of immigrant communities and a sense of "otherness" pervade some groups within those societies.

Canada enters its 150th year in uncertainty, in an unpredictable world, with rising populism, nationalism, and isolationism. At the same time, the current uncertain global order represents an important opportunity for Canada to find a new path. To achieve that goal means looking back to the key principles that have driven this country forward on the global stage, and embracing change openly and willingly.

Fisheries and the World

**William Cheung, Daniel Pauly,
and Rashid Sumaila**

ABUNDANT FISHERIES RESOURCES have played a prominent role in
Canada's economic, social, and political history over the past 150 years.
On Canada's east coast, the Grand Banks once supported a huge biomass of Atlantic cod and other marine life. While First Nations peoples
used these resources sustainably for centuries, the systematic exploitation of the emblematic Atlantic cod shaped the settler populations from
France and the British Isles in what was to become Canada. Indeed, the
perennial pre-Confederation conflicts between France and Britain along
the Grand Banks and similar locations were largely driven by competition over fisheries resources, with Britain gradually reducing France to
a small foothold in Saint-Pierre and Miquelon.

Overfishing—fuelled by subsidies, mismanagement, and incomplete
scientific understanding of ocean ecosystems—drove the once world-
renowned Atlantic cod fisheries into collapse (Figure 1A). It is estimated
that the cod fishery likely provided sustainable yields of 100,000 to
200,000 tonnes per year until industrial trawlers from Europe began to
massively increase the catch, substantially reducing the size of the stock.
Then, the Canadians took over and unleashed their own trawlers onto this
diminished cod stock, which predictably and famously crashed in 1992.

The rise and fall of fisheries on Canada's Pacific coast mimicked
the disaster of the east coast fishery. For tens of thousands of years,
the coastal First Nations in British Columbia have been dependent,

nutritionally and culturally, on salmon and other fish such as herring. After contact with Europeans, First Nations populations decreased substantially, resulting in a marked decline in their participation in the fisheries. Simultaneously, the expansion of industrial non-Indigenous fisheries resulted in dramatic increases in salmon and herring catches (Figure 1B). Many of the First Nations found themselves working alongside Asian immigrants in the salmon canneries dotting the early-twentieth-century coast of British Columbia. However, the salmon and herring stocks did not last long, and catches soon diminished to a small fraction of historical levels. British Columbians, like other Canadians, must now import much of the fish they consume.

In the Canadian Arctic, fisheries have remained small-scale, mainly supporting the livelihood of Inuit and other small coastal communities (Figure 1C). Before the early 1950s, the Inuit were mostly nomadic, and substantial amounts of fish were used to feed sled dogs needed for hunting and transportation. Because fisheries catches by the Arctic communities continue to be used mostly for subsistence purposes, more recent catches reflect the changing population size and consumption pattern of northern residents and their transition away from dogsleds to more modern forms of transport.

Canada currently finds itself with the majority of its commercial fish stocks needing to be rebuilt. Yet, in contrast to the US, Canada has no enabling legislation—indeed, not even a plan for action.

Any plan to rebuild Canadian fisheries stocks will take place in a highly globalized reality of resource markets. Although Canada sources a large amount of the fish it consumes from its three major Exclusive Economic Zones (EEZs), we also export a large proportion of our fisheries catch, while simultaneously importing a sizable amount of the fish consumed domestically. Based on data extracted from the United Nations Comtrade Database, in 2008, 47 percent of Canada's seafood imports came from the United States, followed by Thailand, China, Peru, and Chile. This means that the price of fish available to Canadians depends partly on the supply of fish from foreign waters.

The import and export and values of seafood products to and from Canada have increased enormously from 1965 to 2015. According to the UN Comtrade data mentioned above, over this period, which

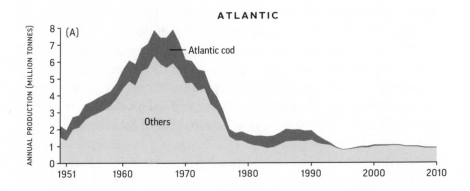

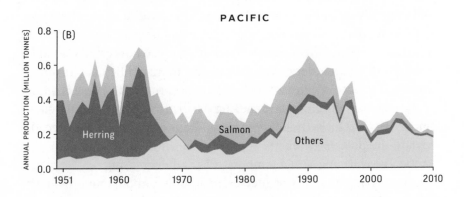

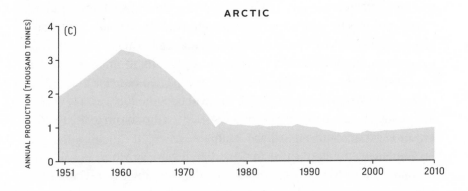

FIGURE 1. Fisheries catches within Canadian Exclusive Economic Zones in the Atlantic (A), Pacific (B), and Arctic (C) oceans. *Source: Sea Around Us; www.seaaroundus.org*

brackets the centennial and sesquicentennial anniversaries of Confederation, export value increased from $137 million to $4,692 million, while imports rose from only $17 million to $2,522 million (all figures in USD). Over time, the proportion of imports to total exports has increased from about 11 percent to 35 percent. These data demonstrate the increasing globalization of Canada's seafood production and consumption, and the need for Canadians to think of fisheries in a more international context.

Any future consideration of Canadian fisheries is also set against a backdrop of global climate change. The waters along Canada's three coasts are currently experiencing effects of a changing climate that will intensify over the coming decades. This poses a major challenge to the Canadian government, and to society at large, in mitigation and adaptation. The world's oceans—including those bordering Canada—are getting warmer, less oxygenated, and more acidic (as a result of increased surface ocean carbon dioxide concentrations). These changes in the ocean environment are causing the distribution of commercially important fish stocks to shift tens to hundreds of kilometres per decade toward the pole, and into areas and depths with cooler waters. In the Arctic, the warming ocean temperatures and decreasing sea-ice coverage are driving an influx of species, including salmon, that previously inhabited only lower latitudes. On the Pacific and Atlantic coasts, our fish and invertebrates are gradually shifting their distribution ranges northward toward Alaska in the west and the Arctic coast in the east. Moreover, species from south of the Canada-US border are also becoming increasingly abundant in Canadian waters. Salmon, and species with similar characteristics, will be particularly impacted because the mouths of the rivers to which they must return will become too warm for them, as already observed in the case of the sockeye salmon run in the mighty Fraser River of southern British Columbia.

Climate-dependent shifts in Canadian fisheries resources will have dramatic effects on the lives of all Canadians. Many coastal communities, particularly First Nations, are nutritionally dependent on fish and shellfish. Decreases in traditional food fishes such as salmon will have a significant effect on these communities. And there will also be strong financial implications that will affect us all—even those living thousands of miles from the coast. Computer models developed by the authors of this article project the biological and economic responses of fish stocks to climate change and suggest that potential fisheries revenues in Canada could decrease by up to 30 percent by 2050 under business-as-usual carbon emissions scenarios. Catches of Pacific salmon and herring, for example, are projected to further decrease by more than 30 percent.

Through the globalized seafood supply chain, Canadians will feel the impacts of climate change on fisheries in tropical regions far from home. As a small but perhaps symbolically important example, the decrease in catch of tropical tuna could increase the price of sushi in restaurants in Vancouver. Farming of Atlantic salmon is also dependent on fish feed originating from other parts of the world, especially anchovies taken in the waters off Peru. The changing distribution of fish stocks has additional geopolitical implications and can destabilize management of fisheries resources that are shared between countries (e.g., Atlantic cod or Pacific salmon stocks that are shared between the US and Canada). In the Arctic, local fisheries for "new" species that move into new habitats made available by climate change may attract competition from the developed industrial fisheries of the US, Russia, and East Asian countries. These developments will further increase the likelihood for mismanagement and overexploitation of fish stocks, and thus exacerbate the impacts of climate change on seafood supply.

In the face of these myriad challenges and complexities, Canada needs concrete policy to rebuild its depleted domestic stocks and conserve current fisheries. In 1996, the Canadian government passed the Oceans Act, which outlines a strategy to conserve marine biodiversity and resources. It is now critical that this act be translated into action in order to meet the grand challenges to the future sustainability of Canadian and global fisheries. For example, Canada should meet its international commitment of setting aside 10 percent of its waters as protected areas, with monitoring programs that track effectiveness toward meeting conservation goals. For overexploited or endangered fish stocks, concrete recovery strategies that include protection of critical habitats are needed. Canada already has the legislative tool to do this through the Species at Risk Act (SARA). What we still lack is a means to effectively implement this important legislation.

To achieve these goals, we need government resources, the intellectual capacity of government and academia, and fair and equitable policies and processes that are supported by an engaged citizenry. Given the importance of the oceans and fisheries to Canada, as the past and present demonstrate, this will be a good long-term investment for Canada.

Internationally, Canada must be an important player in solving the global challenges to oceans and fisheries, and must contribute positively to ensuring the sustainability of global fisheries resources. This can be done by promoting seafood sources from ecologically sustainable fisheries, joining forces to eliminate subsidies that lead to overfishing, and supporting socially equitable fisheries. We must improve our ability to track the sources of seafood and educate the seafood industry and the public about seafood sustainability. Canada can also play an active role in supporting the sustainability of the fisheries of other nations by sharing our wealth of expertise and experience on fisheries and oceans. For example, Canada's researchers played an important role in informing fisheries management in the Asia-Pacific region in the 1980s and 1990s, and this collaborative work has made long-lasting contributions to sustainable fisheries in this region.

The most effective solution to climate change is through the mitigation of greenhouse gas emissions. This requires international co-operation through such mechanisms as the recently ratified Paris Agreement under the United Nations Framework Convention on Climate Change, of which Canada is a signatory. Bi- or multilateral agreements that consider the effects of climate change are also needed to reduce conflict in the sharing of transboundary fisheries resources and to ensure their effective management. Federal and provincial management authorities and local communities need to develop adaptation plans and actions to reduce climate-induced changes in seafood supply. These may include building up resilience of coastal ecosystems through a network of marine protected areas, or diversification of income and livelihood sources for coastal communities.

Fisheries are an integral part of Canada's economy and have been central to our country's evolution into a globally important nation over the past 150 years. However, the future sustainability of fisheries and seafood industries is at a crossroads because of overfishing, climate change, and globalization. Full appreciation of the complex challenges facing sustainable fisheries at home and around the world is key to ensuring that future generations of Canadians have the opportunity to enjoy seafood and healthy oceans. The solutions are available; all of us, from members of the government and private sectors to the public, need to act upon the challenges swiftly before it is too late.

Second Generation

Ayesha Chaudhry

I STARTED WEARING the hijab before consciousness, before I have any memory of putting it on. It is as if I emerged into consciousness with my head already covered. I only know how I came to wear the hijab from stories my mother tells me. She tells me that I started wearing it when I was five years old. She's really proud of this. She says she didn't force me to wear it; to the contrary, I had insisted. I was a strong-willed child. I didn't like "no" as an answer. I still don't. Who does?

She herself started wearing the hijab the year I was born. I was born in Toronto, and my parents, immigrants from Pakistan, had been living in Canada for almost a decade before I showed up. By the time I started kindergarten, I asked if I could wear the hijab, too. My mother tried to dissuade me.

"You're too young. When you're older, you can wear it for sure."

"But I want to wear it now!"

"You're too young! What will people say? They'll think I'm forcing you!"

Apparently, I used to steal my mother's hijabs, wear them at school, and then come home, dragging them behind me, all muddy and dirty. Her hijabs were too big for my tiny body. So she relented and sewed me some hijabs my size: square fabric, which you folded into a triangle and then pinned at your chin, but really your throat, with a safety pin. Given my age, I doubt my mother pinned the hijab at my throat. She probably just tied it at my chin, like a kerchief that elderly Eastern European women wear on their heads. I would graduate to the safety pin.

My earliest memory of the hijab is having forgotten to wear it. I was attending the Islamic School in Toronto, where I would study for two years. Only for two years because my parents pulled me out at the end of the second year. They felt that the Islamic School wasn't "Islamic" enough. They thought it was too Western. There were Muslims from around the world at this school. The principal was Sudanese. He had a thin, white metal rod, four feet long, that he carried around the school with him. He would use it to hit misbehaving children, usually a sharp, stinging strike to their hands. We were terrified of this rod. He believed in public punishment so that the other children would know what to expect if they misbehaved. I saw him hit a young boy once. The child shrieked, his face crumpling with pain and shame, reddening; his eyes squinting as he hopped frantically from one foot to the other. I feel that I was hit by this rod, too. I have a vivid memory of how it felt on my hand. I say I "feel" that I remember this because I'm not sure if I've conjured up this experience with my elaborate childish imagination. Maybe I was hit and I blocked out the details. Either way, we were all terrified of the principal's rod.

But he was also nice. He was very nice to me. One evening after a fundraising event, when people milled about after dinner in a sparse and cavernous community hall, he played with me, lifting me off the floor and twirling me around. I loved the attention. He asked my parents if he could adopt me for a few years. He promised to teach me flawless Arabic.

"Your daughter is special," he told them. "She could become a great scholar."

There were Canadians from all over the world at the Islamic School—South Asians from India and Pakistan; Arabs from Saudi, Syria, and Egypt; converts, European and Japanese. Everyone came with their own cultural background, their own vision of a pristine Islam. All these visions jostled with one another to create a kaleidoscope, an Islamic kaleidoscope, at this school.

But my parents didn't think Islam was a kaleidoscope. They didn't like the way Islam was being practised at the school; it was too compromised, too weak, too Western. There was too much mixing between the genders. Why did this school have coed classes? Did they care nothing for Islam? Besides, I learned far more about Islam at home; the school certainly didn't help me memorize more of the Qur'an. I'd learned to recite the Qur'an very early and had read it in its entirety by the time I was five years old. The Qur'an is divided into thirty sections, and I had memorized the last one by the time I was seven. At the Islamic School, my peers were still learning to recite the Qur'an; they were only memorizing short chapters, and I was way ahead of them. I wasn't learning new chapters. And since the Islamic School was an hour-long bus ride away, the long commute meant that I didn't have time to keep up with my memorization when I got home.

I wonder if my parents also pulled me out of the Islamic School because they couldn't afford to pay the fees. How were they going to send all six children to this school? By third grade, I was back in public school.

But while in the Islamic School, one winter morning—in between grabbing my lunch, wearing my jacket, leg warmers, gloves, and hat—I forgot to also wear my hijab. I didn't realize this until I was on my way to school. As I warmed up on the bus, I went to remove my hat and realized, with horror and shame, that I'd forgotten to wear my hijab! For a moment, I was literally stunned. I became short of breath. My ears started ringing. I didn't know what to do. I quickly replaced the hat on my head, looked around guiltily to make sure no one had seen my hair, and crumpled into the school bus seat. At school I whispered what had happened to my teacher, Sister Nobuko.

"Something really bad has happened." I trembled. "I forgot my hijab."

To my surprise, she was nonchalant. "Oh, well, you don't have to wear it today."

What? Had she lost her mind? I was a Muslim girl; I had to wear the hijab. You couldn't just not wear it. I felt naked without my hijab. Like I'd forgotten to wear pants and everyone was just rolling with it: "Oh well, that happens sometimes. Spend the day without pants and tomorrow you can remember to wear them." What the fuck?

Sister Nobuko saw that I was going to have trouble participating in class, because I stood frozen in place, looking at the floor in shame. She took an exasperated sigh and said, "Well, we can grab one from the bin of extra hijabs we keep for prayer-time. Would you like one of those?"

I gratefully accepted this offer, taking the hijab from her hands with the desperation of a parched traveller in the desert accepting a glass of water. I took the hijab with a mixture of greed and relief. I don't know the last time this hijab had been washed. The smell of many heads mingled in the scent of the hijab to create a pungent, spicy perfume. I didn't care. I'd rather wear a dodgy-smelling hijab than walk shamelessly with my head uncovered all day. As relief washed over me, energy returned to my body. I stood taller, uncrumpling myself. Once again, I felt comfortable at school. I was chatty and enthusiastic. I added my own scent of oiled, thick Pakistani hair to that hijab.

. . .

The hijab became a central part of my identity in public school. Suddenly, it was the first thing that everyone saw about me. They didn't see my adorable face or my oversized eye glasses. I always wanted the biggest glasses; they made me feel like an adult, and this was the '80s. They didn't notice my outgoing, chatty personality. Instead, they noticed and commented on the hijab. Even though I didn't spend every waking moment thinking about the hijab—it was just something I wore, and like all regularly worn things, I forgot I was wearing it—no one else could get over it.

"Why are you wearing that?" they'd ask, reminding me I was wearing something strange.

"Where are you from?" they'd ask, reminding me that I didn't belong, that I couldn't be from Canada.

"Is that from your religion?" they'd ask, reminding me I wasn't Christian.

"What would happen if I saw your hair?"

"Do you wear it when you sleep?"

"Do you have to wear that in the shower?"

"Aren't you too hot?"

"Who made you wear it? Your parents?" Like their parents didn't make them wear the clothes they were wearing.

The questions were ceaseless and incessant. Sometimes they were asked out of curiosity; other times, pity, moral judgment, suspicion.

They always betrayed the privilege of the questioner. To feel that you have the right to walk up to a stranger and ask them why they are wearing what they are wearing—this comfort lies with those who do not have to ask themselves the same questions. Always, the questions made me feel like an outsider, like I didn't belong, demanded that I explain myself, my very existence.

Canada is a cultural mosaic, we were taught in our curriculum. As a country of immigrants, we value everyone's cultural and religious contributions. You don't have to leave your culture and religion behind to belong here; we accept all of you. Your cultural and religious characteristics are small beautiful tiles; each one adds to the beauty of the larger mosaic that is Canada. But some cultures and religions belonged more than others. Some clothes were more "Canadian" than others. The hijab hadn't made it to the cultural mosaic yet.

And it still hasn't. Muslim women's sartorial choices remain a matter of public debate. Anytime we try to define what is Canadian, we somehow wind up talking about what Muslim women should be allowed to wear, whether in classrooms, courtrooms, or the 2015 federal election. Even now, as we stand on the threshold of the 150th anniversary of Canadian Confederation, the National Assembly of Québec convened its first session after a white supremacist gunned down six Muslim men while they were praying in a Quebec City mosque by resuming its debate about Muslim women's clothing. What should Muslim women be allowed to wear? How Islamic is too Islamic? The mosaic tiles that represent Muslim women keep getting rearranged, pried off, stuck back on, only to be pulled off again. The question keeps being asked: Should Muslim women be allowed to wear whatever they want? Our anxieties about Muslim women's clothing—couched in questions that are really accusations, statements of exclusion, "You will not belong if you wear that!"—threaten the mosaic itself. These questions betray a vision of the mosaic robbed of its colour and vibrancy, preferring instead a bland tile-work that makes minorities stand out, vulnerable and exposed, while the majority blends in.

I became good at answering the questions; they were so frequent, so predictable, so... boring. Like everyone was working with the same interchangeable scripts, asking the same questions over and over again.

I was so much more than my hijab. I had ideas about things. But most people couldn't get past the fabric on my head to hear me. Not my class-mates, not my teachers, not strangers in the supermarket. I'd answer patiently, evenly, calmly, mindlessly. Other times, my answers were testy, frustrated, annoyed.

"I wear this because of my religion. I am a Muslim."

"Nothing would happen if you saw my hair."

"No, I don't wear this to sleep."

"No, I don't wear this in the shower. How would that even work?!"

"No, I'm not too hot. But it's hotter in hell."

"I'm from here. I was born in Canada."

Then, in my head: This is what a Canadian looks like, motherfuckers.

A Carbon-Constrained Future

Kathryn Harrison and Sophie Harrison

CANADA FINDS ITSELF at an economic crossroads as it faces the second half of its second century. Our country has prospered by taking advantage of its abundant fossil fuels, and remains committed to further expanding production and exports into the foreseeable future. Yet, Canada also has joined other countries in committing to limit global warming to below 2°C. This presents contradictions at two levels. Domestically, Canada has committed to deep reduction of its own greenhouse gas emissions, a challenge greatly exacerbated by growth in emissions from fossil fuel extraction. Internationally, if global efforts to resolve climate change succeed, markets for Canada's oil exports will disappear.

It is a moment of truth for our country, one at which the authors, a mother and daughter, have arrived, each along a path emblematic of her own generation. Kathryn first learned of the tar sands the year of Canada's 100th anniversary, when a favourite teacher pointed to a classroom map, declaring that Canada's greatest contribution to the world would lie in the tar-embedded sands of northern Alberta. Years later, her first job was helping to design the world's first refinery dedicated to bitumen processing. However, prompted by growing environmental concern, Kathryn changed fields and now works as a climate policy researcher.

A generation later, Kathryn's daughter, Sophie, first learned—and had nightmares—about climate change during elementary school. She understood the immense threat of a warming world from a young age as she watched government after government pass the buck on action, even as emissions from the oil sands doubled over her short lifetime. As a twenty-one-year-old, Sophie attended the twenty-first United Nations climate change negotiations as a Canadian youth delegate. Watching the birth of the Paris Agreement, she felt a glimmer of hope but also a wave of unease, knowing that the success of the treaty will depend on oil-dependent countries like Canada delivering on increasingly ambitious commitments.

The Canadian economy has relied on the export of natural resources since the arrival of European colonists. However, with the discovery of oil at Leduc, Alberta, in 1947, the emphasis shifted from renewable fish, agriculture, and forest products to non-renewable fossil fuels. Canada's oil exports have grown in both volume and economic significance, increasing more than fourfold from 1990 to 2015.[1] As conventional reserves have been depleted, production has shifted to heavy oil and tar sands, which require more energy-intensive extraction processes. Although these processes are more costly, increasing oil prices rendered unconventional oil economically viable until a sudden drop in the price of oil in 2013. Still, in June 2016, the Canadian Association of Petroleum Producers (CAPP) forecasted that a rebound in global oil prices will yield continued growth in heavy oil production from 2.5 million barrels/day in 2015 to 4 million barrels/day by 2030.

The growth in Canada's oil production will have strong negative environmental impacts both within Canada and internationally. Fossil fuels generate greenhouse gas emissions across their life cycle: upstream emissions during production and refining, and downstream emissions at the point of combustion. Both present a challenge in the Canadian context. Canada has taken advantage of its resource endowments to build an economy that is especially dependent on fossil fuel combustion. Manufacturers rely on inexpensive energy, while individual Canadians typically live in spacious homes with one or more cars in the driveway. Yet there are signs that things are beginning to change. Regulation of motor vehicle emissions and transition away from coal in electricity production have already yielded emissions reductions, and federal and provincial governments have committed to additional measures that will continue to reduce Canada's downstream emissions.

The same cannot be said of upstream emissions. Canada exports three-quarters of its oil production, which has two implications. The first is that we contribute to and profit from the downstream emissions that occur in the countries to which we export our oil, an issue to which we return below. The second is that Canada is responsible for upstream greenhouse gas emissions associated with production of a much larger volume of oil than it burns domestically. Those emissions have steadily increased in response to both growing export volumes and a shift toward more emissions-intensive extraction and refining processes.

Over the past three decades, Canadian governments have adopted a series of targets to reduce Canada's greenhouse gas emissions, including the Chrétien government's Kyoto commitment, the Harper government's Copenhagen commitment, and the Trudeau government's Paris commitment. As failure has become inevitable, successive governments have moved the goalposts further into the future. In the meantime, Canada's emissions have steadily increased (with the exception of a period during the recent global recession), with the oil and gas industry accounting for three-quarters of the growth from 1990 to 2014.[2] Moreover, Environment Canada's 2014 report on Canada's emission trends suggests that while other sectors' emissions have started to decline, the oil industry is the one sector from which emissions are expected to continue increasing.

This presents a significant challenge if Canada is to meet its Paris target to reduce its emissions to 30 percent below 2005 levels by 2030. In 2015, the Government of Alberta committed for the first time to capping emissions from the tar sands. Yet, this celebrated cap nonetheless represents a tripling of tar sands production–related emissions from 2005 to 2030, and would require a compensating reduction of 41 percent from all other emission sources nationally in order to meet Canada's Paris target.[3] And that 2030 target is merely the first step. The Government of Canada has proposed an 80 percent reduction by 2050, which will require a continued commitment to de-carbonization of the economy.

In December 2016, the Canadian federal government and all provinces but Saskatchewan and Manitoba agreed to a pan-Canadian plan to address climate change. This plan includes a number of laudable measures, such as provincial commitments to cap emissions, a $50/ tonne national price on CO2 emissions, new building codes, and an accelerated phase-out of coal-fired electricity. However, the ambitious plan still falls short of the reductions needed to meet Canada's 2030 target by an amount comparable to the anticipated increase in tar sands emissions by 2030.

It is one thing to acknowledge that the transition away from fossil fuels necessarily will be gradual. However, the proposed expansion of fossil fuel production and investment in new oil extraction infrastructure are a step in the wrong direction, yielding increases in Canada's greenhouse emissions for decades to come.

Turning to the international context, the Paris Agreement provides another option for Canada to achieve the anticipated shortfall relative to our 2030 target: reliance on the purchase of "Internationally Transferred Mitigation Outcomes." In fact, the 2016 pan-Canadian plan anticipates reliance on such international reductions credits but is tellingly silent on the degree to which that will occur.

In theory, international credits offer a cost-effective mechanism for countries to meet their emissions reduction targets. However, their credibility is questionable given the bottom-up approach of the Paris Agreement, in which signatory countries commit to revisit their ambitions every five years. In that context, countries may be tempted to commit to less ambitious targets so that they are in a position to profit from the sale of international credits. It is also deeply ironic that Canada would pay other countries to reduce their emissions in order to compensate for its own growing emissions associated with fossil fuel exports. At the limit, Canada will be paying other countries not to buy our oil.

Even without international credit trading, other countries' efforts to reduce their own emissions can be expected to reduce global demand for oil. When that occurs, it is likely that Canada's heavy oil exports will be particularly vulnerable. As global demand declines, the price of oil can be expected to fall, rendering relatively costly unconventional sources such as Canada's bitumen less competitive. In addition, regulation or taxation of Canada's extraction emissions will disproportionately affect the price of Canada's oil, since its production is more emissions-intensive.

The International Energy Agency (IEA) has modelled global oil markets under several scenarios, including a current policy scenario and a scenario with more ambitious policies consistent with the 2°C commitment. The current policy scenario, which is reasonably consistent with projections by CAPP, anticipates steadily increasing oil demand. It is also a scenario that promises global warming of 3.6 to 4°C, which IEA projected in its *World Energy Outlook 2014* would lead to "substantial species extinction and large risks to global and regional food security."

In contrast, IEA's 2°C scenario anticipates that oil demand would need to peak in 2018 and decline thereafter. Modelling of a 2°C scenario by McGlade and Ekins projects that the market for Canada's bitumen would disappear after 2020, given the option to satisfy declining demand with less costly sources.[4]

Put bluntly, the business case for tar sands expansion and new pipelines is inconsistent with the international commitment to limit climate change to 2°C. While there is no guarantee the world will meet that target, since current national commitments fall well short of what is needed, it is clear that approving infrastructure to increase Canada's bitumen exports for decades to come is placing an economic bet against the success of the Paris climate agreement.

What is to be done?

In releasing the Pan-Canadian Framework on Clean Growth and Climate Change, Prime Minister Trudeau offered an optimistic vision in which expansion of Canada's fossil fuel exports will ensure continued prosperity, even as policies to reduce greenhouse gas emissions prompt emergence of a new clean energy sector. This reassuring rhetoric fails to acknowledge the incompatibility between increased fossil fuel production and the urgent need to reduce fossil fuel consumption in order to stabilize the global climate.

Transitioning Canada's oil-dependent economy away from fossil fuels is no easy task, and for decades our governments have proven unwilling to rise to that challenge. Politicians have exploited the public's misunderstanding and near-term preoccupations to peddle politically popular yet largely ineffectual policies, such as tax credits for transit passes and a voluntary "one tonne challenge." Even as they have obfuscated their failure with shifting baselines and hidden offsets, consecutive federal governments have deepened Canada's dependence on fossil fuels—at the expense of our international obligations, our economic resilience in an increasingly carbon-constrained world, and the livability of the planet.

If elected officials are unwilling to implement the necessary policies to facilitate the transition away from fossil fuels, what are we to do?

Although mother and daughter have arrived at this national crossroads by different routes, we are committed to applying our complementary skills to ensure that, going forward, Canada chooses a path of sustainability and climate justice.

As the gap between academic advice and government inaction has grown, Kathryn has increasingly engaged in public scholarship, reaching beyond publications aimed at fellow researchers and political elites to help inform voters at large through media interviews and op-eds. Yet it is clear that expert research and public lectures will not be enough.

Sophie has gone beyond her mother's academic footsteps to engage directly in grassroots politics. As a community organizer, she seeks to increase citizen participation in the political process—cutting through empty rhetoric and providing clear opportunities for citizens, especially young voters like herself, to hold their governments to account on climate change.

While we have committed our energy, expertise, and hopes to what we see as complementary strategies, we fear that our efforts and those of other concerned citizens will not be enough in a new world of misrepresentation and false news. Yet, we see no alternative but to speak the truth: Canada's expansion of fossil fuel production is not compatible with our moral obligation to address climate change.

The Hygiene Hangover

Brett Finlay, Perry Kendall,
and David Patrick

EVER SINCE ROBERT Koch and Louis Pasteur showed 125 years ago that germs cause infectious diseases society has been at war with microbes. Sewer and sanitation systems were developed and garbage collection established. Life-saving antibiotics became available near the end of the Second World War. In the 1950s, Toronto-based Connaught produced 1.8 million doses of the Salk polio vaccine, which were used to prove that we could control the scourge of paralytic polio, and several other vaccines have now been developed in the war on infections. In 1966, universal health care became a reality in Canada, providing access to sanitary medicine for all. In 2003, with SARS threatening Canada, Canadian scientists were the first in the world to sequence the genome of this new infectious agent, and develop potential vaccines that could be used to combat this viral threat. Collectively, this major hygiene campaign did a good job ridding the developed world of disease-carrying germs: "Cleanliness is next to godliness." "The only good microbe is a dead one." "Cover your mouth when you cough." This remarkable hygiene battle resulted in spectacular health benefits to Canadians: life expectancy has risen dramatically, and infant mortality plummeted, over the past century, dropping from about one in ten to one in two hundred. Parents have a bottle of hand sanitizer in their diaper bag, "bubble wrapping" their kids to avoid infections as much as possible. All good, right?

Wrong. Extraordinary cleanliness has come at a cost. We now see remarkable increases in non-infectious diseases throughout Canada. Asthma rates have gone from about 1 percent to over 10 percent of all children. In the past five years, we have witnessed unprecedented growth in childhood obesity, in addition to the continuing adult obesity epidemic. The rates of inflammatory bowel diseases and brain issues such as depression, anxiety, stress, and even autism continue to increase rapidly. While the rates of nearly all infectious diseases continue to decline, the opposite is occurring in the non-infectious diseases that so many Canadians currently suffer from. What has happened? We really haven't changed genetically in fifty years. It turns out that our war on microbes is having unforeseen consequences (collateral damage!).

If one looks at a list of the top ten reasons Canadians die today (yes, a morbid task), there is only one that is an infectious disease (influenza and pneumonia). Yet, research in the past decade has shown that there are microbial links to nine of these ten causes, including strokes, cancer, and heart attacks. Other than accidents, every single leading cause of death for Canadians is linked in some way to the microbes we carry around in and on us. Recently, there has been a stunning revolution in our knowledge about microbes, which include bacteria, viruses, and other invisible single-cell organisms, with the realization that we actually need microbes to develop normally, lead healthy lives, and age well. This revolution is standing biomedical knowledge on its head and shows great promise for the future of Canadians' health and well-being.

Despite all the work being done on the "human" genome and epigenetics, there are at least as many microbes in and on you as there are human cells, and they encode greater than 93 percent of the DNA in and on us. We are more microbe than human: *H. sapiens* DNA comprise less than 7 percent of the total genes in a human being! Even personalized medicine is in trouble; humans are more than 99.9 percent identical genetically, yet we each have a unique set of microbes, sharing less than half with any other person. We are colonized at birth, and even that first birthday present—fecal and vaginal microbiota from Mom—is critical for setting us up for life. If you are born by C-section, as over one-quarter of Canadian children now are, you will miss out on these important microbes, and this increases one's chances for allergies and asthma by 20 percent later in life. This 20 percent difference also applies to those who were breastfed versus bottle-fed, and those who live on a farm versus in a city. These factors result in exposure to different specific microbes. Even owning a dog drops the chance of getting asthma by 20 percent (sorry, cats have no effect).

There is no doubt that antibiotics are one of, if not the, most beneficial medical invention of the twentieth century. They have saved countless lives and are a major reason infant mortality rates have plummeted. However, we now realize that there are problems with these wonder drugs. Like many good things, we overuse them, and antimicrobial resistance rates continue to rise, leading the more regular appearance of new "superbugs" (e.g., microbes resistant to all known antibiotics). We now realize that antibiotics "carpet bomb" microbes, killing both the good and bad ones indiscriminately and yielding unexpected negative consequences. For example, antibiotic use in the first year of life causes significant increases in asthma, allergies, and obesity in later life. Similarly, a recent large study in the UK has shown a direct correlation between the number of courses of antibiotics and depression and anxiety. In Canada and the US, over 80 percent of antibiotic use occurs in agriculture as growth supplements, which causes up to 9 percent increase in weight in farm animals and livestock. Unfortunately, there is a similar effect on children; dumping tons of antibiotics into the environment may ultimately contribute to childhood obesity by affecting environmental microbes, in addition to increasing levels of antimicrobial resistance. The use of antibiotics as agricultural growth supplements was banned years ago in Europe. Fortunately, both the FDA and Health Canada are now working with producers to phase out antibiotics as growth promoters of livestock in North America by the end of 2017.

Lessons learned over the past several decades suggest a future where we can use microbes for our benefit. Studies have shown that a simple fecal transfer (yes, this means transferring feces from one person to another!) could cure a life-threatening disease caused by *Clostridium difficile*, which has resulted in many deaths in Ontario and Quebec. This demonstrates that there could be great medical value in identifying and using these beneficial microbes. There are incredibly exciting new studies showing that microbial composition affects cancer chemotherapy, or that "drugging the bugs" in animals can virtually block atherosclerosis, a condition that accounts for heart attacks and strokes in humans.

In one of Canada's best-known medical triumphs, Banting and Best showed in the 1920s that insulin could be used to control diabetes. The most common drug currently used to treat type 2 diabetes is metformin, and we now know that it only works through our microbes. While we know that healthy diets affect nutrients, we also now realize that they have a huge impact on the gut microbiome. Energy from processed foods, including white sugar and white flour, is absorbed very quickly in the small intestine before it can reach the microbes in the large bowel, effectively starving our body's microbes. They need high-fibre foods, fruit, hard-to-digest plant material, and nuts. Without this nourishment, our microbes become less diverse (dysbiotic), which is associated with obesity, diabetes, and the other Western-lifestyle diseases. Personalized diets based on an individual's microbes are being developed that show great promise for weight reduction.

We must rethink our relationship with our microbes and establish a balance between hygiene and exposure to beneficial microbes. Each generation gets cleaner, but the diversity and kinds of microbes in and on our bodies are decreasing rapidly. We are depriving the body of a critical part of its normal function, and the results are reflected in both health and disease. Ironically, because of our assault on microbes, some microbes could become endangered species, yet they have been an essential part of our evolution for millennia. We can't return to the wider range of microbes (and infectious diseases) of our great-grandparents. We can, however, embrace microbes for our own good as we rebalance hygiene with healthy microbes.

What can we do about this? We should think about how our communities, playgrounds, and time at school are designed to allow children access to ground-level play and outdoor learning. Antibiotics should be reserved for infectious diseases that clearly require treatment, and not squandered on colds, flus, and other conditions for which they are of no benefit. Attention to this is required ecosystem-wide: in medical care, dentistry, veterinary medicine, and agriculture. Finally, serious research is required to get us past our current superficial approach to probiotics. We need to understand which microbes are of health benefit, and how and when they can be successfully introduced to best benefit health.

The future of health, wellness, and medical care for Canadians will include our microbes, providing new tools to hopefully increase our health and longevity, long after major threats from germs have been mostly banished.

Theatre, What's Next?

George Belliveau, Tetsuro Shigematsu,
and Jerry Wasserman

PEOPLE COME TO the theatre because they want to think, feel, and witness an artistic representation of the social world that surrounds them. The theatre provides a space where collective groups can engage in a shared experience, and where audiences can be entertained with ideas and witness the turmoil and triumphs of characters on the stage. This has been the case for over two millennia, and the core of theatre has not changed much. As an art form, theatre has survived the advent of film, television, and even the Internet, and it will certainly continue to exhibit tenacity and necessity as it adapts and reinvents itself over the coming decades.

In Canada, we typically trace the birth of theatre to First Nations performance, and Euro-Canadian theatre to 1606 when Champlain's French explorers staged a theatrical pageant by Marc Lescarbot called the *Le Theatre de Neptune* on the shores of present-day Nova Scotia. Since then, Canada has been host to a variety of forms of theatre, with much of the work informed by Western European traditions. Yet over the last hundred years, a distinct Canadian voice has emerged on stages across the country. Our playwrights have revisited pivotal moments in Canadian history (e.g., the Riel Rebellion, Confederation, the Quiet Revolution) and engaged with contemporary concerns and issues (e.g., war, AIDS, Aboriginal rights, sexual identity). On the anniversary of

Canadian Confederation, we want to consider the place of theatre in the Canada of tomorrow.

Because Canada is a vast and sparsely populated country, we anticipate Canadian theatre will likely remain local in its developmental phases; new companies will get their start with support coming primarily from their local communities. As there is no equivalent to Broadway or the West End in Canada, the strength of theatre in this country will continue to derive from local productions and gain momentum through co-productions across the nation, and international touring. The nature of local or more regional productions can be traced back to the Royal Commission on the National Development in the Arts, Letters and Sciences, led by Vincent Massey and completed in 1951. A key aspect of the commission was to look at cultural development in the country, and some of the outcomes included strengthening the CBC (national and regional), establishing the Canada Council for the Arts, and developing a bilingual National Theatre School. The commission also helped mobilize resources for the building of theatres (and companies) across the country by proposing a network of regional theatres, rather than a more centralized approach. To this day, regional theatres continue to be important in the development and nurturing of Canadian theatre.

A growing Canadian trend over the last couple of decades has been partnerships between the various theatres across the country. For instance, *Empire of the Son* (2016) written and performed by Tetsuro Shigematsu, represents an example of this co-production trend. After an extensive development period, the play premiered, in 2015, with a successful run at the Vancouver East Cultural Centre. It returned for a remount in 2016 at the same theatre, kicking off a tour across Canada, including a run at the National Arts Centre in Ottawa, Montreal's Centaur Theatre, Toronto's Factory Theatre, and the High Performance Rodeo in Calgary.

Through social media, an ambient awareness of new productions has emerged that now travels across our country like never before. Through tweets and Facebook, a Vancouver production is shared with friends in Montreal and Toronto during intermission, connecting local work to national followers in a matter of seconds. This phenomenon has drastically increased awareness of Canadian theatre in this digital age, both within Canada and beyond our borders. Social media will continue to impact how potential audience members hear about theatre and whether they will attend. The marketing and packaging of theatre is constantly shifting to trends in social media, and companies without this particular savvy will likely be left behind.

As an example, the Factory Theatre in Toronto used the hashtag #seasonselfie to publicize its historic 2016/17 season, during which Artistic Director Nina Lee Aquino programmed all of the Factory Theatre shows entirely with playwrights of colour. This was an important first for a theatre of this size and stature in Canada. In order to support and celebrate such diversity, theatregoers and theatre artists across Canada could buy a season subscription to the Factory Theatre. Although purchasing theatre subscriptions is almost always a local affair, people outside Toronto who wanted to participate in this campaign could opt to use the hashtag to gift a subscription to a friend in Toronto or to make a financial donation. By uploading a selfie posing next to a computer or phone displaying the Factory Theatre's website, members of the Canadian theatre community could participate in what sociologists call "virtue signalling," the same phenomenon by which social media users overlay their profile picture with the colours of the French flag or vertical rainbow stripes to display their sympathy with victims of terrorism or their support of LGBTQ rights. This is an innovative example of how a local theatre company can effectively leverage the affordances of social media culture to garner community support across the country.

Theatre's great strength is to tell stories that are character-driven. This trend will continue in Canada, as there is a desire and an audience for Canadian plays that engage in cultural and ethnic diversity. In a constantly growing multicultural Canada, we are producing more and more theatre that explores how diverse communities engage with various issues. In fact, more and more marginalized groups within Canada have seen, and will see, theatre's utility as a means to effectively share their stories and offer counternarratives to the dominant culture. For instance, Vancouver's Theatre for Living produced *šxʷʔam'et (home)* in 2017, a play that challenges audiences to make real and honourable reconciliation with Canada's Indigenous populations. Created and performed by Indigenous and non-Indigenous artists, the interactive play weaves together stories on the theme of Truth and Reconciliation that are based on real life.

Moreover, funding mandates are influencing companies to prioritize diversity as part of their outreach, and this is happening across the country. The Canada Council for the Arts and other governmental funding agencies actively seek to support companies and artists that promote diversity as a central value of their artistic practice. In addition, the research community in Canada has also seen shifts in the ways knowledge is mobilized, with an increasing trend toward more dynamic and diverse approaches to dissemination. For instance, it is becoming more commonplace for scholars to share data findings through the use of theatre, and this arts-based dissemination approach is supported through our national research funding agencies. An example of an ongoing funded national project has returning Canadian veterans engage in theatre to mobilize research on effective ways to help military personnel combat psychological stress injuries.[1]

As the stories we tell through theatre have evolved over the past several decades, so too has the form of Canadian theatre. The traditional five-, three-, or even two-act play structure has been replaced with shorter forms of theatre, both in Canada and in other countries. The extended one-act play is on the horizon as a mainstay, because audiences, for the most part, conditioned by film and online video streaming, prefer the eighty- to ninety-minute play with no intermission. This form has forced playwrights to write in more concise ways and increased the need for dramaturgical expertise to navigate scripts toward the essential. Another growing trend in Canada is the proliferation of site-specific theatre, where audiences are brought to non-traditional spaces to witness live plays. For instance, in Electric Company's *The Wake*, the audience travelled to eleven outdoor sites on Vancouver's historic Granville Island. In the unusual use of spaces for theatre (i.e., tennis court, ferry, factory), the audience discovered the island's history, which went from fishing village to an industrial, factory hub during the Second World War. Particular theatre training institutions in Canada, such as Langara College's Studio 58, are developing theatre artists with multiple skills, so that they can create theatre that expands boundaries, using lively, collective approaches within non-traditional spaces.

As in the outdoor production of *The Wake*, theatre's strength rests on the liveness of the work. Despite constant advancements in technology, theatre will continue to distinguish itself through presenting live human actors and holding a mirror up to the community. The traditional play format, with an imaginary barrier between actors and audience, may become less popular as audiences develop an appetite for unique experiences that blur the illusionary divide between audience and performer. Canadian theatre companies are increasingly exposing audiences to productions where the real and imagined, past and present, are simultaneously played out. As such, audiences are asked to become actively engaged, even complicit at times, to the innovative dramas unfolding before/among them.

More common, too, is the production of plays by writer/performers such as Shigematsu (*Empire of the Son*), whose autobiographical stories are presented by the creators themselves and shared in a testimonial-like fashion. Although the genre of the autobiographical monologue is not new, it is presently reaching a new level of authenticity. Audiences want to see stories of real people unfold in front of them. The liveness of an actor telling their story is uniquely compelling, as at any moment the illusion can be broken by a stumble or missed line. It's like watching a tightrope walker; anything can happen when it's live!

The numerous ruins of Roman and Greek theatres from over two millennia ago serve as a reminder of how theatre has always been a vital component of society. The physical space of theatre has changed, and will continue to change, yet the desire for live audiences to hear human stories unfold before their eyes will live on in Canada. As our society evolves and confronts the myriad social, political, and environmental issues facing Canada and the global community, the stories and struggles of our nation will continue to be told in stages from sea to sea to sea.

Uplifting Voices

**Pam Brown, Jennifer Carpenter, Gerry Lawson,
Kim Lawson, Lisa Nathan, and Mark Turin**

IN HER 2010 film, *Spelling Bee*, Zoe Leigh Hopkins—member of the Heiltsuk First Nation—envisions British Columbia as a province with thirty-four official languages, thirty-two of which are Indigenous.[1] Her film is a powerful visualization of a dream. Many Canadians are unaware not only of the dream but also of the rich linguistic diversity of Indigenous nations in Canada, of the knowledge encoded within Indigenous languages and their importance to Indigenous communities. Connected to territory through traditional ecological knowledge and ceremony, Indigenous languages have vast historical depth and are, at the same time, entirely modern. Visible on social media, and mobilized through online dictionaries, radio, art, and music, these languages are spoken and taught in communities across Canada.

The story of the resilience of Indigenous languages across Canada over the last 150 years is one of local endurance and immense perseverance against opposition by Canada itself. Although they have been spoken, sung, and shared for thousands of years, many Indigenous languages are now critically endangered. English and French became established and prevailed in Canada while Indigenous languages and culture were actively supressed through the many processes of colonization. Not the least of these strategies was forcing Indigenous children to attend residential schools, where punishment for speaking their mother tongue was a traumatic reality. Nevertheless, Indigenous languages survived through secrecy and the deep commitment of Elders and community members. Until 1952, Canadian legislation prevented Indigenous people from turning to the Canadian courts for help with government injustices. Indigenous advocates and community leaders worked hard to bring legal action and gain public attention to residential schools and language loss.

Belief in the superiority of Western culture is the basis of the assumption that Indigenous cultures were destined to die out. Because Indigenous people did not abandon their culture and language, drastic measures such as residential schools and criminalization of Indigenous cultural practices were developed to disrupt intergenerational transmission of knowledge. Research that valued Indigenous cultural and linguistic knowledge, but assumed it was destined for extinction, was oriented to preserving fragments of knowledge outside communities, rather than supporting cultural vitality within communities.[2]

In contrast, Indigenous individuals and groups have sought to uplift Indigenous languages and fluent speakers. Indigenous-led organizations—whether national organizations such as the First Nations Confederacy of Cultural Education Centres (FNCCEC), Crown corporations such as the BC-based First Peoples' Cultural Council, or local First Nations cultural centres and Band schools—continue to engage in groundbreaking and urgent work to collect, protect, and connect living languages and cultural traditions in ways that are ethical and sustaining. For example, all of us (authors of this piece) work to support the dissemination, acknowledgement, and use of language research and documentation undertaken by and for the Heiltsuk Nation in Bella Bella. This began in earnest in 1973 when the Band Council welcomed a linguist, John Rath, a PhD student at Leiden University, to come to Bella Bella and work with our fluent speakers. John stayed for many years, working out of the Heiltsuk Cultural Education Centre, and developed a writing system, grammar, dictionary, and many learning aids. Two of his students, Lillian Gladstone and Evelyn Windsor, completed the Native Indian Language Diploma Program at the University of Victoria and returned to Bella Bella to establish the Heiltsuk language program in the Bella Bella Community School (BBCS). Since 1978, the language program has been a formal part of the school curriculum, and it has

focused on curriculum development, Heiltsuk language teacher certi-
fication, and the pursuit of effective language-teaching strategies. The
Heiltsuk College has supported mentorship and provides opportunities
for adult Heiltsuk language learning.

Indigenous language revitalization speaks as much to hard indicators of health and well-being as it does to soft indicators of culture and
identity. As the Sto:lo/Xaxli'p educator and writer Q'um Q'um Xiiem
(Jo-ann Archibald) said to Aboriginal educators at Oral Traditions: The
Fifth Provincial Conference on Aboriginal Education in 1999, while "we
need to preserve our oral traditions, we also need to let them preserve
us." Recent studies demonstrate both the central relevance of language
to many aspects of community well-being and how the transformative
healing nature and holistic benefits of language revitalization have an
impact beyond nurturing linguistic vitality alone. Underscoring the
interrelatedness of language and community well-being, Hallet, Chan-
dler, and Lalonde's 2007 study in *Cognitive Development*, showed a
compelling correlation between Indigenous language use and reduced
Aboriginal youth suicide rates in BC.

How can the Canada 150 commemoration help us understand this
moment in time and understand what can be done now? In contrast to
calls of celebration, we call out the need for more Canadians to recognize the deep grief and incredible resilience that have long been a part
of Indigenous language stewardship in Canada, a need to acknowledge
loss, survival, and enduring damage from colonization.

How can people on these lands transform the residential schools
experience of a "Hundred Years of Loss" for Canada 150 into a story of
support, building the linguistic diversity for which Canada is internationally recognized?[3] As ever, leadership is coming from the grassroots.
Since September 2015, all students in kindergarten through grade
four in Prince Rupert, BC, have been learning Sm'algyax. "We are on
traditional Tsimshian territory and Sm'algyax is the language of the
territory," Roberta Edzerza (Aboriginal Education Principal for her
district) told CBC Radio One.[4] "We are so proud and we would like
to share our language and culture with everybody. It's one avenue to
address racism. Education is key. Learning the language and sharing
in the learning and the culture." Indigenous leaders have committed

decades of careful thinking, advocacy, and heart into work such as the Task Force on Aboriginal Languages and Culture's 2005 report *Towards a New Beginning*,[5] on strategies to revitalize Indigenous languages, as well as the development of the United Nations Declaration on the Rights of Indigenous Peoples (UNDRIP).

How will non-Indigenous people in Canada respond to Indigenous languages becoming visible again? In 2011, when həm̓ləsəm̓ and q̓ələχən Houses opened at UBC's Totem Park Residence, the hən̓q̓əmin̓əm̓ names were met with a mix of hostility, acceptance, and pride. The names are significant to the Musqueam Nation—on whose traditional, ancestral, and unceded territories the Vancouver campus of the University of British Columbia is built—and were gifted to the university by the Musqueam Nation through a transparent and collaborative process. In 2009, Canada's commissioner of official languages, Graham Fraser, was quoted as saying: "In the same way that race is at the core of... an American experience and class is at the core of British experience, I think that language is at the core of Canadian experience."[6] While Fraser was referring to the friction inherent in the relationship between English and French, we believe the powerful tensions between Indigenous and official languages are also central to Canadian experience. Indigenous leaders have long advocated for Indigenous language revitalization to be a national issue. While English and French have federal support and protection as official languages, what place do Indigenous languages hold in the national consciousness? Moreover, what place, acceptance, and support will be found for Indigenous communities that choose to protect their language without sharing it?

What governmental response will we see? Will we see Indigenous languages gain federal support and protection as official languages? Will the federal government and its research councils provide targeted resources to explore the intersection of language, well-being, and health? Prime Minister Justin Trudeau spoke to the Assembly of First Nations in December 2016, pledging to introduce a federal law to protect, preserve, and revitalize First Nations, Inuit, and Metis languages: "We know... how residential schools and other decisions by government were used... to eliminate Indigenous languages... We must undo the lasting damage that resulted... Today I commit to you our government will enact an Indigenous languages act."[7] The bitter irony of the current context is inescapable: colonial governments have for centuries marshalled their economic, military, and administrative might to extinguish Indigenous voices. Now, in the eleventh hour, they are looking to resource that which they first set out to destroy. Benign neglect would have been less damaging than two centuries of violence followed by a last-minute U-turn. Will Canada's citizens hold their government to account and demand that an Indigenous languages act be enacted in this Parliament? Rather than reinventing the wheel—or worse, the flat tire—the Truth and Reconciliation Commission of Canada's 2015 Calls to Action offered the federal government a tangible set of action points, with a clear road map on how they can be achieved.

Elders and youth in Indigenous communities are actively using and appropriating emerging technologies to strengthen their traditions and languages; Indigenous peoples are creators and innovators (not just recipients or clients) of new technologies, particularly in the domain of cultural and linguistic heritage. While technological efforts in the 1970s included specially modified typewriters and custom-made fonts to represent Indigenous writing systems, communities are now making use of digital tools—online, text, Internet radio, and mobile devices—to nurture the continued development of their respective diverse Indigenous languages and cultures. Yet, such interventions are not without risks and consequences. Digital technologies cannot and will not save languages. Speakers keep languages alive. A digital dictionary itself won't revitalize an endangered language, but it could assist the speakers who will. At the same time, technology can be as symbolically powerful as it is practically useful, and can carry considerable political weight. In the English-dominant world of cyberspace, Indigenous communities are engaging with, disrupting, and reimagining digital practices. By generating digital visibility and legibility, Indigenous communities claim a presence online and exert control over the terms of Indigenous representation rather than risk misrepresentation.

Since 2016, the Heiltsuk Cultural Education Centre; Bella Bella Community School; and the University of British Columbia's First Nations and Endangered Languages Program, Museum of Anthropology, and School of Library, Archival, and Information Studies have been working together to expand, deepen, and mobilize existing community language revitalization and cultural documentation initiatives in a digital environment. We envision Indigenous communities participating in and co-creating a shared digital future, which requires an ongoing investment in the common digital backbone. Infrastructure and capital costs are rarely one-off; technology investments must be long term and equitable, not just for communities themselves but also for the organizations that support them. We need to understand how digital tools can support endangered language learning. As yet, there is little evaluation of their use. Longitudinal case studies can help assess the success and review the impact of emerging technologies on Indigenous language learning using criteria that are community-developed and methods that are locally appropriate. Respectful research can offer insights for all of us—communities, policy-makers, and academics—about which tools are proving to be most effective, where, why, and how.

We call upon others, both individuals and organizations, who seek to uplift Indigenous languages to listen to and learn from Indigenous communities, and support community-led revitalization programs through respectful partnership. Indigenous communities know their needs better than anyone, and acknowledging this place-based expertise is a step toward reconciliation. Indigenous communities need better resourcing for language instructors to promote stronger learning outcomes, language retention, and trust. They are proposing that learning goals be set by the community, as these are more attainable and more credible, and have a higher chance of fulfillment. Indigenous communities need more funding, dispersed in a better way, to plan strategically over the long term. Communities must not be positioned as competitors for resources and visibility, but rather have dedicated funding streams that will enable long-term sustainability.

A defining element in Canada's next 150 years will be the extent to which Canadians and their governments respond to the language sections of UNDRIP and the TRC Calls to Action. Another defining element will be the resurgence and celebration of First Nations and Indigenous languages and culture in print and on air, in person and online.

Will the rest of Canadian society accept, listen to, and value Indigenous languages and join us in uplifting them?

facing: Vancouver, British
Columbia | CLARE YOW

above: Burnaby, British
Columbia | CLARE YOW

Cunningham estuary, Northwest Territories | ROBIE MACDONALD

Again at the Crossroads

Seth Klein

So far as it is possible, Canada's effort in this war must be a planned and concerted national effort... In order to have the tremendous quantities of supplies available at the right time, and in the right place, it is imperative that the economic life of Canada be reorganized, but not disorganized... This task can be performed, in the main, only by the national government. Its adequate performance, however, demands the co-operation of provincial and municipal authorities, as well as of business, labour, the farmers and other primary producers, and of voluntary organizations of all kinds.
Prime Minister WILLIAM LYON MACKENZIE KING, October 1939 (one month after Canada entered the Second World War)

THE CANADA LED by Prime Minister Mackenzie King was a country at a crossroads. A lifetime later, on Canada's 150th anniversary, we find ourselves there again. This time it is a climate crossroads that poses an existential threat, and, once again, it is a crisis that demands a comprehensive remaking of our economy.

At the same time, we are witnessing a distressing return of neo-fascism (a term I prefer to the more sanitized "alt right") and the emergence of political leaders both in Canada and elsewhere who are happy to give public expression to our ugliest tendencies. As in the 1930s, the rise of the far right emerges from a toxic stew of racism and xenophobia played out against and catalyzed by a backdrop of growing inequality and economic insecurity.

In such a context, we need solutions rooted in climate justice—a bold political and policy response that links ambitious climate plans with actions that tackle inequality and job insecurity. In a time of ecological, economic, and political crises, we need a well-coordinated plan that incorporates equity and fairness in asking the public to rally in common cause behind the grand task of saving our world from the worse ravages of climate change. And in confronting such vexing challenges, there are lessons to be learned from the last time we were at such a crossroads.

Climate science forcefully tells us that we effectively have three decades to fully wean ourselves off fossil fuels. Consequently, much of the known fossil fuel reserves in Canada's domain will have to remain in the ground. This is a daunting task, the scope of which, at times, feels overwhelming. Yet, as the quote from Mackenzie King reminds us, we have fundamentally retooled our economy before, and done so in far less time.

Of course, the wartime record of the Mackenzie King government had an ugly side, too. Its treatment of Japanese Canadians, Jewish refugees, and Indigenous people, among others, haunts and shames us to this day. As we mobilize in the face of today's crises, we have a chance at reconciliation and are called upon to not repeat the same mistakes.

I write this a few weeks after our American neighbours have inaugurated Donald Trump as their new president. Months after a most unlikely election, many are still in disbelief that such an abhorrent and blatantly racist and misogynist candidate could have won the most powerful political office in the world.

As President Trump assembles his cabinet and issues his first executive orders, it has become clear that his campaign bluster was no mere act. Trump falls somewhere on the neo-fascist spectrum. He shows either ignorance of or contempt for core provisions of the US Constitution. His rhetoric appeals to violence and scapegoating. His early actions suggest he has every intention of turning his ugly rhetoric into policy. And his climate denial is real; this man appears ready to condemn us all as he seeks to trip up the baby steps taken thus far on climate action.

But what lessons does Trump's election have for Canada?

A particularly ill-advised reaction is the smug claim that "it couldn't happen here." Yet, we in Canada are not immune. To claim we are is to deny the deep racial inequities in our own society, particularly for Indigenous people. It is to pretend that the election of Rob Ford as mayor of Canada's largest city didn't push many of the same buttons as Trump is now pushing in the US. It is to ignore that we face many of the same urban-rural divides. It is to forget that a major federal political party in the 2015 election employed racist dog-whistle calls with their "barbaric cultural practices" tip line and politically targeted women who wear the niqab.

In short, the same toxic interplay between working-class alienation and deep-seated racism that elected Trump finds a home here, and we, too, face the risk that the politics of hate will occupy centre stage.

So, a first lesson is to stand on guard against rising xenophobia, Islamophobia, racism, sexism, and anti-immigrant politics and assaults. We must name and challenge these ideas, acknowledging that they exist but refusing to let them spread.

A second lesson is a warning about policies that widen the economic divide.

Since the first Canada-US free trade deal in the late 1980s, Canada, like the US, has seen the hollowing out of working-class manufacturing jobs and the rise of precarious employment. Our economic system has left hundreds of thousands of people behind, bringing more economic insecurity and family stress to their lives. Recent immigrants, women, Indigenous people, people with disabilities, and other vulnerable groups bear the brunt of this economic insecurity. However, a growing pool of white working-class men feel it, too. Building common cause is harder than sowing division and hate, but now is not the time to shy away from this important work.

So, could a Trump-like electoral upset happen here? Yes, it damn well could! It could happen anywhere that masses of working-class people are treated as economically expendable, and where racist and anti-immigrant views lie just below the cultural and political surface, awaiting activation by unscrupulous political demagogues eager to exploit ignorance and alienation.

The great economist John Maynard Keynes warned of the dangers of economic abandonment a hundred years ago. In 1919, Keynes (then a youngish economist, years before his groundbreaking *General Theory of Employment, Interest, and Money*) was part of the British delegation sent to negotiate the Treaty of Versailles at the end of the First World War.

But Keynes did not stay. Appalled by what he witnessed—by how ordinary German people were being made to pay odious reparation debts that would cripple their economy—he quit the meeting in disgust. He returned home and penned a short book called *The Economic Consequences of the Peace*. In it, he warned the treaty would not allow the German economy to recover postwar, leaving a population resentful and vengeful, and, with chilling prescience, he predicted another war.

Trump's election victory should be a wake-up call to rethink all those neo-liberal policies that have given rise to economic insecurity and job precarity: corporate trade deals, tax cuts for the wealthy and corporations, cuts to social programs and protections for those who have fallen on hard times (such as welfare and employment insurance), the erosion of employee rights, the undermining of workers' ability to act collectively through unions, and the increasing use of temporary foreign workers (rather than granting immigrants full status so they can exercise their full employment rights).

And what of climate change in a Trumpian era? For a Canadian government that claims to take climate action seriously, now comes its greatest test. Will we expand oil exports to a country that is walking away from its global climate treaty commitments? Will we invest in new fossil fuel infrastructure when our neighbours seem hell-bent on blowing through what remains of their small share of a global carbon budget?

Early pipeline and liquefied natural gas plant approvals by the Trudeau government provide little comfort. Our new federal government talks a good line on climate, and on Indigenous title and rights, but acts in a manner that indicates it is in denial about both—unable to make policy that is in compliance with either climate science or Indigenous rights, no more so than when these realities run up against the corporate interests of the fossil fuel sector.

This moment calls for a climate leadership reset—the new terrain demands that we redouble our efforts. After all, in the face of another existential threat, when Nazism was on the march in the 1930s, Canada did not wait until the US finally joined the war effort in 1941; we threw ourselves into the fight two years earlier.

The US election does, however, reinforce an important warning when it comes to climate action. Canada must avoid the backlash so dangerously manifested to the south. As with the trade deals, if governmental climate actions consign many working-class people to the economic scrap heap, if their economic security is seen as expendable by "elites" making the decisions, if it feels that "not everyone is doing their fair share," then climate action risks heralding the same spectacular political dysfunction currently playing out in the US.

And, so, as we redouble our climate action efforts, we must also redouble our commitment to climate justice.

We need comprehensive and just transition policies for workers in the fossil fuel sector (ensuring they receive training and income support as they shift to new clean energy industries). We need a government-led job creation program that will produce thousands of new jobs in green infrastructure and the low-carbon economy. And we need to marry our climate action policies with those that redress inequality—and tackle the growing gap with equal vigour.

Let us now return to the more hopeful economic lessons from the Second World War.

Canada's experience in the Second World War reminds us that our society has managed a dramatic restructuring of the economy before: Victory Bonds were sold, profits were restricted to prevent wartime profiteering, new taxes were levied, household consumption shifted, quotas were applied on some goods, people grew "Victory Gardens" and dramatically switched their transportation from private automobiles to public transit—coincidentally, actions that also reduced emissions. Core industries were directed to produce the goods and services needed; there remained a large role for the private sector in the economy, but the for-profit sector did not get to decide how scarce and needed resources would be deployed.

Thus far, the climate policies we have seen from Canada's federal and provincial governments are simply not going to cut it. Our governments' relatively modest carbon-pricing and infrastructure plans to date are woefully insufficient.

How can we scale up and finance the investments need to transition our economy?

One logical option is a national carbon price that quickly escalates. The federal government has thus far committed to a national carbon price of $50/tonne by 2022. That's not much. It's modestly more than BC's current carbon tax of $30 and would represent only about 11.5 cents/litre at the gas pump.

In order to achieve the consumption, investment, and structural changes necessary, the carbon price is going to need to increase more quickly. Consider this: a national carbon price of $200/tonne would raise approximately $80 billion a year. Half of this could be directed toward a low- and middle-income tax credit that offsets the cost for these households and ensures progressivity, while the other half could be directed toward a bold green and social infrastructure plan that sees us undertake—

- a massive program to retrofit buildings for energy efficiency;
- huge investments in renewable electricity;
- a dramatic expansion of public transit;
- high-speed rail between our major cities;
- just transition programs for workers currently employed in the fossil fuel sector; and
- social infrastructure investments in housing, residential care, and child care—the caring economy that is already low-emission.

These are measures that address our climate challenges that will, at the same time, address the social and economic marginalization of vulnerable populations.

Again, the World War II analogy is apt—as we experienced then, an ambitious plan can produce full employment, not to mention a renewed sense of national purpose in undertaking a common project.

The climate reality requires that our governments talk honestly about the future of Canada's fossil fuel industries. We need our leaders to acknowledge that we cannot continue to expand these sectors; these industries will need to be managed for wind-down. This transition need not be as jarring and anxiety-producing as what some communities are already facing given low oil prices. Rather, as during the

Second World War, a planned adjustment with just transition systems in place can work.

It may be difficult to imagine a world that isn't dependent on fossil fuels. But just as children today have never known smoking to be permitted in restaurants or driving without mandatory seatbelt laws (both changes that were fiercely resisted by industry but are now fairly universally accepted as the new normal), those born in the coming decades likely won't know what a gas station is, except for what they see in old movies.

We've been at the crossroads before—a choice between fascism, the suppression of core rights, and the devastation of societies down one path; joining together across race and class to make common cause in an existential fight down the other. We are approaching such a crossroads again. There remains a progressive majority in Canada, even if it too often operates in silos. Both the climate crisis and the Trump victory call on all of us to animate and mobilize our best selves, and to work together across specific causes for a safer and more just world.

Historical Perspective on Environmental Change

Diane Srivastava, Jenny McCune, and Heike Lotze

IF WE COULD step back in time to the year of Confederation, 1867, what would Canada's environment look like? It was a time when most of the nation's natural resources appeared inexhaustible.[1] In Nova Scotia and Newfoundland, the catch of Atlantic cod seemed endless and reliable, with little forewarning that this species would decline by 97 percent by the end of the twentieth century. In the Great Lakes, overfishing of salmon and sturgeon was already changing the food web, but no one expected the dramatic shift that would happen a century later with the introduction of invasive mussels. As we paused our westward journey in Manitoba, we could choose a picnic site from six thousand square kilometres of tallgrass prairie, where now only one hundred square kilometres remain. On southern Vancouver Island, we would find hundreds of acres of land already plowed for crops, replacing oak savannahs that had been nurtured for millennia by the Coast Salish peoples. Loggers, having already felled many of the easily accessible large trees in Atlantic Canada, would be trekking west to start exploiting those in the rest of Canada. Over the next 150 years, they would reduce old-growth forest in coastal British Columbia by about a third. The human population of all of Confederation Canada and Newfoundland was 3.6 million, only a tenth of what it would become by 2017.

History tells us a lot about what Canada's land and seas looked like 150 years ago, but there are many gaps. For example, there are no published estimates of how many wolves, bears, and caribou roamed pre-Confederation Canada, or whether recent explosions in snow goose populations have any historical precedent. While the answers to some of these questions may be orally passed down within Indigenous culture, Canadian scientists have been slow to access and quantify such knowledge. Without accurate records of the state of the environment in the past, we have to rely on our imperfect human memory and perceptions. This leads to the problem of shifting baselines, where the degree of environmental change over time is underestimated as knowledge is lost over generations. Most of our recorded ecological data is relatively recent: it was not until Robert Borden became prime minister (1911-20) that the federal government got serious about scientific data collection, and not until the 1960s that ministries—especially fisheries—began research monitoring programs. We are now facing a period of intensifying global change, yet we still have very few monitoring programs to help us evaluate change—especially for those species that are not exploited commercially. There is an urgent need to establish both historical baselines and long-term monitoring programs to understand change from the past to the present and into the future.

Because scientific monitoring programs in Canada are, at most, only a few decades old, ecologists have to find creative ways to look into the past. An important element in this is to move beyond the confines of Western science by incorporating the traditional ecological knowledge of Canada's Indigenous peoples. For example, oral interviews of Inuit Elders have been used to estimate change in Arctic caribou populations going back many generations. Similarly, beaver population sizes in northern Quebec have been estimated by the Cree by combining their local knowledge on occupancy rates of beaver lodges with the provincial government's aerial photographs of lodges.

There are also large amounts of untapped information in historical records and artifacts. Revisiting forest plots or repeating fish or plankton surveys, when the old data and locations can be found, can take us back decades. Old fisheries statistics, logbooks, and trade or market records reach back a century or more. For example, the Hudson's Bay Company's trapping data, from 1820 to the early 1900s, reveal decadal population cycles of snowshoe hares and their predator, the Canada lynx. Historical paintings, photographs, and writings tell tales of centuries past when there were oysters the size of plates and salmon runs so loud that people couldn't sleep.

Organisms can also serve as natural repositories of historical data. Tree rings record environmental history encompassing the lifespan of the oldest trees, which in some cases can be many centuries (Canada's oldest tree on record was eighteen hundred years old when felled). Over longer time scales, archaeology and paleoecology can help determine what plants and animals were present and used by humans thousands of years ago. We can use specimens of dried plants and preserved animals in herbaria and museums to associate species with times and places; for example, such records have been used to show changes in butterfly distributions across Canada over the last century.

Collectively, all these sources of historical data can be combined to reconstruct Canada's ecological past and help plan for future resource management, restoration, and conservation. Yet, so far, this has only occurred in a few cases. We'll use two examples to demonstrate the importance of a historical perspective to better plan for the future.

First, consider Atlantic cod. The historical size (Figure 1) and density of cod is legendary, with John Cabot in 1497 commenting that his men could scoop cod up in baskets, and Nicholas Deny (1672) describing an abundance of large cod in every cove and bay. Over time, catches of cod steadily increased to an all-time high in the late 1960s, although much of this catch was from foreign trawlers fishing close to Canada's shores. In 1970, government scientists began to use research trawls to monitor cod stocks on the Grand Banks and Scotian Shelf. The first years of data looked positive, pointing to a doubling in cod biomass on the Scotian Shelf to almost 400,000 metric tonnes by the mid-1980s. Indeed, there was a small uptick in cod catches over that period, related to increases in national fishing fleets after foreign trawlers were excluded within 200 miles of Canada's coast. However, as national fishing fleets were building up, the unimaginable happened: cod populations on both the Grand Banks and Scotian Shelf collapsed in the early 1990s and the fisheries were effectively closed. Over forty thousand people lost their jobs as a result. What happened?

The story of the Atlantic cod is like the parable about a man who looks for his lost watch by a street light, because that is where it is easiest to see rather than where it is most likely to be. Part of the story is bias in the population models used to analyze research trawl data since the 1970s. When these model biases are corrected, the resulting analyses show declines decades earlier. Another part of the story is political interpretation of scientific uncertainty, which continually took the most optimistic view of stock estimates. But most of the story is that we took too short a historical view of this stock. Although the years before 1970 are away from the "street light" of research trawl data, that is precisely where we should have been looking.

To understand the longer-term history of cod, two innovative approaches have been used to reconstruct past changes in stocks on the Scotian Shelf. The first approach was to estimate the potential "carrying capacity"—that is, the maximum number of individuals the area could support in the absence of fishing. Carrying capacity can be estimated from the relationships between adult spawner density and the abundance of new recruits, and this information can be gleaned from modern fishery survey data. Using this approach, biologist Ransom Myers estimated the carrying capacity of the Scotian Shelf as 1.15 million metric tonnes. The second approach, carried out by a team led by Andrew Rosenberg, was to collate historical catch records from the logs of fishing vessels that fished for cod on the Scotian Shelf in the years 1852–59. The estimate based on this historical data pegged the Scotian Shelf cod biomass at 1.26 million metric tonnes in 1852, remarkably similar to the carrying capacity estimate. This result implies that by the time fisheries scientists began monitoring the Scotian Shelf cod population in 1970, the stock was already only 8 percent of its pre-Confederation size. Had this been realized at the time, we might have been motivated to reduce fishing pressure earlier and prevent further decline to 3 percent of its pre-Confederation size, the point of economic collapse.

Our second example is the Garry oak savannah of southwestern British Columbia. These savannahs have distinctive grass and wildflower communities interspersed with graceful oak trees. They represent one of the most threatened ecosystems in Canada, with dozens of rare and endangered species. It is estimated that 90 percent of the original savannah habitat has been lost to agriculture and housing since the city of Victoria was founded in 1843. But to fully understand what has happened to the Garry oak savannahs, we have to go much further back in time.

Pollen records extending to the end of the last glaciation twelve thousand years ago show abundant savannah between eight and six thousand years ago, when the climate was warmer and drier than today. The onset of cooler, wetter conditions about six thousand years ago favoured the conversion of open savannahs to denser coniferous forests, but many savannahs were nonetheless able to persist locally, likely through the action of Indigenous communities. We know that, up until the time of European colonization, Coast Salish communities purposefully set fire to Garry oak savannahs in fertile, low-lying areas to prevent forest succession and to ensure high densities of camas plants, which were a staple in their diet.

This all changed with the arrival of Europeans, who outlawed the fires and brought diseases that decimated Indigenous populations. A comparison of land survey records from the mid-1800s with modern resurveys shows that forest density has roughly doubled and has shifted to fire-sensitive species like Western red cedar. Tree-ring analysis shows a spike in tree seedlings immediately following European settlement. Interestingly, although only Garry oak savannahs exist today, much of the savannah habitat at the time of European settlement was sprinkled with Douglas-fir trees rather than Garry oaks. Yet, it is the oak that is revered and serves as the flagship species for conservation efforts. Another twist in this story comes from analyses of the geographic distributions of savannahs over the last 150 years. The European settlers claimed the most fertile and flat areas of savannah for agriculture, leaving only the savannah on exposed, steep, and rocky sites, where environmental conditions naturally prevented succession to forests. The savannahs left today are therefore not representative of the range of past savannahs. It is only through this deep historical analysis that ecologists have been able to refute the popular idea that savannahs existed unchanged for millennia before European colonization and were shaped by nature alone.

There are several reasons Canada should take a more historical perspective on resource use, management, and conservation. The first is simply to understand what we have lost—and could potentially restore. Without historical data, we could not have estimated the real declines in savannah ecosystems or Atlantic cod stocks—and this distorts our targets for ecological restoration programs. Nor can we estimate the vulnerability of populations without understanding the magnitude of decline. The further back in time we push reference baselines, the more accurate (and often larger) this estimate of decline becomes. For example, the 9 percent decline of Atlantic cod from Confederation to 1970 suggests that it was already critically endangered by 1867 and therefore facing a high likelihood of extinction. Had Canada realized this at the time, we like to think that the nation would have managed Atlantic cod populations very differently.

The second argument in support of long-term historical approaches is that management and conservation require targets, such as viable population sizes, geographical ranges, and reference communities. Simply using contemporary ecosystems as a reference can bias our targets, given that intact remnants of heavily exploited ecosystems are often in marginal and inaccessible areas. This is not to say that all targets should be set to the state of the country at Confederation. But an intelligent discussion of targets requires understanding the starting points and trajectories of change.

The third reason to look back into our history is to assess current or potential future risks, by considering the natural range in plant or animal population fluctuations over time, or past ecosystems responses to historical climate changes. Such information on long-term trajectories and their underlying driving factors is critical for accurate forecasts of potential future changes in our natural resources and ecosystems. Ecological and ecosystem forecasting is still in its infancy and in urgent need of better historical information. But with this information, we could get a better idea of how Canada's natural environment may be transformed over the next 150 years in the face of environmental change and human activities.

Although compiling and synthesizing historical data is challenging, we urge the wider adoption of this practice in Canada. At the very least, we need to start acknowledging the dangers of incremental thinking in our environmental policies, and to push for baselines that are relevant rather than just expedient. In a country where generational knowledge has been erased by residential schools, there is an urgency to seek Indigenous knowledge of ecosystems before losing another generation of Elders. We also need to invest in basic, long-term monitoring programs of the biodiversity on our lands and in our waters, so that future scientists and managers have the data necessary to understand how things have changed—and why. Such long-term monitoring programs are well-funded south of our border, yet Canada has never systematically invested in the monitoring of non-exploited species. The few programs that individual scientists have been able to establish have been funded through ad hoc mechanisms, rendering them vulnerable to political whims—as evidenced by the destruction wrought by the Harper government on the Polar Environment Atmospheric Research Laboratory (PEARL) time series of Arctic climate data. Another option for monitoring is to use organized networks of citizen volunteers. Data gathered by citizens have been used very effectively in the UK to track changes in species abundances and distributions. For example, citizen monitoring of British butterflies since 1976 has provided some of the most convincing evidence of the biotic effects of climate change. This "public science" would have the added benefit of engaging citizens in the process of discovering Canada's rich biodiversity. The time is ripe to build such monitoring networks to carry us through the next 150 years.

FIGURE 1: Average size of Atlantic cod caught a century ago in Newfoundland. Stocks of Atlantic cod are now less than a tenth of their historical levels. *Photographer unknown. Source: Library and Archives Canada, Neg. No: c76178*

Through the Arctic Looking Glass

Eddy Carmack

CONSIDER TWO FACTS. First, Canada is an Arctic nation. We know that. Second, the Arctic is warming faster than any region on Earth, with sea-ice loss being the leading signal of change. We know that, too. Taken together, these two facts show that the world has been given a time machine, and it is called Canada. An unpredictable, non-linear future has already arrived on our northern shores, and this presents Canada with both a potential crisis and a potential opportunity. As we reflect on the 150th anniversary of Canadian Confederation, it is up to us to select a path to follow. The ways in which we embrace new approaches to turn crisis into opportunity must be shaped by our wisdom as a liberal democratic society and our true—not token—concern for future gener-ations. If we succeed in these experiments, it may influence the world to follow our lead.

Canada, with the world's longest national coastline, is bordered by three magnificent oceans. Let us focus on just one of those borders and look north to the Arctic Ocean. In doing so, we must look well beyond the limits of our own nation and well back in time beyond the 150 years of our Confederation, to almost two billion years ago, when the drifting slabs of Precambrian rock that would someday be called Canada began to unite. From this broader perspective, we will begin to understand that our large but sparsely populated nation carries a grave human responsi-bility for leadership. Will we shoot the puck? Or lose our paddle?

Let's start lightly with a few facts about the Arctic Ocean, why it is special, and why it is our urgent responsibility to govern wisely. This tiny ocean holds only 1 percent of the world's ocean volume and occupies only 3 percent of the world's ocean surface area, but its impact on the global climate system is disproportionately large. Though small in area, it scoops up over 10 percent of global river runoff and claims twenty of the world's one hundred longest rivers.[1] The Arctic marine domain comprises about a third of the world's coastline and one-quarter of the world's continental shelf, both of immense socio-ecological importance.[2] On all counts, the little Arctic Ocean holds its own on the global stage.

And yet, an economist might point out that the High Arctic is a remote, sparsely populated, and costly playing field, of minor importance to the global economy. Likewise, politicians typically view the small number of voters and move on—there are only 3 (out of 335) seats in the Canadian Parliament from communities above 60 degrees north latitude. So why should we focus any attention on the Arctic at all? First, the potential economic importance of the Arctic is disproportionate; while only 0.05 percent of the world's population lives north of the Arctic Circle (and only 0.25 percent of Canadians), 15 percent of global petroleum production and around 20 percent of undiscovered of petroleum stores are found in the Arctic.[3] About 10 percent of metal resources and global shipping activity also occurs there.[4] At present, only a small fraction of global ecotourism occurs in the Arctic, but this activity has the potential to rapidly expand, as does the potential for major Arctic fisheries catches.[5] If we choose to use or extract any of these resources, then we must also launch the necessary adaptive management experiments to track the consequences; before, not after. Second, there is mounting scientific evidence for the interconnectedness between the Arctic system, mid-latitude weather, and global climate. Third, ecological and socio-economic systems in the Arctic region are undergoing an observable and southward spreading transformation, and this provides a proverbial "looking glass" into the future.

To understand the future, we must first understand the present. What governs the dynamics of this remarkable little ocean, with its disproportionate global ownership of freshwater, continental shelves, and coastlines? The ultimate driver—which renders the Arctic Ocean far different from its polar opposite in the southern hemisphere—is the global hydrological cycle, which determines the distribution of water around the planet. This driver begins in warmer climes far to the south, with the equatorial trade winds and mid-latitude westerlies. It is refined and shaped by the global distribution of land masses that, in the northern hemisphere, collect precipitation and direct it poleward in massive subarctic rivers, including the mighty Mackenzie, which flows over four thousand kilometres from its headwaters in northeastern British Columbia to the Beaufort Sea. These rivers introduce substantial amounts of fresh water into the upper layers of the Arctic Ocean, providing the required conditions for an ice cover to form, and regulating nutrient supplies and biological productivity. Changes in global temperature, hydrological cycles, and sea-ice cover have all had significant and eminently observable effects on the Arctic Ocean. Over the past two decades alone, summer sea-ice extent in the Arctic Ocean has decreased by over two million square kilometres. This represents a surface area somewhere in between the size of Mexico and Argentina, and larger than all but about a dozen countries in the world.

But the little Arctic Ocean is not just a passive victim of anthropogenic change: it is reaching back to the global system in ways that were overlooked even a decade ago. Though the exact mechanisms are still debated, Arctic sea-ice loss may be affecting both ocean currents and mid-latitude weather patterns along our southern borders. And the processes occurring in the Arctic play a vital role in connecting Canada's two other coastal regions in the Pacific and the Atlantic. The fabled Northwest Passage is more than a destination for explorers and commercial ship traffic; it is an oceanographic freight train that ties together and influences all of Canada's maritime regions, and other aspects of the global climate system.

Observations from the three oceans surrounding Canada during the International Polar Year illustrate the principle of interconnection. Oceans currents link all three of Canada's oceans, allowing heat, salt, and organisms to flow from one to another, with interconnected consequences. Envision a row of dominoes, each representing a specific component of an intertwined ocean system; changes to one may set off a cascade of falling dominoes with far-reaching "downstream" effects.

For example, warming of inflowing Atlantic and Pacific waters may drive sea-ice loss in the Beaufort, which may lead to surface freshening, which may limit the resupply of nutrients to marine plankton, and so on. Each step along the way may have its own set of feedbacks and limits. As individual dominoes begin to lean, they may surpass their own "tipping points" and thus organize in new and sometimes unexpected ways. Some outcomes may be beneficial to existing ecosystems and humans, but others will likely be detrimental. Welcome to the non-linear future!

The past holds clues to what a non-linear future might look like in the Arctic. Geology and climate are impatient with our tiny ocean, as sea-level fluctuations during glacial-interglacial climate cycles have repeatedly exposed and flooded the expansive continental shelves of the Arctic. During the last glacial maximum, about twenty thousand years ago, massive ice sheets covered the northern half of our continent, and the transfer of water from the oceans to continental glaciers exposed the Arctic continental shelf to form the Bering land bridge. This exposed land blocked the flow of low-salinity and nutrient-rich Pacific water into the Arctic Ocean, but allowed animal and human migration and settlement between Eurasia and North America. During the subsequent interglacial warming period, ice sheets melted, sea level rose (sound familiar?), and the Arctic continental shelves were flooded once again. In this manner, the Arctic's "oceanographic clock" was reset a mere ten thousand years ago, making its current ecosystem a work in progress.

We can trace our story even further back across geological time. Scientists now recognize that, over the past 445 million years, there have been five major extinctions and dozens of lesser ones. Each of these events was defined by a rapid and worldwide loss of animal species, as was captured in Canada's vast geological record. Such extinctions are forever. Proposed triggers include massive volcanic events, comets and asteroids striking Earth, and mega-glaciations—the "snowball Earth" scenarios. While such triggers have been identified, they do not work directly; rather, they disrupt system properties essential to life, and when these change, the rules for the game of life change. Despite their various triggers, all extinctions come down to changes in relatively few parameters: temperature, salinity, oxygen, acidity, nutrients, CO_2 concentrations, etc.—the very same parameters that are currently undergoing significant perturbations in the Arctic Ocean and beyond. The message in the story of all extinctions is that life is an interconnected system, subject to rapid disruption, and this demands an Earth ecosystem perspective.

In the Arctic Ocean, big changes in sea-ice cover, freshwater supply, nutrient availability, and underwater light climate are taking place at an accelerated pace, with associated shifts in seawater chemistry and biological activity, and alterations to habitat and food-web structure that are affecting an entire ocean. Ocean waters are growing more acidic, and oxygen concentrations have decreased by nearly 8 percent over the past fifty years alone.[6] Concerns now exist for the catastrophic release of methane, a potent greenhouse gas, from both marine and terrestrial environments.[7] From this perspective, it seems inevitable that the ongoing and rapid changes in the physical environment of the marine Arctic will push existing socio-ecological systems—small and large—beyond tipping points and into new regimes.

But how can we avoid unwelcome surprises, and what comprises responsible vigilance? Some steps are obvious when viewed in reverse order: you won't protect what you don't appreciate; you won't appreciate what you don't understand; and you can't understand what you haven't taken the effort to observe and study. At the very least, we need to study and monitor the basic "life variables" mentioned above, including temperature, dissolved oxygen, nutrients, and components of the carbon cycle, just as a physician would monitor the blood pressure of the patient. When early warning signs of disruptive overconsumption of ecosystem services do appear, it will be wise to have well-thought-out adaptive and intervention plans in our back pockets, ready to implement if necessary. With the pace of Arctic change, such plans may be needed sooner in Canada than elsewhere in the world. With work and planning, Canada can choose to lead the pan-Arctic nations and the globe with a strategy of detection and intervention.

To look ahead, Canada must recognize and celebrate its status as an Arctic nation, and think well beyond local problems and self-interests. Even if the world is able to limit anthropogenic warming to 2°C, Arctic amplification will push Arctic temperatures to twice that amount or more. Now, more than ever, it is imperative to close the gap between the knowledge of a rapidly changing Arctic and the corresponding development of new ideas and innovative policies to sustain resilience of the Arctic through that change. We must recognize the capacity of the Arctic system to change, and yet maintain identity in the face of significant disturbance. To do so, we must seek—through observation, modelling, and open debate—the leading indicators of regime change, and then act responsibly to maintain resilience through adaptation-oriented policy. The challenge of turning crisis into opportunity may be better met if we pursue an approach that will allow northern Canadian residents living in small coastal communities to join in observing, adapting, and—if necessary—transforming socio-ecological systems. The work that we do as an Arctic nation will result in ideas that are transferable around the world, so that everyone can benefit from Canada's clear-eyed assessment of its Arctic time machine.

Notes

Practising Reconciliation

1. Duncan Campbell Scott, Canada's deputy superintendent general of Indian Affairs from 1913 to 1932, quoted in Adam Shortt, *The Dominion: Political Evolution*, vol. 6, sec 4, pt I of *Canada and Its Provinces: A History of the Canadian People and Their Institutions* (Toronto, ON: Publishers' Association of Canada, 1914), 615.

Anniversary Reading

1. "Turn Down the Volume," *The Globe and Mail*, April 1, 1994, A19.

A Greener Future

1. Intergovernmental Panel on Climate Change, *Climate Change 2014: Impacts, Adaptation, and Vulnerability*, Working Group II contribution to the *Fifth Assessment Report of the IPCC*, ed. Christopher B. Field et al. (New York: Cambridge University Press, 2014).

2. Gary Pickering, "Barriers to Change: Climate Change Scepticism and Uncertainty in Canada" (working paper ERSC-2016-001, Environmental Sustainability Research Centre Working Paper Series, 2016). See also Environment and Climate Change Canada, *Canadian Environmental Sustainability Indicators: Greenhouse Gas Emissions by Canadian Economic Sector*, 2016, www.ec.gc.ca/indicateurs-indicators/F60DB708-6243-4A71-896B-6C7FB5CC7D01/GHGEmissions_EN.pdf.

3. Nicole Mortillaro, "Arctic Temperatures Soar to 30°C Above Normal," CBC News, December 23, 2016, www.cbc.ca/news/technology/arctic-temperatures-warmth-1.3910765.

4. Benjamin Israel and Erin Flanagan, *Out with the Coal, in with the New: National Benefits of an Accelerated Phase-out of Coal-fired Power*, Pembina Institute, 2016, www.pembina.org/reports/out-with-the-coal-in-with-the-new-final-.pdf; Office of the Minister of Environment and Climate Change, "The Government of Canada Accelerates Investments in Clean Electricity," November 21, 2016, news.gc.ca/web/article-en.do?nid=1157989.

5. International Institute for Sustainable Development, *Unpacking Canada's Fossil Fuel Subsidies: Their Size, Impacts, and What Should Happen Next*, www.iisd.org/faq/unpacking-canadas-fossil-fuel-subsidies/; Yanick Touchette, *G20 Subsidies to Oil, Gas,*

and Coal Production: Canada, 2015, www.iisd.org/library/g20-subsidies-oil-gas-and-coal-production-canada; IPCC, *Climate Change 2014*, *supra* note 1; Elizabeth Bast et al., *Empty Promises: G20 Subsidies to Oil, Gas, and Coal Production*, 2015, www.odi.org/publications/10058-empty-promises-g20-subsidies-oil-gas-and-coal-production.

6. Janis Sarra, « *Rectifier la Trajectoire—L'Equité, les Marchés Financiers, et l'Adaptation au Changement Climatique* », *La Revue Internationale des Services Financiers* (forthcoming, 2017).

7. Nicholas Rivers and Brandon Schaufele "Carbon Tax Salience and Gasoline Demand" (working paper 1211E, University of Ottawa, Department of Economics, 2012); Stewart Elgie, "British Columbia's Carbon Tax Shift: An Environmental and Economic Success," World Bank Climate: Development in Changing Climate (October 9, 2014); and Mark Jaccard et al., "Is Win-Win Possible? Can Canada's Government Achieve its Paris Commitment... and Get Reelected?" (Simon Fraser University, School of Resource and Environmental Management, September 2016).

8. Scott Nystrom and Patrick Luckow, "The Economic, Climate, Fiscal, Power, and Demographic Impact of a National Fee-and-Dividend Carbon Tax," Regional Economic Models, Inc. and Synapse Energy Economics, Inc. (June 9, 2014), citizensclimatelobby.org/wp-content/uploads/2014/06/REMI-carbon-tax-report-62141.pdf; Brian C. Murray and Nicholas Rivers, "British Columbia's Revenue-Neutral Carbon Tax: A Review of the Latest 'Grand Experiment' in Environmental Policy" (working paper NI-WP-15-04, Duke University, 2015).

Better Democracy

1. Wendy Brown, *Undoing the Demos: Neoliberalism's Stealth Revolution* (New York: Zone Books, 2015).

2. John F. Helliwell, Richard Layard, and Jeffrey Sachs, eds., *World Happiness Report 2015* (New York: Sustainable Development Solutions Network, 2015).

Two Stories

1. Andrew Jackson, "The Return of the Gilded Age: Consequences, Causes and Solutions," Broadbent Institute, April 8, 2015, d3n8a8pro7vhmx.cloudfront.net/broadbent/pages/3987/attachments/original/1431376127/The_Return_of_the_Gilded_Age.pdf?1431376127.

2. Janine Brodie, "Reforming Social Justice in Neoliberal Times," *Studies in Social Justice* 1, no. 2 (2007): 93–107.

3. Martha Jackman, "Constitutional Castaways: Poverty and the McLachlin Court," *Supreme Court Law Review* (2d) 50 (2010).

4. Keith Banting and John Myles, "Introduction: Inequality and the Fading of Redistributive Politics," in Keith Banting and John Myles, eds., *Inequality and the Fading of Redistributive Politics* (Vancouver, BC: UBC Press, 2013): 1–42, 27.

5. The Conference Board of Canada, *Acceptance of Diversity*, 2013, www.conferenceboard.ca/hcp/details/society/acceptance-of-diversity.aspx.

6. Nick Nanos, "What Makes Canadians Proud of Their Country? Equality and Respect, Poll Says," *The Globe and Mail*, October 25, 2016, spon.ca/what-makes-canadians-proud-of-their-country-equality-and-respect-poll-says/2016/10/27.

7. Boluwaji Ogunyemi, "Why We Must Maintain Tolerance as a Canadian Value," *The Huffington Post*, January 23, 2017, www.huffingtonpost.ca/boluwaji-ogunyemi/tolerance-canadian-value_b_14328168.html.

8. Jackson, "Gilded Age," *supra* note 1.

A Quantum Parable

1. Brenda Bouw, "Satellite Maker MDA's Outgoing CEO Looks Back on 80 Profitable Quarters," *The Globe and Mail*, July 27, 2016, www.theglobeandmail.com/report-on-business/rob-magazine/satellite-maker-mdas-outgoing-ceo-looks-back-on-80-profitable-quarters/article30520060; David Pugliese, "EDC Financing Satellite Construction in California Because of 'Direct Benefit' to Canada," *National Post*, October 17, 2016, news.nationalpost.com/news/canada/canadian-politics/canadian-tax-dollars-paying-for-u-s-high-tech-workers-to-build-satellites-in-california.

2. *Aerospace Review Report* as described in Janet Davison, "What is Canada's Future in Space?" CBC News, December 17, 2012, www.cbc.ca/news/canada/what-is-canada-s-future-in-space-1.1146918.

Welcome to the Revolution

1. For more information on Louise Armaindo, see « *Coup de Chapeau à Louise Armaindo* », *Le Petit Braquet*, 2005, www.lepetitbraquet.fr/chron70_louise_armaindo.html; M. Ann Hall, *Immodest and Sensational: 150 Years of Canadian Women in Sport* (Toronto, ON: James Lorimer and Company Ltd., 2008); David V. Herlihy, *Bicycle: The History* (New Haven, CT: Yale University Press, 2004), 205; "About," Kentucky Wheelman, www.kentucky-wheelmen.org/about.html.

2. Historica Canada, *Addie Aylestock*, Black History Canada, www.blackhistorycanada.ca/profiles.php?themeid=20&id=12; Susan Hill Lindley and Eleanor J. Stebner, eds., *The Westminster Handbook to Women in American Religious History* (Louisville, KY: Westminster John Knox Press, 2008), 9; and Barrington Walker, ed., *The History of Immigration and Racism in Canada: Essential Readings* (Toronto, ON: Canadian Scholars, 2008), 240.

3. Paul-Émile Borduas, « *Refus Global* », 1948, www.dantaylor.com/pages/refusglobal.html; Gilles Daigneault, « *Récipiendaire: Ferron, Marcelle* », *Les Prix du Quebec*, www.prix-duquebec.gouv.qc.ca.

4. Consuelo Solar, "Newcomers: Baljit Sethi—Role Model," *Canadian Newcomer Magazine* (2011), www.cnmag.ca/issue-40/1054-n11-newcomers-baljit-sethi-role-model.

5. Speak Truth to Power Canada, "Mary Simon: Cultural Identity and Education," 2017, sttp-canada.ctf-fce.ca/lessons/mary-simon.

Caring for Health

1. Canadian Institute for Health Information, *International Comparisons: A Focus on Diabetes* (Ottawa, ON: CIHI, 2015).

2. Paul J. Allison et al., *Improving Access to Oral Health Care for Vulnerable People Living in Canada*, The Canadian Academy of Health Sciences, 2014, cahs-acss.ca/wp-content/uploads/2015/07/Access_to_Oral_Care_FINAL_REPORT_EN.pdf.

3. Louise Nasmith et al., *Transforming Care for Canadians with Chronic Health Conditions: Put People First, Expect the Best, Manage for Results*, The Canadian Academy of Health Sciences, 2010, www.cahs-acss.ca/wp-content/uploads/2011/09/cdm-final-English.pdf.

4. Sioban Nelson et al., *Optimizing Scopes of Practice: New Models of Care for a New Health Care System*, The Canadian Academy of Health Sciences, 2014, www.cahs-acss.ca/wp-content/uploads/2015/07/Optimizing-Scopes-of-Practice_REPORT-English.pdf.

The Future Arctic

1. World Tourism Organization, *Global Report on Adventure Tourism*, AM Reports, vol. 9 (2014), skift.com/wp-content/uploads/2014/11/unwto-global-report-on-adventure-tourism.pdf.

Medicare

1. Marc-André Gagnon, *The Economic Case for Universal Pharmacare: Costs and Benefits of Publicly Funded Drug Coverage for All Canadians*, Canadian Centre for Policy Alternatives 2010, s3.amazonaws.com/policyalternatives.ca/sites/default/files/uploads/publications/National%20Office/2010/09/Universal_Pharmacare.pdf.

Un avenir confédéral

1. Pensons à la répression des Métis (1869-1870) et la pendaison de leur chef Louis Riel (1885), aux crises de conscription durant les deux Guerres mondiales ou encore à l'abolition de l'enseignement du français au Manitoba (1890), en Ontario (1912), et au Nouveau-Brunswick (1871).
2. Will Kymlicka, "Marketing Canadian Pluralism in the International Arena," *International Journal* 59, no. 4 (2004): 829-52.
3. Ministre de l'Industrie, « Caractéristiques linguistiques des Canadiens: Langue, Recensement de la Population de 2011 », Statistique Canada (2012).
4. Guy Lawson, "Trudeau's Canada Again," *The New York Times*, December 8, 2015, www.nytimes.com/2015/12/13/magazine/trudeaus-canada-again.html.
5. Hubert Aquin, « La Fatigue Culturelle du Canada Français », *Liberté* 4:23 (1962): 299-325.
6. Dont témoigne, « Le Livre Blanc de 1969, la Politique Indienne du Gouvernement du Canada », Indigenous and Northern Affairs Canada (The White Paper, 1969).
7. François Rocher et al., « Le Concept d'Interculturalisme en Contexte Québécois: Généalogie d'un Néologisme », rapport présenté à la Commission de consultation sur les pratiques d'accommodement reliées aux différences culturelles (December 21, 2007).
8. Marco Bélair-Cirino, « La Foi Souverainiste en Recul », *Le Devoir*, October 28, 2015, www.ledevoir.com/non-classe/453715/le-projet-de-pays-du-quebec-rebute.

A Confederal Future

1. For example, the repression of Métis (1869-1870) and the hanging of their leader Louis Riel (1885), the conscription crisis during the two World Wars, or the abolition of public French schooling in many provinces.
2. Ministre de l'Industrie, « Caractéristiques linguistiques des Canadiens: Langue, Recensement de la Population de 2011 », Statistique Canada (2012).
3. Guy Lawson, "Trudeau's Canada Again," *The New York Times*, December 8, 2015, www.nytimes.com/2015/12/13/magazine/trudeaus-canada-again.html.
4. Hubert Aquin "The Cultural Fatigue of French Canada," in *Writing Quebec: Selected Essays by Hubert Aquin*, ed. Anthony Purdy (Edmonton: University of Alberta Press, 1988): 19-48.
5. Dont témoigne, « Le Livre Blanc de 1969, la Politique Indienne du Gouvernement du Canada » Indigenous and Northern Affairs Canada (The White Paper, 1969).
6. Gérard Bouchard, "What is Interculturalism?" *McGill Law Journal* 56, no. 2 (2011): 435-68.
7. Marco Bélair-Cirino, « La Foi Souverainiste en Recul », *Le Devoir*, October 28, 2015, www.ledevoir.com/non-classe/453715/le-projet-de-pays-du-quebec-rebute.

Hard of Herring

1. M. Stocker, "Recent Management of the British Columbia Herring Fishery: Perspectives on Canadian Marine Fisheries Management," *Canadian Bulletin of Fisheries and Aquatic Sciences* 226 (1993): 267-93; D. Pauly and D. Zeller, eds., *Global Atlas of Marine Fisheries: A Critical Appraisal of Catches and Ecosystem Impacts* (Washington, DC: Island Press, 2016); Cameron Ainsworth, "Research Note: British Columbia Marine Fisheries Catch Reconstruction: 1873 to 2011," *BC Studies* 188 (2016): 81-90.

2. Russ Jones, Catherine Rigg, and Evelyn Pinkerton, "Strategies for Assertion of Conservation and Local Management Rights: A Haida Gwaii Herring Story," *Marine Policy* 80 (2017); and S. Raman et al., "Science Matters and the Public Interest: The Role of Minority Engagement," in B. Nerlich, S. Hartley, S. Raman, and A. Smith, eds., *Science and the Politics of Openness: Here Be Monsters* (Manchester, UK: Manchester University Press, forthcoming).

3. Mimi E. Lam et al., "A Values- and Ecosystem-Based Management Approach: The Pacific Herring Fishery Conflict in Haida Gwaii, Canada" (manuscript in preparation, on file with author); and Mimi E. Lam, "Opinion: Herring Fishery Needs Integrated Management Plan," *Vancouver Sun*, 2015, www.vancouversun.com/technology/ Opinion+Herring+fishery+needs+integrated+management+plan/11505147/ story.html.

4. Szymon Surma et al., "The Role of Pacific Herring and Its Fisheries in a Northeast Pacific Food Web: Insights from Ecosystem Modelling and Closed-Loop Simulation" (manuscript in preparation, on file with author).

Indigenous Land and Food

1. Valerie Tarasuk, Andy Mitchell, and Naomi Dachner, *Household Food Insecurity in Canada, 2012* (Toronto, ON: Research to Identify Policy Options to Reduce Food Insecurity [PROOF], 2014).

Privacy and Technology

1. John Naughton, "Tim Wu: 'The Internet Is Like a Classic Story of the Party That Went Sour,'" *The Guardian*, January 8, 2017, www.theguardian.com/technology/2017/jan/08/ tim-wu-interview-internet-classic-party-went-sour-attention-merchants.

2. John Perry Barlow, "A Declaration of Independence of Cyberspace," Electronic Frontier Foundation, 1996, www.eff.org/cyberspace-independence.

3. Samuel Warren and Louis Brandeis, "The Right to Privacy," *Harvard Law Review* 4 (1890): 193–220.

4. Anna Minton and Jody Aked, "'Fortress Britain': High Security, Insecurity and the Challenge of Preventing Harm" (working paper, New Economics Foundation, November 2012), www.annaminton.com/single-post/2016/03/21/ New-report-Fortress-Britain.

5. David Lyon, ed., *Surveillance and Social Sorting: Privacy, Risk, and Digital Discrimination* (New York: Routledge, 2003).

6. Elle Hunt, "Facial Recognition to Replace Passports in Security Overhaul at Australian Airports," *The Guardian*, January 22, 2017, www.theguardian.com/australia-news/2017/ jan/22/facial-recognition-to-replace-passports-in-security-overhaul-at-australian-airports.

The Next Energy Transition

1. CPAC Public Record, "Navdeep Bains and John Manley," October 12, 2016, www.cpac.ca/ en/programs/public-record/episodes/49294461/.

Claiming the 21st Century

1. John Hancock, "Will the BRICS Countries Become World Powers? Don't Hold Your Breath," *The Globe and Mail*, March 27, 2013, www.theglobeandmail.com/ opinion/will-the-brics-countries-become-world-powers-dont-hold-your-breath/ article10428666/.

A Carbon-Constrained Future

1. Statistics Canada, *Table 126-0001: Historical Supply and Disposition of Crude Oil and Equivalent*, CANSIM database (2017), www5.statcan.gc.ca/cansim/a26?lang=eng&id=1260001.
2. Environment and Climate Change Canada, "Figure S-3," *National Inventory Report 1990–2015: Greenhouse Gas Sources and Sinks in Canada: Executive Summary* (2016), www.ec.gc.ca/ges-ghg/default.asp?lang=En&n=662F9C56-1.
3. Ibid.
4. Christophe McGlade and Paul Ekins, "The Geographical Distribution of Fossil Fuels Unused When Limiting Global Warming to 2°C," *Nature* 517 (2015): 187–90.

Theatre, What's Next?

1. George Belliveau and Marvin Westwood, "Soldiers Performing Self," *Contact! Unload: Innovations in Theatre and Counselling* (Vancouver, BC: UBC Faculty of Education, 2016).

Uplifting Voices

1. Bliss Pictures Inc., *Spelling Bee*, Catrina Megumi Longmuir, Marilyn Thomas, Sharon Bliss (producers) and Zoe Hopkins (director), in *Our First Voices* (Moving Images Distribution, 2010).
2. For information about Indigenous approaches to maintaining traditional knowledge within communities, disruption of traditional knowledge systems, and the complexity of managing Indigenous collections in non-Indigenous institutions, see Kim L. Lawson, *Precious Fragments: First Nations Materials in Archives, Libraries and Museums* (thesis, UBC, 2004).
3. The Legacy of Hope Foundation, "100 Years of Loss: Healing the Legacy of the Residential Schools," 2011, 100yearsofloss.ca.
4. *Daybreak North*, "Prince Rupert Students Must Learn Indigenous Language from September," CBC News, June 11, 2015, www.cbc.ca/news/canada/british-columbia/prince-rupert-students-must-learn-indigenous-language-from-september-1.3108193.
5. Task Force on Aboriginal Languages and Culture, *Towards a New Beginning: A Foundational Report for a Strategy to Revitalize First Nation, Inuit, and Métis Languages and Cultures*, Report CH4-96/2005 (Ottawa, ON: Ministry of Canadian Heritage, 2005), www.afn.ca/uploads/files/education2/towardanewbeginning.pdf.
6. Official Languages Commissioner Graham Fraser, quoted in *The Hill Times*, August 31, 2009, 14.
7. Prime Minister Justin Trudeau, "Prime Minister Justin Trudeau's Speech to the Assembly of First Nations Special Chiefs Assembly," transcript (Gatineau, QC: December 6, 2016), pm.gc.ca/eng/news/2016/12/06/prime-minister-justin-trudeaus-speech-assembly-first-nations-special-chiefs-assembly.

Historical Perspective on Environmental Change

1. Readers interested in the scientific basis to this article are referred to the bibliography deposited at DOI: 10.5281/zenodo.400373.

Through the Arctic Looking Glass

1. E.C. Carmack et al., "Fresh Water and Its Role in the Arctic Marine System: Sources, Delivery, Disposition, Storage, Export, and Physical and Biogeochemical Consequences in the Arctic and Global Oceans," *Journal of Geophysical Research-Biogeosciences* 121, no. 3 (2016): 675–717, 675.

2. Dorte Krause-Jensen and Carlos M. Duarte, "Expansion of Vegetated Coastal Ecosystems in the Future Arctic," *Frontiers in Marine Science* 1 (2014), journal.frontiersin.org/article/10.3389/fmars.2014.00077/full.

3. Donald L. Gautier et al., "Assessment of Undiscovered Oil and Gas in the Arctic," *Science* 324, no. 5931 (2009): 1175–79; Christophe McGlade and Paul Ekins, "The Geographical Distribution of Fossil Fuels Unused When Limiting Global Warming to 2°C," *Nature* 517 (2015): 187–90.

4. Roger Howard, *The Arctic Gold Rush: The New Race for Tomorrow's Natural Resources* (New York: Bloomsbury Publishing, 2009); Victor M. Eguíluz, Juan Fernández-Gracia, Xabier Irigoien, and Carlos M. Duarte, "A Quantitative Assessment of Arctic Shipping in 2010–2014," *Scientific Reports* 6 (2016).

5. Jørgen S. Christiansen, Catherine W. Mecklenburg, and Oleg V. Karamushko, "Arctic Marine Fishes and Their Fisheries in Light of Global Change," *Global Change Biology* 20, no. 2 (2013): 352–59.

6. Sunke Schmidtko, Lothar Stramma, and Martin Visbeck, "Decline in Global Oceanic Oxygen Content During the Past Five Decades," *Nature* 542 (2017): 335–39.

7. E.A.G. Schuur et al., "Climate Change and the Permafrost Carbon Feedback," *Nature* 520 (2015): 171–79.

Author Affiliations

Sally Aitken is a Professor of Forest and Conservation Sciences at the University of British Columbia.

Paul Allison is a Professor and the Dean of the Faculty of Dentistry at McGill University.

Peter Arcese is a Professor in the Department of Forest and Conservation Science at the University of British Columbia.

George Belliveau is a Professor in the Department of Language and Literacy Education at the University of British Columbia.

Joseph Bennett is an Assistant Professor in the Department of Biology at Carleton University.

Marc-André Blanchard is the Canadian Ambassador to the United Nations.

Michael Brauer is a Professor in the School of Population and Public Health at the University of British Columbia.

Ed Broadbent is a political scientist and the former leader of the New Democratic Party of Canada, from 1975 to 1989.

Kim Brooks is a Professor at the Schulich School of Law at Dalhousie University.

Pam Brown is a Heiltsuk community member and the Pacific Northwest Curator at the Museum of Anthropology at the University of British Columbia.

Maxwell Cameron is a Professor of Political Science at the University of British Columbia.

Chris Carlsten is an Associate Professor in the Department of Medicine and the School of Population and Public Health at the University of British Columbia.

Eddy Carmack is a Senior Scientist Emeritus at the Institute of Ocean Sciences, Fisheries and Oceans Canada.

David Carment is a Professor of International Affairs at Carleton University.

Jennifer Carpenter is a Heiltsuk community member and Director of the Heiltsuk Cultural Education Centre.

Ayesha Chaudhry is an Associate Professor of Religion, Law and Social Justice at the University of British Columbia.

William Cheung is an Associate Professor in the Institute for the Oceans and Fisheries at the University of British Columbia.

George Elliott Clarke is a Professor of Canadian Literature at the University of Toronto, and Parliamentary Poet Laureate of Canada (2016–17).

Joseph Dahmen is an Assistant Professor in the School of Architecture and Landscape Architecture at the University of British Columbia.

Ron Darvin is a lecturer at the Faculty of Education at the University of British Columbia.

Liam Doherty is a PhD candidate in the Department of Language and Literacy Education at the University of British Columbia.

Margaret Early is an Associate Professor in the Department of Language and Literacy Education at the University of British Columbia.

Robert Evans is a Professor Emeritus at the Centre for Health Services and Policy Research at the Vancouver School of Economics at the University of British Columbia.

Margot Filipenko is a Professor of Teaching in the Department of Language and Literacy Education at the University of British Columbia.

Brett Finlay is a Peter Wall Distinguished Professor at the University of British Columbia.

Esther Geva is a Professor in the Department of Applied Psychology and Human Development at the Ontario Institute for Studies in Education at the University of Toronto.

Naveen Girn is the Director of Community Relations for the Mayor's Office, City of Vancouver.

Sherrill Grace is a Professor Emerita in the Department of English at the University of British Columbia.

Jean Gray is a Professor Emerita of Medical Education, Medicine, and Pharmacology at Dalhousie University.

Jan Hare is an Anishinaabe scholar and Associate Dean of Indigenous Education at the University of British Columbia.

Jillian Harris is a former Chief and Councillor of the Penelakut Tribe.

Leila Harris is an Associate Professor in the Institute for Resources, Environment and Sustainability and in the Institute for Gender, Race, Sexuality and Social Justice at the University of British Columbia.

Kathryn Harrison is a Professor of Political Science at the University of British Columbia.

Sophie Harrison is a climate and pipeline campaigner in Vancouver, BC, unceded Coast Salish territories.

Carol Herbert is a Professor Emerita, Schulich School of Medicine and Dentistry at Western University.

Christiane Hoppmann is an Associate Professor in Psychology at the University of British Columbia.

Laura Hurd Clarke is a Professor in the School of Kinesiology at the University of British Columbia.

Matthias Kaiser is the Director of the Centre for the Study of the Sciences and Humanities at the University of Bergen, Norway.

Perry Kendall is the British Columbia Health Officer and a Clinical Professor in the Faculty of Medicine at the University of British Columbia.

Seth Klein is the British Columbia Director of the Canadian Centre for Policy Alternatives.

Mimi Lam is a Marie Curie Fellow in the Centre for the Study of the Sciences and Humanities at the University of Bergen, Norway.

Joe Landry is a PhD candidate at the Norman Paterson School of International Affairs, Carleton University.

Diana Lary is a Professor Emerita in the Department of History at the University of British Columbia.

Gerry Lawson is a Heiltsuk community member and the Coordinator of the Oral History and Language Lab at the Museum of Anthropology of the University of British Columbia.

Kim Lawson is a Heiltsuk community member and a librarian at Xwi7xwa Library, First Nations House of Learning at the University of British Columbia.

David Ley is a Professor in the Department of Geography at the University of British Columbia.

Heike Lotze is a Professor in the Biology Department at Dalhousie University.

Alex Maass is the former Research Project Manager for Missing Children and Unmarked Graves, Truth and Reconciliation Commission of Canada, and a current policy advisor for Indigenous and Northern Affairs, Canada.

Robie Macdonald is an Emeritus scientist at the Institute of Ocean Sciences, Department of Fisheries and Oceans.

Mark Mallory is an Associate Professor in Biology at Acadia University.

Andrew Martindale is an Associate Professor in the Department of Anthropology at the University of British Columbia.

Anne Martin-Matthews is a Professor in the Department of Sociology at the University of British Columbia.

Jenny McCune is a Postdoctoral Fellow in the Department of Biology at Carleton University.

Heather McKay is a Professor in the Departments of Orthopaedics and Family Practice at the University of British Columbia.

Walter Mérida is the Director of the Clean Energy Research Centre at the University of British Columbia.

Dawn Morrison, Secwepmec, is the Founder and Director of the Working Group on Indigenous Food Sovereignty.

Anne Murphy is an Associate Professor in the Department of Asian Studies at the University of British Columbia.

Louise Nasmith is a Professor in the Department of Family Practice at the University of British Columbia.

Lisa Nathan is an Assistant Professor in the School of Library, Archival and Information Studies, at the University of British Columbia.

Christian Naus is a Professor in the Department of Cellular and Physiological Sciences at the University of British Columbia.

Sioban Nelson is a Professor of Nursing at the University of Toronto.

Peter Nemetz is a Professor Emeritus in the Sauder School of Business at the University of British Columbia.

Bonny Norton is a Professor in the Department of Language and Literacy Education at the University of British Columbia.

Deborah O'Connor is a Professor in the School of Social Work at the University of British Columbia.

Evgeny Pakhomov is the Director of the Institute for the Oceans and Fisheries at the University of British Columbia.

Robert Paquin is a poet, songwriter, and literary translator of novels and films, including works by many of Canada's leading artists.

David Patrick is a Professor in the School of Population and Public Health at the University of British Columbia.

Daniel Pauly is a Professor in the Institute for the Oceans and Fisheries at the University of British Columbia.

Alison Phinney is a Professor in the School of Nursing at the University of British Columbia.

Tony Pitcher is a Professor in the Institute for the Oceans and Fisheries at the University of British Columbia.

Elaine Power is an Associate Professor in the School of Kinesiology and Health Studies at Queen's University.

Raghavendra Rao K.V. is a conceptual artist and a Research Associate at the Centre for India and South Asia Research at the University of British Columbia.

Philip Resnick is a Professor Emeritus in the Department of Political Science at the University of British Columbia.

John Richardson is a Professor in the Department of Forest and Conservation Sciences at the University of British Columbia.

Amanda Rodewald is the Director of Conservation Science at Cornell University's Lab of Ornithology and Department of Natural Resources.

David Sanschagrin is a PhD candidate in the Department of Political Science at l'Université du Québec à Montréal.

Janis Sarra is a Presidential Distinguished Professor and Professor of Law at the University of British Columbia.

Hans Schreier is a Professor Emeritus in the Faculty of Land and Food Systems at the University of British Columbia.

Richard Schuster is a Liber Ero Post-doctoral Fellow in the Department of Biology at Carleton University.

Anthony Alan Shelton is the Director of the Museum of Anthropology, and a Professor of Art History, Visual Art and Theory at the University of British Columbia.

Tetsuro Shigematsu is an artist and PhD candidate in the Department of Language and Literacy Education at the University of British Columbia.

Linda Siegel is a Professor Emerita in the Department of Educational and Counselling Psychology and Special Education at the University of British Columbia.

Joanie Sims-Gould is an Assistant Professor in the Department of Family Practice at the University of British Columbia.

Milan Singh is a Research Fellow at the Centre for Policy Studies on Culture and Communities at Simon Fraser University.

Paneet Singh is an Instructor in the Theatre and Music Department at Arts Umbrella, Vancouver.

Darshan Soni is a student in the Integrated Engineering program at the University of British Columbia.

South Asian Canadian Histories Association is a collective of scholars, artists, and community leaders undertaking the Canada 150+ project "Trauma, Memory, and the Story of Canada."

Diane Srivastava is a Professor in the Department of Zoology at the University of British Columbia.

Philip Stamp is the Director of the Pacific Institute of Theoretical Physics at the University of British Columbia.

Espen Stranger-Johannessen is a PhD candidate in the Department of Language and Literacy at the University of British Columbia.

Edward Struzik is a fellow at the Institute for Energy and Environmental Policy at Queen's University.

Rashid Sumaila is a Professor in the Institute for the Oceans and Fisheries, and Liu Institute for Global Issues at the University of British Columbia.

Philippe Tortell is the Director of the Peter Wall Institute for Advanced Studies at the University of British Columbia.

Mark Turin is an Associate Professor of Anthropology at the University of British Columbia.

Oscar Venter is an Associate Professor in the Department of Ecosystem Science and Management at the University of Northern British Columbia.

Michael Vonn is a lawyer and the Policy Director of the British Columbia Civil Liberties Association.

Jerry Wasserman is a Professor Emeritus, Department of Theatre and Film at the University of British Columbia.

April SGaana Jaad White is a Haida geologist and artist, the Director of Wind Spirit Art, Powell River, BC, and Old Massett, Haida Gwaii.

Catharine Whiteside is a Professor Emerita, Faculty of Medicine, University of Toronto.

Judith Wiener is a Professor in the Department of Applied Psychology and Human Development at the Ontario Institute for Studies in Education, University of Toronto.

Hannah Wittman is an Associate Professor in the Centre for Sustainable Food Systems at the University of British Columbia.

Alexander Woodside is a Professor Emeritus in the Department of History at the University of British Columbia.

Margot Young is a Professor in the Allard School of Law at the University of British Columbia.

THE PETER WALL INSTITUTE FOR ADVANCED STUDIES
at the University of British Columbia provides an intellectual environment where leading scholars address fundamental research questions through collaborations that transcend disciplinary boundaries. Our work stimulates new thinking and intellectual risk-taking, leading to important advances in knowledge that are shared through community engagement programs.

You can find out more at www.pwias.ubc.ca

PETER
INSTITUTE FOR ADVANCED STUDIES
THE UNIVERSITY OF BRITISH COLUMBIA VANCOUVER